DISCARD

POLICE FOR THE FUTURE

STUDIES IN CRIME AND PUBLIC POLICY
Michael Tonry and Norval Morris, *General Editors*

Police for the Future
David H. Bayley

Incapacitation: Penal Confinement and the Restraint of Crime
Franklin E. Zimring and Gordon Hawkins

The American Street Gang: Its Nature, Prevalence, and Control
Malcolm W. Klein

POLICE FOR THE FUTURE

David H. Bayley

New York   Oxford
OXFORD UNIVERSITY PRESS
1994

Oxford University Press

Oxford New York Toronto
Delhi Bombay Calcutta Madras Karachi
Petaling Jaya Singapore Hong Kong Tokyo
Nairobi Dar es Salaam Cape Town
Melbourne Auckland Madrid

and associated companies in
Berlin Ibadan

Library of Congress Cataloging-in-Publication Data
Bayley, David H.
    Police for the future / David H. Bayley.
        p. cm.—(Studies in crime and public policy)
    Includes bibliographical references and index.
    ISBN 0-19-509116-7
    1. Police—Cross-cultural studies.   2. Law enforcement—Cross-
    cultural studies.   I. Title.   II. Series.
HV7921.B36   1994
363.2—dc20   93-46099

9 8 7 6 5 4 3 2

Printed in the United States of America
on acid-free paper

To Chris
Companion of a lifetime

Preface

This book presents a theory of policing. Not a theory in the scientific sense of explaining why police act as they do (although there is some of that), but a theory that explains the choices democratic societies face about the police. Are the police doing what they should? If not, what are the possibilities for improvement? In particular, what are the advantages and disadvantages of continuing as we are or of pressing forward in different ways? This book presents a theory of policy choices. It presents what people need to consider in order to frame police policies intelligently.

The book is based on four years of intensive reserch in five countries—Australia, Great Britain, Canada, Japan, and the United States. These countries are not a representative sample. They were chosen because they are similar politically and economically and are accessible for research on the police. They are countries that can learn from one another, and indeed have often done so. Moreover, I have worked in all of them, and in addition to having useful contacts in these countries, I am familiar with their histories, patterns of development, and national cultures. I did not go to them as a novice.

More generally, the book reflects almost a lifetime of study of the police around the world. My interest began almost by accident in India in 1963 and since then has involved fieldwork on four continents. Over time I have studied strategies, tactical behavior, accountability, misbehavior, formal organization, and innovation. It was time, I thought, to try to see the police institution as a whole. What has it become? What does it need? I wanted to work out whether it is doing what the citizens of democratic countries require and can reasonably expect.

Over the past four years the research in each of the five countries followed a tripartite plan. First, I collected information on the performance of a sample of individual police forces over the past twenty years. None of the countries have centralized systems, although Japan comes close. Detailed data protocols were submitted to each force. The forces were not asked to perform original research but to provide as much of the data as could readily be found in existing records and files. The information that I report, therefore, is a reflection of what police managers themselves have at hand as they make decisions about police activities. The information was then coded and entered into a large database. Altogether, I studied 28 forces: 7 in Australia, 3 in Britain, 6 in Canada, 3 in Japan, and 9 in the United States.

Second, within each police force I collected information about the activities of a cross section of police stations—precincts in the United States, sub-divisions in Britain, and police stations in Australia, Canada, and Japan. Because police operations vary considerably from place to place, I wanted to determine whether there are patterns that are related to socioeconomic conditions. I thought it might be possible to discover whether variations in policing are systematic. The stations were selected on the basis of location—urban, suburban, and rural. The results of this exercise were disappointing. Only gross differences in patterns of policing could be discovered; it was rarely possible to connect them to variations in context because contextual information is either not readily available for local areas or the units of analysis fail to coincide with police-station boundaries. Information about police performance was collected for 47 front-line stations: 12 in Australia, 9 in Britain, 3 in Canada, 12 in Japan, and 11 in the United States.

Third, I observed police operations in the field and interviewed police managers and supervisors at all levels. Besides getting an impression of what policing is like in practice, I wanted to find out what managers think needs to be done in order to improve policing in the near term. I wanted to understand the perspective, the worldview, of the people who are responsible for leading the police. I made a special point of visiting commands where something explicitly new or experimental is taking place.

In this book I sometimes describe the police in unflattering terms. I believe my characterizations to be correct. However, I don't believe the defects of the police are unique or personal. Police are no worse than many other institutions in our society, and certainly no worse than American universities, which is where I work and for which I bear some responsibility. In several respects, universities may be even less rational than the police, despite their pretensions about intellectual superiority, idealism, and selfless service.

When James Thurber, the American humorist, was asked, "How's your wife?" he replied, "Compared with what?" That is exactly the question that should be asked about the inadequacies of the police. Society should hold professors and police officers responsible for whether their institutions contribute as effectively as they might to the objectives of education and public safety. Unfortunately, these very institutions often make it difficult for talented, dedicated, and farsighted faculty and police officers to be responsible for what they are doing in ways that they and their communities would want them to be.

Acknowledgments

Research as extensive as this cannot be carried out without assistance from a host of institutions and individuals. All the forces I visited, as well as the separate commands within them, were invariably welcoming and helpful. Even though I often showed up on short notice, people went to extraordinary lengths to see that my visit accomplished what I hoped. I was often embarrassed, in fact, because I could not devote more time to study their particular activity after they had gone to so much trouble to help me understand it. Their effort often deserved more attention than I could give. Time after time, officers would take my address so that they could send me some additional item of information that was not immediately available. Furthermore, my physical needs were more than amply taken care of. If not wined and dined, at least "coffee'd and lunched." Nor was a chance ever missed to give me a guided tour of the local sights.

With an enormous sense of gratitude, I acknowledge the generous assistance and hospitality of the following police forces: (Australia) New South Wales, Northern Territory, Queensland, South Australia, Victoria, and Western Australia; (Britain) Leicestershire, London, and Northumbria; (Canada) Edmonton, Montreal, Ontario Province, Peel Regional, Royal Canadian Mounted Police, and Vancouver; (Japan) Kochi, Osaka, and Tokyo; and (United States) Aurora, Colorado; Houston, Texas; Los Angeles, California; New York, New York; New York State Police; Portland, Oregon; Rutland, Vermont; Santa Ana, California; Seattle, Washington; and Suffolk County, New York.

The research was supported by grants from several institutions: the Japan Foundation, Tokyo, and the Japanese Federation of Crime Prevention Associations, Tokyo; the National Police Research Unit, Adelaide, South Australia; Office of Research and Demonstration, Ministry of the Solicitor General, Ottawa; the Law and Society Program, National Science Foundation, Washington, DC, grant number SES-9121950; and the Earhart Foundation, Ann Arbor, Michigan. None of the grants would have been prepared or dispersed successfully without the expert support of Sharon Wright and the Hindelang Criminal Justice Research Center, State University of New York at Albany.

I am also very grateful for the reseach assistance I received from K. Hoshino and the staff of the National Institute for Police Research, Tokyo; the National Police Research Unit, Adelaide, South Australia; and Kathleen Maguire and the staff of the *Sourcebook on Criminal Justice Statistics*, State University of New York at Albany.

At the risk of omitting someone who truly "made my day" in some farflung place over the past four years, I am especially grateful to the following people: Jim Albrecht, John Alderson, John Avery, Michael and Marianne Banton, Margaret Beare, John Beck, Des Berwyck, Lenna Bradburn, Chris Braiden, John Braithwaite, Colin Brittan, Lee Brown, John Broughton, Brian Bull, Michael Bullock, David Burge, Bob Burgreen, Tony and Elizabeth Butler, Peter Campbell, L. Chahley, Tom Clewes, Thomas Constantine, Marcia and Ken Dam, Laurence Davidoff, Jim Deschane, P.J. Duggan, David Dunn, John Eck, Nick Eley, Barb (Murphy) Etter, Pat Fitzsimons, Kate Flannery, I. Futaba, Daryl Gates, Kel Glare, Rita Goutam, Peter Grabosky, Dan Guido, K. Hirasawa, Bob and Robyn Holmes, David Hunt, Michael Hurst, Icqbal Jamal, Jeff Jarratt, Peter Jordan, T. Kanemoto, Y. Kaneshige, A. Kanazawa, T. Kato, Les Kennedy, Duncan King, Jim King, Wilf Laidler, Leah Lambert, Clare Lewis, Joann Litven, Robert Lunney, Craig Masterson, Tom and Anne McGranahan, Jr., Gerry McGraw, John McMillan, Doug McNally, Nancy McPherson, Bob Mellia, Michelle Micklethwaite, Ed and Wanda Miles, Setsuo Miyazawa, Dave Moore, Peter and Leonie Morrison, Steve Morrow, Satyanshu Mukherjee, Chris Murphy, Pat Murphy, Toni Murray, N. Nakagawa, I. Nitta, T. Nomura, A. Oosthoek, Tim Ottmeier, Mick Palmer, Linda Papadimitrious, Tom Pine, David Potter, Robert Reiner, Claude Rochon, Jim Ryder, S.H. Shultz, Clifford Shearing, M. Shikita, James Slater, David H. Smith, David J. and Ann Smith, Phillip Stenning, John Stevens, Bob Stewart, Dan Thies, Bob Trojanowicz, Bob Vernon, Bruce and Elen Wyatt, Paul Walters, Alan Warloe, Betsy Watson, Dan Watson, Mollie Weatheritt, Grant Whorlow, Gerald Williams, Peter Winship, Bob Winton, Jerry Woods, Ed Wright, and John Wylie.

During the course of the research I was blessed with having two of the finest graduate research assistants I could imagine: Eric Riksheim and Edward Maguire. They managed the masses of statistical material collected in the five countries, devised the database format, and put the information into machine-readable form. Ed Maguire prepared the codebook and did all the statistical analysis. Both of these talented young men were expert, willing, and responsible. They were also fun to work with.

As usual, I am deeply indebted to my wife, Chris. She makes the work enjoyable and worthwhile, while enduring my gripes, silent preoccupations, and general lunacies, not all of which can be blamed on being a scholar.

Albany, New York   D.H.B.
March 1994

Contents

POLICE FOR THE FUTURE

1

The Myth of the Police

The police do not prevent crime. This is one of the best kept secrets of modern life. Experts know it, the police know it, but the public does not know it. Yet the police pretend that they are society's best defense against crime and continually argue that if they are given more resources, especially personnel, they will be able to protect communities against crime. This is a myth.

What is the evidence for this heretical and disturbing assertion? First, repeated analysis has consistently failed to find any connection between the number of police officers and crime rates. Second, the primary strategies adopted by modern police have been shown to have little or no effect on crime.

Studies of the connection between the strength of police forces and crime rates have been done by comparing police jurisdictions with similar social conditions, determining whether differences in the rate of crime vary with the number of police officers employed (Loftin and McDowall 1982; Krahn and Kennedy 1985; Koenig 1991; Laurie 1970; Gurr 1979; Emsley 1983; Silberman 1978; Reiner 1985; Lane 1980; Walker 1989). For example, in 1987 U.S. cities with populations of over one million had the highest ratios of police to people (320 per 100,000), but they also had the highest rates of serious crime (Bureau of Justice Statistics 1987). In other words, cities with more crime had more police. Moreover, cities with more crime also had more police per crime. Police in high-crime cities, therefore, did not have greater criminal case loads. Among cities with populations over one million, Dallas had the highest crime rate (16,282 per 100,000) and Kansas City, Missouri, the lowest (3,789 per 100,000), yet they had almost exactly the same number of police per capita—2.3 per 1,000 in Dallas and 2.4 per 1,000 in Kansas City.[1] The major city with the highest number of police per capita—Chicago, with 4.1 per 1,000—had a crime rate that was only slightly

3

above the city with the lowest number of police per capita—San Diego, with 1.5 per 1,000. Their respective crime rates were 8,638 and 8,483.[2]

In 1990, Seattle and Houston had one third fewer police officers per capita than Los Angeles (409 vs. 282 police per 1,000 people) but one fourth to one third less violent crime per capita (1,507 and 1,388 vs. 2,384 per 100,000).[3] Furthermore, although Los Angeles had more police officers per capita than Houston or Seattle, violent crime in Los Angeles was twice that in Houston and two thirds higher than that in Seattle.

The plain but disconcerting fact is that differences in crime rates cannot be attributed to variations in the number of police. This discovery is not new. The President's Commission on Law Enforcement and the Administration of Justice pointed it out in 1967.

The lack of connection between crime and police numbers can also be found through analysis of historical trends. For example, between 1970 and 1990 the number of full-time police officers in the United States rose by 70.7%, but serious crimes rose by 78.8% and violent crimes by 147%. Adjusting these figures for increases in population, which affect both the number of crimes committed and the number of police that communities think they need, one sees that the number of police rose 70.6%, the number of serious crimes 46%, and the number of violent crimes 101%. A similar lack of correspondence between changes in the number of police and crime rates can be seen in Australia, Britain, and Canada. In Australia between 1970 and 1990, the number of police per capita rose by 25% and the crime rate by 115%. In Britain between 1977 and 1990, police per capita rose by 12% and the crime rate by 67%. In Canada between 1970 and 1990, police per capita rose by 16% and the crime rate by 34%.[4]

Since World War II, increases in the numbers of police have closely paralleled increases in crime rates. Detailed analysis has shown that communities hire more police when they see crime rates rising. But this is a desperate game of catch-up that has no effect on the rate of increase in crime. Additional police officers do not slow, even temporarily, the rate of increase.

A few ingenious studies have explored what happens when the number of police is suddenly reduced in communities—for example, as a result of strikes or significant layoffs due to budgetary crises. Surprisingly, crime rates are again unaffected (Pfuhl 1983, Clarke and Hough 1984).

No one seriously proposes on the basis of these studies that police be disbanded and sent home, although that would save a great deal of money. Although criminals do not seem to notice normal changes in the number of police, they would surely notice if there were no police. It is probably also true that at some point adding police would make a difference in how much crime occurs. If there were a police officer on every corner or on every doorstep, crime would almost surely go down. In other words, there are probably critical thresholds beyond which changing the number of police would affect crime. The problem is that no one knows what these thresholds are. Would half as many, for instance, be too few or would twice as many be just enough to change crime patterns? What are the critical numbers? All that one can reasonably conclude is that the increases and decreases that are likely to occur in the number of police as a result of normal political and budgetary pressures will not make any difference in the incidence of crime. It is unlikely that the bottom will fall out of public safety if we reduce the number of police, even quite substantially, and it is equally unlikely that crime will be reduced if we try to spend our way to safety by adding police officers. Changes in the number of police within any practicable range will have no effect on crime.

Summing up all the evidence, the authoritative Audit Commission (1991, p. 12) in Britain recently wrote: "The terms of public debate need to move off the assumption that more police officers and more police expenditures lead to a commensurate increase in the quantity and quality of police outputs." Or as one distinguished U.S. police executive said, U.S. police chiefs should stop acting like urban generals "who keep throwing men into battles without any evidence that this will win the war" (Bouza 1990, pp. 130–131).

The second sort of evidence that demonstrates the ineffectiveness of the police in preventing crime comes from evaluations of the impact on crime of the three core strategies of contemporary policing: street patrolling by uniformed officers, rapid response to emergency calls, and expert investigation of crime by detectives. These are the activities that police themselves believe to be essential for protecting public safety. These are the functions they say will prevent crime. Unfortunately, there is no evidence that they do.

Research has consistently failed to show that the intensity of random motorized patrolling by uniformed officers has any effect on crime rates, victimization, or even public satisfaction (Kelling et al. 1974, Kelling 1985, Morris and Heal 1981).[5] The number of patrols in an area may be doubled, halved, or even removed altogether without changing crime levels. Saturation patrolling—flooding areas with uniformed police officers—does have an effect on crime, but it is too expensive to be more than a short-term expedient. The general conclusion is that some routine motorized patrolling is probably better than none, but that more is not better than some—at least not within practicable limits. Police in Edmonton, Canada, point out that one of the city's high-crime areas, notorious for prostitution and rowdy bars, is also one of the most heavily patrolled areas because it is just down the street from police headquarters. Patrolling, as Samuel Walker has said, is like mayonnaise: a little goes a long way (Walker 1989).

Patrolling on foot by uniformed officers appears to be slightly more useful. Although it does not affect the amount of crime, it does reassure the public psychologically, reducing their fear of crime and increasing their satisfaction with police service (Police Foundation 1981; Kelling 1985). In other words, police foot patrols make people feel better, but they do not prevent crime.

Rapid response by the police to emergency calls, usually over the well-publicized emergency telephone number, are supposed to help prevent crime by increasing the chances that criminals will be caught and punished. Emergency response is supposed to enhance the capacity of the criminal justice system as a whole to deter crime through punishment. Again, unfortunately, although many studies have sought to find it, there is no evidence that reducing the time the police take to get to crime scenes increases the chances that criminals will be caught (Tien, Simon, and Larson 1978; Bieck and Kessler 1977; Spelman and Brown 1981). One qualification needs to be made: If police can arrive within one minute of the commission of an offense, they are more likely to catch the suspect. Any later and the chances of capture are very small, probably less than one in ten. As a general matter, however, this fast a response rarely occurs. Although the police can sometimes "stake out" likely criminal locations, waiting for crime to happen, this strategy is costly. Whereas crime in the aggregate is fairly predictably distributed over large areas, specific criminal events are not, so that the chances are very small a police patrol will be nearby when a crime is committed. The familiar complaint, "Why isn't there a police officer around when you need one?" expresses a fundamental truth. Unless police are everywhere, they will almost never be where they are needed. Consequently, they will almost never arrive quickly enough to make a difference in the probability of arrest.

Police initiatives to reduce the time of response to crime calls are undermined, no matter how expertly they are implemented, by a factor outside police control—namely, the time taken by victims or witnesses to notify the police. In most cases of theft or burglary, criminals are long gone by the time the victim discovers the loss. Even in confrontational crimes, when victim and criminal are face to face, it commonly takes as long as twenty minutes for police to be notified. The reasons are understandable. Crime is traumatic, and victims are likely to seek support from family members, friends, and neighbors before they call the police. They are apt to be disoriented, making it difficult to find a phone, find the number to call, or report the crime coherently. What this means is that although the police may work heroically to reduce response time, their best efforts will not make a big enough difference to change the outcome. Criminals will almost always have a big head start.

Contrary to what most police think, rapid response is not even a key element in satisfying the public (Percey 1980, Bieck and Kessler 1977). Most of the time a predictable response is more important than a speedy one. The exception, of course, is when there is a genuine emergency and a crime is in progress at the moment of notification. Then a speedy response is critical. But such calls are comparatively rare, probably representing no more than 5–7% of all the calls made to the police over the emergency number (interviews with police departments 1990–1992, Reiss 1971). In all other cases, crime victims seem to understand that a quick response is not going to be particularly helpful. Therefore, what they want to know is when the police are really going to show up so that they don't have to sit around waiting but can start to put their lives back in order. It is more important, then, for the police to make reasonable promises they can keep than to reduce average response times by several minutes.

Finally, the success the police have in criminal investigations has no appreciable effect on public security. When crimes occur the responsibility of the police is to find and apprehend the suspect and then to collect evidence that can be used in subsequent prosecution and trial. Police success is measured by clearance rates—that is, the ratio of crimes solved to the number of crimes reported to the police. In the United States this is somewhat misleadingly referred to as the arrest rate, because arrest is what usually happens when the police complete their investigation and pass matters on to prosecutors. In any case, arrest or clearance rates have not been found to be related to crime rates. Strange as it may seem, the crime rate is not affected by the rate of success the police have in solving crimes. For instance, although the percentage of violent crimes cleared by arrest in the United States between 1980 and 1990 rose from 43.6% to 45.6%, the rate for violent crimes also increased—and by a whopping 22.7% during the same period (*Sourcebook* 1991, Tables 3.127 and 4.21). If criminals noticed the increased efficiency of the police, they certainly didn't seem to care.

In all probability, the relationship does not run from clearances to crime but from crime to clearances. That is, success in making arrests for known offenses does not reduce crime, but the amount and nature of crime determine how successful the police are likely to be in solving crime (Laurie 1970, Burrows 1986). Contrary to what people expect and hope, crime patterns have a greater effect on the success of criminal investigations than the success of criminal investigations has on crime patterns.

Studies have found that the critical ingredient in solving crimes is whether the public—victims and witnesses—provide information to the police that helps identify the suspect (Greenwood, Petersilia, and Chaiken 1977, Eck 1982). This information might be a name, an address, a license plate, or a presumed relationship to the victim. Neither the amount of attention given to an investigation nor the way in which a police force is organized for criminal investigation affects clearance rates. Contrary to the picture painted by movies, television, and detective novels, successful investigations do not usually begin with the collection of small physical clues that lead to the identification of the suspect. Instead, successful investigations most often begin with the presumed identity of a suspect, which allows the investigators to collect information that will support prosecution. Studies show that unless the public can specifically identify suspects to the police, the chances that a crime will be solved fall to about 10% (Greenwood, Petersilia, and Chaiken 1977, Eck 1982, Royal Commission on Criminal Procedure 1981). On their own, police are relatively helpless, regardless of the resources they devote to criminal investigation.[6]

Police might argue that it isn't their fault that clearance rates do not affect the crime rate, believing that their best efforts are being undermined by the failure of the rest of the criminal justice system, especially the courts, to follow through by convicting and punishing. Police are often highly critical of "turnstile justice," with known felons either being immediately released on bail or given what seem to be slaps on the wrist. They complain bitterly about defendants being found innocent on procedural technicalities; plea bargains that reduce serious charges to minor offenses; and the liberal use of probation, fines, and community service, which allows criminals to avoid prison.

Police are undoubtedly right in arguing that the preventive effect of their work depends on actions by prosecutors, judges, parole officers, and corrections officials that are beyond their control. But they are wrong in thinking that if the system backed them more solidly fewer crimes would be committed and society would be safer. Neither the deterrent—fear producing—nor incapacitating—criminal removing— effects of criminal sanctions have been proven (Walker 1989, Chap. 6). The United States, which has the highest crime rates of any developed democratic country, also has the largest proportion of its population in either jail or prison. In 1990, for every 100,000 people in the United States, 426 were behind bars (Canada, Correctional Services 1991). This number was over ten times that of the Netherlands, the country with the lowest rate. Canada, Britain, and Australia, all with crime rates lower than that of the United States, had much lower incarceration rates. The Canadian rate was 112.7, approximately one fourth the U.S. rate; Britain's was 97.4, Australia's 78.8, and Japan's 42. As a panel of the National Academy of Sciences noted, prison time for every violent offense tripled in the United States between 1975 and 1989, yet crime rates continued to rise ("Biological and Genetic Factors in Violence," *New York Times* 13 November 1992). And though the United States steadily puts people to death for heinous crimes, almost uniquely among democratic countries, the deterrent effect of the death penalty is still hotly debated, with the preponderance of evidence on the side of no effect (Walker 1989).[7] In other words, despite the fact that the United States has the toughest criminal sanctions among the countries with which it likes to be compared, its crime rates are also the highest and show no signs of dropping.

The plain fact is that police actions cannot be shown to reduce the amount of crime. Whose fault this may be is largely beside the point because it is doubtful that even if the criminal justice system became substantially more sure or more severe, crime rates would respond as we would wish. With respect to police policy, therefore, Patrick V. Murphy, a former police commissioner in New York City, was surely right when he said that "police executives can rest assured that whatever they do is not going to make the situation worse."

The damning conclusion that the police are not preventing crime rests entirely on a large body of research undertaken for the most part during the 1970s. Try as they might, researchers were unable, often at considerable cost, to show that the number of police, the amount of money spent on police, or the methods police use had any effect on crime. This is still the consensus among experts. But was this research good enough to support the sweeping conclusion that police are largely ineffective against crime? Most of the studies cited contained flaws of some sort. Some have been severely criticized. Moreover, it has become a truism that such evaluations, whether they are applied to police practices or to those of other criminal justice agencies, generally fail to find compelling evidence of effectiveness. It could be, therefore, either that better studies might produce favorable evidence or that the conditions for detecting crime-preventive effects are too demanding for the research techniques of social science. In either case, the police may be more useful than it appears.

Athough the research done so far may not be the last word, it places the burden of proof squarely on the police. Police everywhere promise to "serve and protect." Robert Peel, who created the London Metropolitan Police in 1829—the first modern force in the English-speaking world— said, "I want to teach people that liberty does not consist in having your house robbed by organized gangs of thieves, and in leaving the principal streets of London in nightly possession of drunken women and vagabonds" (Critchley 1967, p. 54). These words sound contemporary, don't they? If this is what police promise, then it's reasonable to ask them to show that they are doing what they say. But they haven't. The "evidence" they produce is entirely a matter of anecdote, intuition, and gut instinct. The academic research may be flawed, but it is more rigorous and systematic than what the police have relied on so far. The public has a right to be skeptical about the claims of the police when it has been so difficult to show even the slightest effect of police actions on crime.

The best that can be argued is that the impact the police are having on crime may be so subtle that it is difficult to detect. But this isn't what the police promise. They promise a real, perceptible improvement in public safety as a result of their actions.

It is time for the police to "put up or shut up." If the studies are true, then police practices should change. If the studies are unacceptable, then new research needs to be undertaken. The importance of protecting society from crime is too important to leave unexamined. The police shouldn't be expected to do it because the results are potentially too threatening. Academics might take on such research, but they haven't the financial resources. The responsibility rests, then, with governments. Governments should either resolve the doubts about the usefulness of the police or face up to the conclusion that preventing crime requires a great deal more than pouring money into law enforcement.

That the police are not able to prevent crime should not come as a big surprise to thoughtful people. It is generally understood that social conditions outside the control of the police, as well as outside the control of the criminal justice system as a whole, determine crime levels in communities. Police themselves recognize this, often complaining that they are expected to protect communities from the consequences of their own neglect. In a phrase police often use, they see themselves as a "band-aid on cancer."

Crime experts generally accept that the best predictors of crime are factors such as employment status, income, education levels, gender, age, ethnic mix, and family composition. A precise figure can't be put on it, but most—perhaps as much as 90%—of the differences in crime rates among communities can be explained by differences in such factors (Sampson 1987, Avison and Loring 1986, Williams 1984, Skogan 1990, McGahey 1986, Wilks 1967, Cohen 1985, Braithwaite 1989, Bennett 1983, Currie 1985, Walker 1989, Silberman 1978, pp. 171–172, Furstenberg and Wellford 1973, Wellford 1974, Chaiken and Chaiken 1983). To give only one example from a voluminous literature, Cohen, Felson, and Land (1983) found that between 1947 and 1977 such factors could account for 96.5% of the differences in robbery rates, 99% of the differences in burglary rates, and 99.3% of the differences in auto-theft rates throughout the United States.[8] It is not really surprising, then, that finding evidence the police prevent crime is so difficult. Police shouldn't be expected to prevent crime: They are outgunned by circumstances.

There are indications, however, that the public has begun to figure out that the police do not prevent crime and cannot be expected to. One indication is the growth of the private security industry over the past thirty years. In the United States in 1990 there were three times as many private security agents as public police—2 million versus 650,000 (Mangan and Shanahan 1990, *Sourcebook* 1991). From 1960 through 1990, relative to population, the number of private security personnel has increased faster than the number of police officers—174% versus 103% (Nalla and Newman 1991, Table 1). It has been projected that during the 1990s private security agents will grow annually at double the rate of public police (Cunningham et al. 1991).

The situation is similar in Britain and Canada, where there are twice as many private security agents as public police, and the rate of growth for the private sector is again faster than for the public (Fielding 1991, Toronto Police Department 1990, p. 36).

This means that as crime rates have risen, and with them the public's fear and apprehension, the police monopoly on public safety has eroded. Police have quietly been supplanted in shopping malls, stores, banks, office buildings, apartment houses, single-family residential communities, urban cul-de-sacs, schools and colleges, and factories. The police have been pushed out of what has been called "private public space," that is, premises owned by private individuals but routinely accessible to the public or at least the public with a reason to be there (Shearing and Stenning 1980). Although the police continue to have legal jurisdiction in such places, tangible protection is increasingly provided by private security guards, who have become the first line of practical defense against crime in much of modern life (Stenning 1989, Miyazawa 1991).

There are other signs that public confidence in the police is declining. During the last few years organized self-protection activities on the part of communities have mushroomed. Almost every city has block watches; citizen foot patrols; escort services for senior citizens; radio-alert networks for buses, taxis, and commercial trucks; and citizen-band (CB) radio automobile patrols. In New York City, for example, by 1985 over 151,000 people were involved in crime-prevention programs (New York State 1985, p. 89). In Washington, DC, over 100 neighborhood patrols were created between 1988 and 1991, involving over 6,000 people (*Washington Post*, 17 January 1991, p. 1). Serving primarily as extra eyes and ears for the police, these patrols actively try to discourage criminal activity, especially drug dealing, that takes place on the streets. This widespread trend toward citizen involvement, often actively encouraged by the police, reflects a deeply felt need to supplement the usual police protection (Grabosky 1992).

In democratic countries all over the world, then, there is a sense of crisis about public security. And at the center of this crisis are the police, who promise to protect us but do not appear to be able to do so. We want them to be effective, but increasingly we have doubts that they are. Police are expensive, and we don't know whether they should be replaced—even though this is quietly occurring.

The purpose of this book is to discuss this crisis in policing and the choices available to us. If law enforcement as currently constituted is not preventing crime, what can be done, and what might be the role of the police? The fundamental issue is whether we really want the police to prevent crime more effectively. In order to determine this, three questions need to be answered: (1) Why haven't the police been effective in preventing crime? (2) What might the police do to become effective crime deterrents? and (3) Considering the requirements, do we want the police to be effective? These questions are taken up in the three major parts of the book—"Problems," "Possibilities," and "Solutions."

Part I, "Problems," begins with Chapter 2, "What Do the Police Do?" and describes what the police are doing and whether they can reasonably be expected to reduce crime. Chapter 3, "How Much Is Enough?" analyzes whether the police are getting enough resources to prevent crime, how decisions about resource allocations are made, and what the police do with their resources. Chapter 4, "The View from Inside," examines the organizational structure and culture of the police, with particular attention to the way these factors affect the ability of police officers to respond creatively to new challenges.

In Part II, "Possibilities," Chapter 5, "Agendas for Change," describes the organizational reforms in contemporary police forces that might have an impact on their ability to protect society from crime. Chapter 6, "Taking Crime Prevention Seriously," examines the strategic efforts police are making to become more effective at crime prevention.

Part III, "Solutions," has two chapters. Chapter 7, "Options for Policing," discusses the choices democratic communities have with respect to the crime-prevention role of the police. Chapter 8, "A Blueprint for the Future," presents a plan for an effective crime-prevention police force that is compatible with democratic institutions and values.

I

PROBLEMS

2

What Do the Police Do?

The radio call came to the patrol officer late on a warm spring afternoon, directing him to investigate an automobile accident in a suburban residential neighborhood. At the scene he found a tow truck and its disgruntled operator gazing at the remains of an accident. According to the tow-truck driver, the driver of a 20-year-old Plymouth sedan had lost control of the vehicle at the intersection, crashed into a street sign, knocked over two newspaper vending machines, and careened through a bush onto the front lawn of a house. Muddy car tracks could be seen, and the broken vending machines were lying on the lawn. The driver of the car, who was drunk and abusive, had refused to wait for the police after the tow truck arrived. He and his car disappeared down the street and around a corner. The tow-truck operator supplied the license plate number and a full description of the car and driver. Checking by radio with radio dispatch, the police officer confirmed what he had suspected: The driver lived only a few blocks away.

Arriving at a modest, single-story, stucco house, the officer saw that a car matching the description he had was parked in the driveway. It had a dented front end, two broken headlights, and dirt on the hood. No one answered the door when the officer knocked, even though he could see through a large picture window a young woman working in the kitchen; he also caught a glimpse of an older woman in a wheelchair moving out of sight down a hall. Angry that he was being ignored, the officer pushed open the letter drop in the door and shouted that if the door wasn't opened immediately, the car was going to be towed away and impounded. At that, a disheveled man moved out from behind the door, pulled back the bolts, and mutely beckoned the officer in.

The suspect, who was 70 years old, according to his automobile registration information, collected the woman in the wheelchair and pushed her into the middle of the living room. The man was unshaven

15

and slovenly dressed in old shoes, a work shirt, and brown slacks. He lowered himself heavily onto the couch, cursing and wondering aloud "what the fuck this officer is doing here." The officer explained the situation to the bright-eyed, white-haired elderly woman in the wheelchair and told her that he would have to arrest her husband for driving while intoxicated and for leaving the scene of an accident. "I'm not his wife," the old woman said in a quavery voice, "I'm his mother, and I'm 100 years old."

While the officer wrote out the traffic citation, the mother, tearful and agitated, pleaded with the officer not to take her son away. She was 100 years old, she said again and again, because "I have lived with the Lord and he has lived with me." Proud of her age, she insisted on rolling her chair up to the officer to demonstrate that she could actually stand up. Against the pleas of the officer, who was afraid she would keel over and die on the spot, she grasped the arms of the wheelchair and slowly levered herself up to a half crouch. "See," she said triumphantly, "I can half stand up."

Recognizing that he could not possibly arrest the slovenly old drunk and take him to jail as he richly deserved, the officer gave the man the traffic citation and shook hands with the aged mother. As the officer moved toward the door, he commented brightly that he hoped she would continue in good health so she could celebrate her 110th birthday. The grizzled son muttered disgustedly from the couch, "Oh God!"

The officer got wearily back into the patrol car and reported himself "in service."

This is what the police do. This is real police work. The reason the police are not preventing crime is because what they do in practice has little relation to crime or to the conditions that produce crime.

Patrolling

Sixty percent of police officers are assigned so they may do the kind of work just described. These are patrol officers, working around the clock every day of the year, in uniform, usually in marked radio patrol cars. Patrol is by far the biggest assignment in policing. From my study of 28 forces, 65% of police officers are assigned to patrol work in the United States, 64% in Canada, 56% in Britain, 54% in Australia, and 40% in Japan.[1]

Patrol work is determined almost entirely by what the public asks the police to do. Driving slowly around their assigned beats, patrol officers wait for radio dispatchers to relay calls that have come over the well-publicized police emergency telephone numbers (911 in the United States and Canada, 999 in Britain, 000 in Australia, and 110 in Japan).

Since the radio determines almost all that patrol officers do, they become almost magically attentive to it. Experienced patrol officers can pick their particular call sign out of static and the chatter of other calls despite engine noise or the hum of air conditioning or while conversing with partners or members of the public. Many officers even listen to two radios—one tuned to dispatch, the other to a popular music station.

In cities, over 90% of the work of patrol officers is generated by dispatch. Self-initiated, or proactive, work, in police jargon, occurs more frequently in less developed and rural areas (Reiss 1971, Southgate and Eckblom 1984, President's Commission on Law Enforcement and the Administration of Justice 1967a, McCabe and Sutcliffe 1978, Ericson 1982, Bayley 1985). Stopping motor vehicles that have violated traffic laws accounts for the largest portion of self-generated work, at least in Australia, Canada, and the United States. Patrol officers spend the rest of their time discouraging behavior that officers view as disruptive or unseemly, such as drunks sleeping in front of doorways, teenage boys lollygagging on a street corner, prostitutes soliciting in a blue-collar residential neighborhood, or men urinating against a wall around the corner from a busy bar.

Contrary to what many people think, the police do not enforce their own conception of order on an unwilling populace. Almost all they do is undertaken at the request of some member of the public. If the public stopped calling the police, the police would have to reinvent their job.

Very little of the work patrol officers do has to do with crime. British and U.S. studies have consistently shown that not more than 25% of all calls to the police are about crime; more often the figure is 15–20%. (Whitaker et al. 1981, Southgate and Ekblom 1984, Scott 1980, Morris and Heal 1981, Thames Valley Police 1991). In Tokyo in 1990, the figure was less than 25%. A survey of calls to police in Britain during one eight-hour period in February 1991 showed that of 30,000 incidents reported throughout the country, 17% were crime related. Eighty-five percent of these reports had to do with property crime, such as burglary or theft (reported in *The Independent*, 18 June 1992). Moreover, what is initially reported by the public as crime is often found not to be crime by the police who respond (Gilsinian 1989, Reiss 1971). Residents of a low-income apartment building may tell the police dispatcher that there is "a man with a gun on the fourth floor"—when, in fact, a child has been trapped in an elevator that is stuck between floors. Lonely elderly people may report burglaries in progress so that police will come and talk with them for a while. Thus the real proportion of requests to the police that involve crime may be more like 7–10%.

Most of the genuine crime that police are called upon to handle is distinctly minor. Not unimportant necessarily—certainly not to the people involved—but a far cry from the senseless violence and mayhem that newpapers and television lead the public to expect. Using the categories provided by the well-known Uniform Crime Reports, one finds that from 1984 to 1990 violent crime (homicide, forcible rape, aggravated assault, robbery) averaged 12.6% of total serious crime (violent crime plus burglary, larceny theft, and auto theft) in the United States (*Sourcebook*, 1991, Table 3.127). In Australia, violent crime accounts for about 2.3% of serious crime (Mukherjee and Dagger 1991).[2] The ratio of violent to serious crime tends to be higher in large cities, but violent crime still represents only 25% of total crime in New York City, 12% in Houston, 26% in Los Angeles, 16% in Montreal, and 16.7% in Toronto.

If one compared violent crime to all crime, no matter how trivial, such as minor shoplifting, disturbing the peace, vandalism, minor property theft, and so on, the proportion would be much lower indeed. During 1990 the proportion was 11% in New York City, 6% in Houston, 10% in Seattle, and 18% in Los Angeles. The proportion of serious or violent crime to total crime cannot be computed for the United States as a whole because no national figure on total crime is published. In 1990, violent crimes were 0.76% of all crime in Australia, 8.5% in Canada, 4.7% in Britain, and 1% in Japan.

In order to demonstrate the dimensions of the "real" crime problem, the Leicestershire police force in the industrial Midlands of Britain estimated that the most common serious crime was auto crime. There were 6.94 such crimes for every 100 people, 60% of which was thefts from unattended motor vehicles. Indeed, in Britain as a whole, auto crime accounted for one third of all reported crime, according to an article in *The Guardian*, 22 May 1992. In Leicestershire, burglary was the next most common crime (3.65 per 100 persons), followed by other thefts (2.3), other crimes (1.75), and, lastly, crimes against the person (0.56). In other words, people fear most what is least likely to happen to them.

Not only is crime a minor part of patrol work and often not especially serious, the trail is almost always cold by the time the police arrive, with the culprit having been gone for hours and often days. This is typical of crimes against property, the largest category of serious crimes. A typical example was the summons to police in the north of England to a car whose driver's-side window had been smashed. Glass was lying in the car, and the contents of the vehicle appeared to have been rifled. The patrol officer quickly identified the owner of the car from the license number, a doctor who worked at a nearby hospital. After having asked that the doctor be telephoned about what had happened, the officer waited thirty minutes for him to appear. Finding that only an old pair of tennis shoes had been stolen, the officer briskly advised the doctor how to get the police case number in order to file an insurance claim and went on his way.

If the majority of police officers are not directly fighting crime, what are they doing? The answer is that they are restoring order and providing general assistance. In the apt words of Egon Bittner (1970), the key function of the police is to stop "something-that-ought-not-to-be-happening-and-about-which-someone-had-better-do-something-now." Police interrupt and pacify situations of potential or ongoing conflict. Typical instances are young men drinking beer on a street corner and making rude remarks; people playing rock music at a high volume late at night in an apartment; kids turning on a fire hydrant to provide a shower on a hot summer day; homeless people begging and sleeping in the corridors of a busy bus terminal; slippery mud accumulating on a highway where trucks turn out from a gravel pit; tenants refusing to leave an apartment from which they have been evicted; a dog barking persistently late at night; a truculent and inconsiderate neighbor obstructing a driveway with his car; kids playing on a tractor trailer parked overnight in a vacant lot; teenagers sitting in booths at a fast-food restaurant, not placing orders but using the paper cups for wine they have brought with them; a thirty-ish couple refusing a theater manager's request to leave after they have insisted on bringing in their own homemade popcorn.

The most common, as well as the most difficult, conflict situations police handle are disputes within families. Officers around the world claim that such disturbances are more common on the days when public assistance checks are delivered, because then people have money to drink. Police everywhere are also convinced that disturbances of all sorts increase when the moon is full.

Police believe that family disputes are very dangerous and risky to them, although research indicates that this is not true. Apart from auto accidents, police are most likely to be killed or injured dealing with armed robberies and arresting persons carrying concealed weapons (Garner and Clemmer 1986, Margarita 1980). Most of the time fighting stops when the police show up; police rarely have to intervene physically (Bayley and Garafolo 1988). Nonetheless, police officers like to tell stories about especially clever things they have done to pacify conflict. For example, a young but experienced female officer swears she stopped a fight in a "biker" bar by saying, "Has anybody got a cigarette? I've spaced mine out and left them in the car." The hard-bitten bikers were so distracted in finding a cigarette that they forgot what they were fighting about. Another officer got so irritated at a married couple who refused to stop shouting at each other that he blew his whistle as loud as he could, threw his pocket handkerchief in the air, and proclaimed, "Fifteen yard penalty for unsportsmanlike conduct," mimicking a National Football League official. Startled, the couple broke down laughing. Another officer took advantage of the display of religious decor in a house by asking a young husband and wife, "What would the Lord want you to do?" They made up and asked him to shut the front door behind him as they made their way up the stairs, arms entwined.

When officers are called to actual or potential conflicts they try to "sort out," as the British say, what has been going on and to produce a truce that will last until the officer gets away. Is there an offense? Who is the victim? Who is the culprit? This searching for the truth is often very difficult. People lie brazenly, which explains in large part why the police become cynical and hard to convince. For example, a 40-year-old woman with blonde, bouffant hair insisted that she had not been driving the Cadillac that hit and demolished a parked red sports car, despite the fact that four eyewitnesses reported that they saw her get out of the car. Or people tell self-serving, partially true stories. One example is the middle-aged black man in a three-piece suit who said he was an off-duty security guard and wanted help from two police officers in finding an alleged assailant. After an exhausting chase on a stifling hot day, it turned out the two were brothers; they had been dealing narcotics, and the complainant had never been a security guard.

The police "sort out" situations by listening patiently to endless stories about fancied slights, old grievances, new insults, mismatched expectations, indifference, infidelity, dishonesty, and abuse. They hear about all the petty, mundane, tedious, hapless, sordid details of individual lives. None of it is earthshaking, or worthy of a line in a newspaper—not the stuff that government policy can address, not even especially spicy: just the begrimed reality of the lives of people who have no one else to take their problems to. Patient listening and gentle counseling are undoubtedly what patrol officers do most of the time.

Most of the time the police do not use the criminal law to restore calm and order. They rarely make arrests, although the threat of doing so always exists. Research into the handling of domestic disputes in the United States has shown that police routinely pursue eight different courses of action (Bayley 1986). Most commonly, they simply leave after listening, without doing anything at all (23.7% of cases). Next, they give friendly advice about how to avoid a repetition of the incident (16.1%). Arrest is the third most frequently used action, occurring in 13.9% of incidents. British police, similarly, make arrests in domestic disputes about 23% of the time. Fifty percent of the time, they only "advise" (Shapland and Hobbs 1989). Police also pointedly warn people about what will happen if they are called back; promise future help if it is needed; give explicit advice to one or the other about what they should do to extricate themselves from the conflict; make sure that one party leaves the scene; or suggest referral to third parties, professional or otherwise (MacIver and Parks 1981)

The infrequency of arrests is not just true of police responses to disputes. In general, patrol officers, who are responsible for most contacts with the general population, rarely make arrests. In the United States in 1990, police officers made an average of 19 arrests a year (*Sourcebook*

1991).[3] That is less than one arrest per officer every 15 working days, and it includes arrests of all sorts. Data from the six largest police forces in the United States in 1986 show that officers make only 1.7 arrests each year for a violent crime and 3.0 arrests each year for a property crime (Pate and Hamilton 1990). In Canada, police officers make one criminal arrest a month and encounter a recordable criminal offense only once a week (Ericson and Shearing 1986).

Although police rarely enforce the law in their manifold encounters with people, it would be wrong to suggest that the power to arrest is not important. The threat is potent, whatever the outcome of particular encounters. The power to arrest gives the police tremendous leverage. It is what makes their intervention authoritative. Police *can* forcibly stop people from doing what they are doing. Police *can* legally throw people on the ground and cuff their hands behind their back; they *can* shackle them to iron benches in police stations; they *can* order people to kneel on sidewalks with their faces pressed against brick walls; they *can* force them to lie prone on dirty sidewalks while police dogs stand guard; and they *can* push people into bare cells with wet concrete floors and slam shut the heavy barred door behind them. As U.S. police officers sometimes say, "Maybe I can't give 'em the rap [a conviction], but I can sure give 'em the ride."

Disputes are not the only situations in which the police are called upon to intervene authoritatively. People come to the police with all sorts of urgent problems, hoping they will be able to help. These requests, which vastly outnumber disturbances, are as varied as the needs of the public. Such calls require service, not force or law enforcement. In the United States requests of this kind are referred to as cats-in-a-tree situations and in Australia as frogs-in-the-drain cases. Such situations vary—from a woman who brought her parakeet to the police station to be weighed because she thought it was sick; to a man who stopped a patrol car in the hope of finding a pair of needle-nosed pliers to repair his stuck trouser zipper; to a girl who called the police to find out her zip code; to a senile woman who lost her blankets, which police found in her deep freeze; to an invalid living alone who fell out of bed and couldn't climb back in without assistance; to a very sick old woman whose family called the police to determine if she needed to go to a hospital; to a middle-aged housewife who couldn't get a response to a phone call or a knock on a neighbor's door; to a secretary locked out of her house; to an apartment resident who wanted a stuck car horn turned off in the parking lot; to a man who wanted the police to notify his sister, who didn't have a phone, that their brother had died.

Contrary to what one normally sees on television, most patrol work is boring, whether it involves restoring order or providing services. A typical evening shift in a patrol car in almost any city in Australia, Britain, Canada, Japan, and the United States is something like this.

3 P.M.: The shift begins with a brief informal roll call, or "parade," as the British say, during which notices are read, wanted persons and vehicles are listed, and important events of the past shift are mentioned.

3:30 P.M.: The pair of officers drive slowly along major commercial streets and up and down alleys, showing the flag, looking for stolen cars, and watching for motoring offenses.

4:30 P.M.: They go to a garage to pick up a police car that had been taken in for repairs.

4:50–5:05 P.M.: They take a statement from a yuppie couple who returned from work to discover that their ground-floor condominium had been burglarized for the fourth time in six months.

5:30–5:45 P.M.: The radio dispatcher sends them to a small grocery store to investigate a shoplifting. The shoplifter turns out to be a six-year-old named Gordon. The proprietress doesn't want to prosecute—indeed, has fed Gordon, whom she thought looked hungry. So the officers take Gordon home. Gordon's mother thanks the police, explaining that Gordon often runs off late in the afternoon.

6:30 P.M.: The officers pick up Chinese food, which they take to the police station, where they also take some extra time to catch up on paperwork.

7:50 P.M.: They resume patrol.

7:55–8:10 P.M.: The radio sends them to the apartment of a single woman living alone, who complains that she is being harassed, this time by having her telephone line cut outside in the hall, perhaps by a drug-addicted woman she had befriended.

8:13–8:20 P.M.: The officers volunteer to cover an ambulance that is attending an injury resulting from a fight at a shelter for homeless alcoholics. When the officers arrive, they find paramedics treating a man who had fallen down outside the shelter. The woman supervising the shelter hasn't called either the ambulance or the police and wonders who did.

8:30 P.M.: Patrolling down a narrow alley, the officers follow a man and a woman who have come out of the gate of a well-known brothel. As they get into a red sports car, the officers stop them and check their identification.

8:35–8:45 P.M.: A middle-aged store owner with a foreign accent stops the patrol car to complain that local derelicts have stolen his heavy-duty plastic refuse bags. The officers find the bright blue bags a block away being used as ground cover by homeless men who are sleeping on a concrete loading platform. The bags are reclaimed, the homeless men claiming that the bags were just lying around.

8:50–9:10 P.M.: The officers are called to take a report from a young couple whose car was lightly damaged in a hit-and-run accident.

9:20 P.M.: Attracted by the flashing dome light of another police car, the officers stop to watch the unit investigate a silent alarm at an Esso service station. The alarm is false.

9:50–9:55 P.M.: Notified that a robbery is in progress, the officers drive in short, fast bursts, according to the traffic, with the dome light flashing but not sounding the siren, to a small milk bar. The report is false. However, there are three sodden 50-year-old black men sitting on the step of the milk bar. One of them truculently stands up and says, "Shoot me, shoot me, too," referring to a well-publicized police shooting earlier in the week. Concluding that the owner probably invented the crime to get the police to come, the officers leave the drunks exactly as they found them.

10:00–10:20 P.M.: The officers are called to public housing. A man is worried about an older woman who lives alone and isn't responding to phone calls. The man and other neighbors agree this has happened before because the woman takes strong sleeping pills. The officers advise the neighbors to call in the morning if she doesn't appear.

10:35 P.M.: They try unsuccessfully to serve a subpoena for a court appearance to a man who isn't home.

10:50 P.M.: The officers return to the station, turn in their equipment, file one or two minor reports, and report off duty.

Most of the incidents to which patrol officers respond are routine and undramatic. A survey of police officers in Canada found that only 6.4% of their contacts with the public could be described as exciting (Ericson 1982, p. 163, Shapland and Hobbs 1989). Los Angeles police estimate that not more than 7% of their dispatched calls require an emergency response. Police in Edmonton, Canada, say the number is 18%; police in Seattle 13%; and the Kent Contabulary, Britain, 4%. As a rule of thumb in the United States, patrol cars drive hell-for-leather, sirens blaring and lights flashing, to about 10% of all mobilizations (Farmer and Furstenberg 1979, Clairmont 1988). Actually, officers soon learn that often what seems like an emergency probably isn't, so they often dawdle in situations that would seem to require a fast response. At other times, they drive fast for no reason except to relieve boredom.

Patrol officers spend a lot of time simply waiting for something to happen—a summons from dispatch, a supervisor to show up, ambulances to arrive, detectives to finish with a crime scene, tow trucks to haul a car away, relatives to be summoned, and the fire department to flush gasoline off the street. When the public sees officers gathered in tight knots in the middle of what seems like great excitement, with flashing lights and emergency vehicles, the police are probably discussing the promotion chart, their next leave, and where to eat lunch.

The working world of the patrol officer is a peculiar combination of impersonal exteriors and intimate interiors. Patrol officers spend most of the time driving methodically around, guided by their extensive knowledge of where incidents are likely to occur. Like tour guides at a museum of human frailty, they can point out houses where they are repeatedly called to mediate family disputes, upscale apartment complexes where young swingers frequently hold noisy parties, troublesome "biker" bars where drugs are sold, business premises patrolled by a vicious dog, street corners where drug dealers collect after 10 P.M., car parks often hit by thieves, warehouses with poor alarm systems, and places where police officers have been shot or injured. This world is dominated by facades of buildings, commercial signs and billboards, badly lighted alleys, deserted parks and playgrounds, all-night service stations, automobiles and delivery vans, endless traffic lights, and fast-food restaurants.

From this tawdry, largely commercial world police officers may be catapulted instantly into the depths of people's private lives, where they must deal with grief, rage, suspicion, and acute embarrassment. They see people utterly unmasked, defenseless before the matter-of-fact gaze and impersonal questions of the police.

By and large, the people police deal with are life's refugees. Uneducated, poor, often unemployed, they are both victims and victimizers. A young black prostitute sits on a bench near a street corner, her lower left leg in a heavy cast, a pair of crutches on the ground beside her. The patrol officer, speaking familiarly from the open patrol-car window, asks whether she is working. "Have to," she replies with a shrug. Or a 37-year-old white man, dressed in a blue parka, off-orange–colored slacks from which a long drawstring hangs, and a kid's imitation football helmet and face mask, refuses to pay for the food he has eaten at Denny's restaurant. Coherent, quiet, almost dignified, the man, a known drunk, promises to pay later. He is cuffed and taken to jail, along with his attaché case filled with soft pornography. Or the two disheveled middle-aged men rooted out from under juniper bushes at 2 A.M. after the woman whose door they were banging on called the police. Covered with dirt and dew, the men are cuffed and put into the back of the patrol car. Asked whether they had ever been arrested before, one of the men says, "Uh huh." "What for?" "Bein' drunk . . . just like I am now."

Hapless, befuddled, beaten by circumstances, people like these turn to the police for the help they can't give themselves. There is little the police can do for them except listen, shrug, and move on. The police try to distinguish the few who are genuinely vicious from the majority who are not and to treat them differently. However, it is often difficult to be patient even with the respectable ones and they are lumped together with the others as "worbs" in Sydney, Australia; "prigs" in Newcastle,

Great Britain; "mutts" in New York City; "pukes" in Toronto; "slag" in London; and "assholes" in Los Angeles. All of them, in one way or another, are incorrigible. All of them have become "police property" (Lee 1901). They are the salvage of modern society, entrusted indifferently and without particular gratitude to the police.

Although patrol work is mostly trivial and noncriminal, it is nonetheless fraught with uncertainty. Patrol officers can never forget that at any moment the boredom of a long shift can be shattered by a call that can be harrowing, traumatic, dangerous, and life threatening. For example, two officers responded urgently to the report of a man with a gun fighting with others at a housing project. The officers found a large middle-aged Native American man standing numbly on the sidewalk, his son on the ground, bleeding from a shoulder wound and a torn ear. Two other men with cut and bruised faces stood nearby, not far from a discarded .22-caliber rifle. They had no idea who the culprits were or whether they were still nearby.

Four officers surrounded a two-story stucco apartment late one afternoon where a working-class black man reported he had been threatened by a boy with a gun. Guns drawn, the officers knocked carefully on the door of a second-floor apartment. When the door was finally opened, they found a badly frightened 14-year-old boy, a weeping mother, and several agitated sisters. The boy said he had only been "playing" with the gun. He was taken into custody.

On a hot midsummer day, two young patrol officers chanced upon the robbery of a Tropicana orange drink delivery van. The driver had been bashed over the head and lay unconscious in a pool of blood. Seeing a youth running away, one of the officers sprinted after him, gun drawn. He charged after the youth up a short flight of stairs and into the entryway of a tenement where several people were relaxing in beach chairs. Grappling with the suspected robber, the officer fell over a beach chair, pulling the youth with him. The officer's gun accidentally discharged, mercifully missing everyone except the robber, who was wounded superficially.

The dilemma for patrol officers is that they must prepare for war even though they are rarely called on to fight. To relax invites risk; to be constantly on guard invites overreaction.

Criminal Investigation

The next biggest job in policing after patrolling is criminal investigation. It accounts for 14% of police personnel in Canada, 15% in Britain and the United States, 16% in Australia, and 20% in Japan. Criminal investigation is done by detectives, who usually do not work in uniform and have more flexible hours than patrol officers. Detectives in small police departments or those assigned to field stations tend to be generalists, investigating whatever crime occurs. The rest, usually working out of headquarters, are assigned to specialty units, such as homicide, robbery, vice, commercial crime, narcotics, auto theft, and burglary. In recent years some forces have added new specialties, such as bias crime, child abuse, sexual assault, and computer crime.

Like patrol, criminal investigation is overwhelmingly reactive. Whatever preventive effect detectives have comes primarily through deterrence—that is, by removing particular offenders from the streets or by demonstrating to would-be offenders that crime does not pay. Detectives rarely anticipate crime and prevent it from happening. Criminal investigators are usually responsible for the collection of information about crime potentials (intelligence), but most of the follow-up law enforcement from this analysis is turned over to patrol officers, to specialty investigation squads, notably narcotics and vice, and to small "strike" forces, sometimes composed of both detectives and patrol officers. Detectives may occasionally "stake out" the sites of likely criminal activity or clandestinely watch known criminals in order to catch them in the act. Both tactics have been shown to be costly relative to the amount of criminal activity discovered (Sherman 1986).

Undercover penetration of criminal conspiracies, featured so often in movies and television, is rare. A more common tactic, especially during the 1980s, was for detectives to pose as people willing to do something illegal, such as buying drugs, receiving stolen property, offering a bribe, soliciting a prostitute, or even killing someone (Marx 1988).

What do the vast majority of detectives who investigate crime do? Basically, they talk to people—victims, suspects, witnesses—in order to find out exactly what happened in particular situations and whether there is enough evidence to arrest and prosecute suspects with a reasonable likelihood of conviction. In most cases detectives make very quick judgments about whether an investigation should be undertaken. It depends on two factors: first, whether a credible perpetrator has been fairly clearly identified and, second, whether the crime is especially serious or repugnant—the sort that attracts public attention. Except when forced to do so by public pressure, police do not invest resources in cases in which they have no idea who the criminal might be. Such cases include almost all burglaries and most robberies.

Contrary to their fictional portrayal, detectives quickly formulate a theory about who committed the crime and then set about collecting the evidence that will support arrest and prosecution. Unlike Sherlock Holmes, they do not maintain a disinterested open mind. Detectives know that if perpetrators cannot be identified by people on the scene, police are not likely to find the criminals on their own. Nor is physical evidence especially important in determining whether a case is pursued. Physical evidence is used as confirmation—to support testimony that identifies suspects. It is seldom used diagnostically, to find suspects. The absence of physical evidence might mean that a case cannot be made; it may also disconfirm a theory. But it hardly ever leads to the identification of persons not already suspected by the police. In premises that have been burglarized, for example, police "dust" for fingerprints if residents insist, but they laugh among themselves at the futility of this public relations exercise. In short, criminal investigators begin with an identification, then collect evidence; they rarely collect evidence and then make an identification.

For the most part, crimes are solved quickly or not at all. Cold cases are not revisited because the essential element—identification of a suspect—is increasingly less likely to occur as time passes (Ericson 1982, Royal Commission on Criminal Procedure 1981). If a crime cannot be solved more or less on the spot, the case will probably be closed and police investigators will move on to more promising cases.

In effect, like doctors in a war zone, criminal investigators employ a triage strategy. Crimes that have been solved on the spot, usually with an arrest, are left to patrol officers to process. At most, detectives may supervise or take over the paperwork. Crimes without victim or bystander witnesses are usually written off as hopeless unless there is strong public pressure for an investigation. Therefore, detectives concentrate on crimes in which an identification has been made or is likely and in which a reasonable amount of questioning and nosing around will confirm the suspicion in a way that courts will accept.

Because most crime suspects cannot be identified readily, most crimes go unsolved. Japan is the exception among developed democratic countries. Its police solve about 58% of all crimes reported to them. The United States has one of the worst records: only 21.6% of even the most serious crimes are solved; in Britain, the number is 35%, in Canada, 45%, and in Australia 30%. The likelihood of solving a crime varies with the nature of an offense, with higher rates for confrontational crimes and lower rates for property crimes. In the United States, for example, police solve 45.6% of violent crimes against people and 18.1% of property crimes (*Sourcebook* 1991, Table 4.20). Among serious (or index) crimes, homicide is most likely to be solved—67.2%—and motor-vehicle theft the least likely—14.6%.

So detectives spend most of their time talking with people strongly suspected of being involved in crimes in an attempt to get them to confess. Contrary to popular opinion, however, interrogations are generally fairly low key and straightforward. Detectives simply confront a suspect with the evidence they have: "We've got you cold," or "Cut the crap, what's going on?" Police do not have to be very clever because most of the time suspects do confess. Perhaps they have been encouraged by remarks like, "You can make it easy and tell us now, or you can tell it to the judge." Sometimes detectives make threats, but threats have much more to do with the ability of the police to persist than with physical force: "We've got all night to talk to you; we get paid for this." Sometimes, too, the police bluff: "The lady across the street saw you clearly and your fingerprints are all over everything." Or they may cajole: "Will your Mum be pleased with what you've been doing?" Occasionally police try an outright scam. For example, one man confessed to burglarizing a friend's house after the police told him that they had developed a new "oscillating magnetic resonance imager" that recognizes individual body patterns in the air months after a person has left. People have confessed after officers have told them to put their hands on a patrol car's mobile computer terminal, pretending that it is a portable lie detector. As detectives often remark, most criminals are not very bright (Greenwood and Petersilia 1976, Ericson 1982, Walker 1989, Bradley et al. 1986).

Detectives also work hard to get "secondary clearances." A secondary clearance occurs when a person who is prosecuted—or sometimes convicted—for one crime confesses to other crimes. Many burglaries are cleared in this way. Studies in Britain and the United States indicate that the only sure way for a police force to raise a low clearance rate is to give more attention to obtaining secondary clearances (Eck 1982, Burrows 1986). Once again, the lesson is that the ability of the police to solve crimes depends on having reasonable suspicions about likely culprits.

Perhaps the most demanding part of a detective's job is developing expertise in the legal requirements for collecting and reporting evidence. Few detectives have had formal legal training, yet they need to understand how prosecutors will use their evidence and the challenges their evidence will face in court. Detectives complain that paperwork is becoming increasingly more intricate and burdensome. In the United States this is because Supreme Court rulings are constantly changing, especially in the areas of search and seizure and taking confessional statements. In Britain the reason is the new Police and Criminal Evidence Act of 1985 and in Canada the enactment of the Charter of Rights and Freedoms of 1982. Research shows that for every hour detectives talk to people and search for evidence, they spend a half hour on paperwork.

Although criminal investigation is regarded as the epitome of policing, it is not at all clear that it requires skills that are peculiar to the police. Many detectives admit off the record that investigation can be done by anyone who is intelligent, persistent, poised, and willing to learn the intricacies of criminal law. As one experienced detective chief inspector in Britain said, "Criminal investigation work is the sort of work that any good Prudential insurance man could do" (McClure 1980, p. 383).

Traffic

The third big job that police undertake is the regulation of motor-vehicle traffic. On average about 8% of officers are assigned to traffic units: 17% in Japan, 10% in Australia, 7% in Britain and the United States, and 6% in Canada. Traffic regulation is important for two reasons. First, the number of people killed or injured in traffic accidents and the monetary damage to property are substantially higher than result from crimes. Second, a larger cross section of the populace comes into contact with the police through the enforcement of traffic laws than in any other way.

Traffic officers generally work in marked cars, patrolling major roads for the purpose of preventing motor-vehicle accidents. They do this by enforcing laws against dangerous driving as well as against defective vehicles and by controlling traffic flow in potentially hazardous situations, such as those associated with accidents, spillage of toxic substances, parades, sporting events, and construction sites. Their work is more self-initiated than that of patrol officers or criminal investigators. They go where the traffic problems are, often guided by detailed analyses of the incidence of serious accidents. A collateral benefit of their patrolling is the assistance they give to motorists whose cars have broken down. Traffic officers also conduct investigations of the causes of motor-vehicle accidents.

Enforcement of traffic regulations, as well as directing traffic, is not done exclusively by traffic specialists. In most jurisdictions, people are as likely to be stopped by patrol officers as traffic officers. Britain may be an exception: Patrol officers ignore all but the most serious driving offenses, leaving traffic matters to the traffic police.

Traffic officers tend to be zealous, convinced that what they are doing is very important. They also feel beleaguered, unappreciated, and understaffed. Their reaction may have to do with the view among police officers that traffic regulation is peripheral to "crime fighting." Actually, a small proportion of traffic stops do result in criminal law enforcement, such as the arrest of wanted persons, the recovery of stolen cars, and the discovery of evidence of criminal wrongdoing. Oddly enough, police departments do not keep track of such cases, so no one really knows how useful crime "hits" by traffic officers are.

Enforcement of traffic laws is a means to an end—maintaining order and safety—not an end in itself. Traffic officers, like patrol officers, use the law as a tool for obtaining compliance. For example, they almost always allow motorists to exceed speed limits to some degree, except around schools. Leniency is also affected by their reading of the character of drivers.

An elderly woman who drove through a stop sign was so shaken by being pulled over that her hands shook on the steering wheel. She was given a mild verbal warning. A teenage boy who treated an officer with "cool" nonchalance, glancing at his friends to see how it was going over, got a ticket and a very stern dressing down. A professional man in an expensive car with an expired driver's license was not excused with a warning because the officer thought a person of his standing should know better. On the other hand, an unemployed working-class man was simply advised to get his expired license renewed. Traffic officers have been known to accept fishing licenses and even library cards as proof of identity from people who could not produce a license but were genuinely apologetic about it. On the other hand, if a driver makes the officer angry, what might have been a simple infraction can become costly. The officer may list all the offenses, rather than simply the worst, and give what one officer calls the "$103 walkaround," meaning that he carefully inspects every inch of the car in order to penalize even the smallest mechanical defect. The moral of the story is that humility goes a long way when dealing with traffic police.

Drivers who speed are more likely to be stopped if they appear furtive, avert their faces from the police car, or are arrogant and sassy. Traffic officers can almost always find an excuse to stop a vehicle, if not for driving mistakes then for mechanical vehicle defects, such as bald tires, a noisy muffler, or a cracked windshield. When all else fails, determined officers have been known to pull a car over, park behind it, and while walking forward to talk to the driver, deliberately strike a rear fender with their hand. The officer then apologizes for stopping the vehicle, remarking that the tail light that wasn't working now seems to be all right. Would the driver mind showing a license and registration?

Traffic patrolling is highly discretionary, requiring officers to make a lot of decisions on the spot about whether the law should be enforced. Research in the United States has shown that when traffic officers stop a car for a driving violation, their options are not simply whether or not to impose a punishment. Rather, they generally choose among five different courses of action: (1) 43% of the time they issue a citation, but (2) they may also release the driver with a warning (20.7%); (3) arrest the driver for being intoxicated or for another crime (14%); (4) simply let the driver go (13.4%); and (5) issue a citation while also giving a stern lecture (12%) (Bayley 1986). In Britain an official penalty is applied in only 25% of traffic stops (Skogan 1990).

Other Work

Patrol, criminal investigation, and traffic regulation are the largest areas of modern operational policing, occupying about 85% of all police personnel. Most of the rest is accounted for by administration: 11% in Japan, 10% in Canada, 9% in the United States, 7% in Britain, and 6% in Australia. Administration includes recruitment, training, public relations, and all the housekeeping functions of purchasing, paying, supervising, and so forth.

All of the other operational units are very small, designed to support patrol, criminal investigation, and traffic regulation in specialized ways. The most well-known special units are probably the dog squad and the special weapons and tactic team—SWAT—or less reverently, "Several weirdos armed to the teeth." Although the SWAT acronym is a U.S. invention, one that some foreign forces deliberately avoid, it is recognized around the world, and most police forces have some unit like it. These units are used in ongoing violent confrontations, such as hostage takings and barricaded suspects. They are often responsible for rescue operations. New York City's Emergency Services Unit, for example, has over 300 officers who handle more than 100,000 calls a year, ranging from heart attacks, suspected bombs, the taking of hostages, and even elevator malfunctions ("Wide Variation in Police Coverage," *New York Times*, 15 March 1992).

Large police forces may also have permanent formations of riot police—the *Kidotai* in Japan, the Mobile Reserves in Britain, and the Task Force in New York City. Small police forces train all officers in controlling crowds, demonstrations, and civil unrest, drawing officers from other assignments when the need arises.

Finally, police forces in cities that are political centers, for example, Tokyo, London, and New York, are called upon to protect important persons.

The people who must give explicit attention to anticipating and preventing crime, apart from routine uniform patrolling and the undercover actions of a few investigators, barely show up on most organizational charts. Specialized crime-prevention units account for 6% of personnel in Japan—by far the largest among the police forces in the sample in this study. In Australia the figure is 4%; in large U.S. forces, 3%; in Canada, 1%; and in Britain, less than 1%. These explicit "crime-prevention" units are relatively new, dating generally from the 1980s.

Describing the work that police do in terms of the formal assignments of officers is not completely satisfactory. Patrol officers may not exclusively patrol—they may also do crime-prevention work. Detectives sometimes patrol; patrol officers also investigate crimes. A more discerning approach is to examine the minute-by-minute work of individual officers. These reports, called work-load studies, are discussed in Chapter 3.

Police forces are also responsible for a number of activities that do not appear on the organization chart. For example, some police inspect and license firearms, bars, liquor stores, and gaming parlors. Police sometimes operate jails, serve warrants and summonses, certify deaths that occur outside medical premises, administer drivers' license tests, maintain a lost-and-found, do background checks on government employees, and transport emergency medical supplies (Bayley 1985). In short, police often perform a host of ancillary tasks given them by government, largely for reasons of convenience.

The point is that although police are expected to prevent crime, people expect them to do many other things—things that are not noticed until they are not available.

Variations in Police Work

Policing is strikingly similar from place to place, at least as indicated by organizational assignments. Among the forces in the present sample, about 60% of police personnel patrol and respond to requests for service, 15% investigate crime, 9% regulate traffic, and 9% administer. Within the countries considered here the proportion of officers assigned to different specialities varies considerably among forces—less in Japan and Britain, more in Australia and the United States.

These differences are not systematic, that is, related to features of social context, such as crime rates or population densities. Two factors are indicative. First, the proportion of officers in the major assignments differs very little among urban, suburban, and rural police stations (see Table 2.1). Rural police stations tend to have slightly more officers proportionately in patrol. The numbers of officers in criminal investigation, traffic, and administration are almost identical. Although the variation in the strength of patrol officers might be explained by context, U.S. research suggests instead that it is due to the size of a police force. Smaller forces have a larger proportion of officers in patrol (Langworthy 1986, Ostrom et al. 1977). Rural police stations might have larger proportions of their officers in patrol, not because of their location but because they are small.

TABLE 2.1

Percentage of Police Officers in Different Assignments among Urban, Suburban, and Rural Police Stations ($N=38$)

	Urban	Suburban	Rural
Patrol	61	66	73
Criminal investigation	13	12	12
Traffic	7	6	5
Administration	7	9	7
Operational support	7	5	5
Crime prevention	3	5	0

Second, the proportion of police officers assigned to different sorts of work has not changed significantly among the forces surveyed in Australia, Britain, Canada, Japan, and the United States during the last twenty years. Among the 18 forces for which historical data were available, the proportion of police in each line of work changed marginally (see Table 2.2). The table shows that patrol declined by about 10%, and crime prevention grew from nothing to 3%. Criminal investigation, administration, and traffic barely changed.

Although these data do not constitute a definitive test, they suggest that police forces are organized to do the same sorts of work regardless of the social circumstances they confront.[4] Crime and social conditions certainly vary among urban, suburban, and rural police jurisdictions, but police organizations are staffed in almost exactly the same way everywhere. Moreover, although social conditions, particularly crime, changed between 1970 and 1990 in Australia, Britain, Canada, Japan, and the United States, police organizations did not. It appears that variations in the relative importance of the work police are prepared to perform is not related to the conditions that generate that work. Police organizations seem to be "loosely coupled" to their environment (Langworthy 1986, Murphy 1986, Hagan 1988, Weick 1976, Meyer and Brown 1977). What they are prepared to do does not change with what needs doing.

There are several reasons for this. The first is bureaucratic politics. Existing organizational units fight hard to maintain their share of resources. Police chiefs are seldom willing to challenge the customary power of the patrol, criminal investigation, and traffic regulation.

A second reason is that police forces are sometimes compelled to adhere to national standards for staffing. In Britain, for example, Her Majesty's Inspectorate of Constabulary, a central government agency,

TABLE 2.2

Average Percentage of Police Officers in Different
Assignments, Aggregated Across Countries (*N*=18)

	1970–1975	1986–1990
Patrol	70	59
Criminal investigation	11	15
Traffic	9	8
Administration	7	8
Operational support	13	11
Crime prevention	0	3

Note: Averages have been computed as the starting and end points because information was not always available for the same beginning and ending years. This also explains why the columns total more than 100%.

monitors staffing patterns among all forces and recommends adjustments to fit the preferred model. This is also the case in Japan at the behest of the National Police Agency. Although the United States has no mechanism for ensuring similar staffing patterns, the newly created processes of accreditation, so far voluntary, exerts the same homogenizing effect.

Finally, police officers are part of an international professional culture, reinforced by conferences, seminars and workshops, exchanges of personnel, and trade publications. They continually look over their shoulders to determine whether their forces follow what the profession considers "efficient, modern, and progressive." In short, they copy one another, especially a few "flagship" forces, such as Los Angeles and New York City, the London Metropolitan Police, and the Royal Canadian Mounted Police (Murphy 1986).

For all these reasons, police organizations do not adapt to the work they must do. Rather, the work they must do is adapted to the police organization.

Conclusion

Modern police perform two major functions: *authoritative intervention* and *symbolic justice.* Most police officers are engaged in one or the other of these most of the time.

Authoritative intervention is what patrol and traffic officers are primarily responsible for. It is almost wholly reactive, rarely anticipatory. Crime is involved only occasionally or ambiguously. The purpose of authoritative intervention is to restore order. Almost no attempt is made to correct underlying conditions that have led to the need for police intervention.

Symbolic justice is the realm of detectives and traffic officers. Also largely reactive, it is achieved through law enforcement. Its purpose is demonstrative, to show offenders and public that a regime of law exists (Silberman 1978, Reiss 1971). The success of police in rendering symbolic justice is almost entirely dependent on information supplied by the public, just as the mobilization of patrol officers is for authoritative intervention.

Interestingly, traffic police, who are regarded as peripheral to most police forces, participate in both authoritative intervention and symbolic justice. Perhaps alone of all the assignments, traffic police are full-service police. They are different from the rest, however, because their work is limited to a particular venue—namely, public thoroughfares—and to particular people—namely, those who operate motor vehicles. But in terms of work, traffic police are detectives as well as patrol officers.

Few police resources are devoted to anticipating criminal events. Targeting crime prevention is fitful in location and intensity. Furthermore, these minimal anticipatory actions, carried out by a few patrol officers and detectives, concentrate mainly on "residual crimes," or offenses that take place exclusively in public, mostly on streets and roads (Bittner 1990). Most of the crimes people are really afraid of— murders, rapes, assaults—are ignored by the police before they happen.

Chapter 1 noted that the police do not really prevent crime in demonstrable ways and asked why this is so. There are several major reasons. The first, which this chapter has explored, is that the police spend very little of their time dealing with crime, and when they do, it is with crimes that have already occurred. In a few cases police prevent crime from escalating, but by and large they respond to crimes that have taken place. Therefore, any systematic effect police may have on preventing crime must come through deterrence—that is, teaching would-be criminals that crime does not pay. Police actually devote only a minor portion of their resources to this function. Morever, the success of police in deterrence depends on the activities of the larger criminal justice system. Altogether, this deterrent effect appears to be weak.

Even if the police are not effectively preventing crime, what they are doing still has value. Authoritative intervention and symbolic justice are important services in any society. Conflict must be stopped; people who commit crimes must be caught and punished. Somebody needs to do these things. Unfortunately, however, these police activities do not appear to be making society a great deal safer.

Could the police do more? Could they be more effective if they intensified what they are doing or, alternatively, reshaped their activity? To explore these issues we need to know what the police are doing now with the resources they have. In particular, we need to determine whether the police are so overburdened that they cannot do more. These issues are explored in Chapter 3.

3

How Much Is Enough?

Police everywhere complain that they are understaffed and overworked. In the face of rising crime rates, it is unrealistic, they argue, for the public to expect them to be more effective without additional resources. The war on crime is underfinanced. When President Bill Clinton was campaigning for the White House, he repeatedly called for the hiring of 100,000 more police officers. That would, by the way, represent an increase of almost one seventh.

Are resources really the reason police are not more effective in reducing the levels of crime and violence in contemporary society? Are they so overburdened and underfunded that they cannot get the job done? The answer to both questions is no. Spending more on police and hiring more police is unlikely to bring about a perceptible increase in public safety.

In order to demonstrate this heretical view, we need to examine two issues. First, are the police really strapped for resources? Second, do police manage the resources they are given in a rational way?

The first issue is examined in the first three sections, which deal, respectively, with (1) a comparison of patterns of expenditure, (2) the operational burdens of front-line police officers, and (3) the way police organizations manage the demands placed on them. The second issue—the rationality of resource management—is considered in three further sections, which deal with (1) the rationality of allocation processes to the police, (2) the flexibility of allocation processes within the police, and (3) the economics of maintaining a visible street police presence.

Patterns of Investment

By world standards the United States is not underpoliced. Compared with Australia, Britain, Canada, and Japan, the United States has *more* police in relation to population. In 1990, there were 393 Americans for every police officer (*Sourcebook* 1991; *Statistical Abstract of the United States 1992*).[1] But there were 414 Australians, 406 British, 474 Canadians, and 552 Japanese for every police officer.[2] On a per capita basis, the United States was 17% better off than the average for these other countries. Interestingly, Japan has more people per police officer than the other countries, but it also has the lowest crime rate.[3]

Furthermore, the ratio of police to population in the United States has improved faster during the last twenty years than in any of these countries except Australia. Between 1970 and 1990, the U.S. ratio of police to population rose by 26%, compared with an average increase of 19% for the other four countries.[4] Australia increased by 32% and Britain by 24.5%. Japan had the lowest rate of increase (4%), and Canada, at 15.5%, was in between. In absolute terms, the number of police in the United States increased by 64% between 1970 and 1990; in Australia the increase was 97%; in Canada, 47.6%; in Britain, 34.6%; and in Japan, 22%. Only Australia obeyed one of C. Northcote Parkinson's famous "laws," that bureaucracies grow at an average of 4–5% a year. Australia's rate of increase was 4.9% and that of the United States 3.2%. All the others were half or less of what Parkinson predicted.[5]

National figures conceal enormous variations in the concentration of police officers within countries. Differences in the ratios of police to population are greater among forces within countries than between them. Very large cities, as one would expect, have the heaviest concentrations. For example, New York City had 282 persons per officer in 1990, Tokyo 289, London 256, and Montreal 216. Among the 47 police stations (precincts) studied in the five countries, city stations had the highest ratios of police to population, rural stations the least, and suburban stations in between. The same gradient can also be seen in the ratio of police to territory covered: heaviest police concentrations per square mile in cities, lightest concentrations in rural areas, and in between in suburbs.

Investments in police must be examined in relation not only to populations and territory but to the unique responsibilities of the police, especially the numbers of crimes and to citizen calls for service. With respect to crime, Canadian officers have borne the greatest burden relatively and those of Japan the least. This conclusion is based on a comparison of the ratio of police to violent crime—murder, rape, robbery, and aggravated assault. It would be misleading to calculate a ratio of crime to police using figures for total crime because countries include very different sorts of violations.[6] Among the five countries in 1990, the United States was in the middle with respect to the number of violent crimes per officer—2.8 per officer each year as opposed to 4.7 for Canada, 1.7 for Britain, 1.2 for Australia, and 0.11 for Japan.[7] This represents an enormous difference in the crime burdens of police, even if Japan is excluded.

Americans cannot take much comfort from these figures. The high crime rate in the United States cannot be blamed on unfavorable ratios of police to population, territory, or violent crime. The United States is doing much less well than other countries in controlling crime, yet its police are not disadvantaged relatively. To give only one example, the U.S. violent crime rate in 1990, composed of homicide, rape, robbery, and assault, was 728 per 100,000 persons, compared with 301 in Australia, 419 in Britain, and 9.7 in Japan.[8] In general, the rate of victimization for all forms of crime is higher in the United States than in other developed countries. In the United States, as Elliot Currie (1985) has said, crime rates are more like those of a "volatile country of the Third World" than a modern industrial nation.

Violent crime and total crime generally are greater problems for police in urban than in rural or suburban areas. Comparing the 47 police stations of my sample, one sees that city stations had 4.5 violent crimes and 54 crimes of all sorts per officer each year; suburban stations had 1.24 and 47.5; and rural stations 0.03 and 40. At the same time, variations in the burdens of police officers were substantial among forces within rural, suburban, and urban areas. For example, Philadelphia in 1986 reported 2.3 violent crimes per police officer, New York City 5.2, and Los Angeles 9.2 (Pate and Hamilton 1991). Even within a single large police force, crime burdens differed from precinct to precinct. In New York City, for example, violent crimes per officer in 1990 varied from 19.2 in Manhattan South to 1.2 in Staten Island (*New York Times*, 15 December 1990). The general rule is that the number of crimes per officer varies in accordance with the reported incidence of crime. The more crime per capita, the more crime per police officer.

In terms of requests by the public for intervention and assistance, countries differ enormously in the burden placed on police. The U.S. forces in my sample, which ranged from 391 to 28,000 sworn officers, average about 200 calls for service per officer each year.[9] Canada is about the same. Australian police, however, average only about 50–60 calls per officer, and Britain about 30–40. Japan has the lowest ratio, with about 16.3 calls per officer each year. Even if Japan is excluded, the ratio of requests per officer varies by a factor of ten. There are substantial differences within countries as well. For example, Seattle in 1990 had 695 calls per officer; Los Angeles 278; Houston 188; and Aurora, Colorado's third largest city, 366.

Historical data on trends with respect to the calls for service work load are hard to get. Police forces do not keep such information in a readily retrievable form. On the basis of fragmentary evidence, the best I can say is that calls for service per officer appear to have risen slightly between the 1970s and the 1990s. But it is important to note that although the burden of public requests may have increased everywhere, it is from quite different baselines from place to place. Police are not similarly burdened with requests from the public either among or within countries.

Comparing all the police stations in the five countries, again one finds a nice gradient in the proportion of calls per officer from rural to urban areas. Calls average 109 per officer in rural areas, 154 in suburban areas, and 178 in cities.[10] As with violent crime, city police are busier than suburban ones, who in turn are busier than rural police.

Because the regulation of traffic and the prevention of motor-vehicle accidents are important police responsibilities, the incidence of traffic accidents, as well as the density of traffic, affect how much the police have to do. Australian, British, and Japanese police handle many fewer accidents than Canadian and U.S. police. Japan and Britain average 3–4 accidents per officer each year, Australia 5–6, and Canada and the United States 13–15. There are, however, enormous variations among police forces within countries. For example, in Australia police in the states of South Australia and Western Australia handle three to four times the number of motor-vehicle accidents than officers in Queensland and the Northern Territory. In the United States in 1990, there were 17.5 motor-vehicle accidents per officer in Houston compared with 2.7 in New York City. In all the forces for which I have data on traffic accidents (21 of 28), police appear to have been notably successful in reducing the incidence of motor-vehicle accidents during the last ten to twenty years. Traffic accidents have diminished in all jurisdictions, so that there are fewer accidents per officer today than there were several years ago.

Responding to traffic accidents is the biggest burden on police in suburbs, the smallest in cities, and in between in rural areas. The number of traffic accidents per officer mirrors the ratio of motor vehicles to population: The more vehicles per person, the more accidents per police officer.

Summarizing all these measures of police work load, one finds that U.S. police work harder in terms of calls for service and traffic accidents. Although Americans clearly make more requests of their police than do other nationalities, further study is needed to determine whether this really means that U.S. police work harder. They could, for example, be failing to follow through on a larger proportion of these calls than foreign police forces. My impression is that the higher number of calls for service does mean more work, but I cannot provide hard comparative evidence. On the other hand, the United States has more police per capita than Australia, Britain, Canada, or Japan. The violent crime rate per officer in the United States is significantly less than in Canada, for classificational reasons, but significantly higher than in Australia, Britain, and Japan. It is also worth noting that responding to traffic accidents is the least burdensome activity for police in cities, precisely where violent crime is most prevalent. It follows that U.S. police do not usually confront high rates of both violent crime and traffic accidents. Altogether, then, I believe U.S. officers work harder than police in the other four countries.

City police in all countries work harder than police in other locations. At the same time, city police have more personnel in relation to population and territory. Motor-vehicle accidents are the only category of work in which city police do not bear a heavier burden. Suburban police handle more accidents proportionately.[11]

"At the Coal Face"

Aggregate figures provide some indication of the relative amount of work police have to do from place to place, as well as at different periods of time. Such figures, however, do not show what operational personnel are actually confronted with. They do not reveal how tough it is to work "at the coal face," as Australian police say, "on the shop floor," as British police say, or "on the front line," as U.S. police say.[12]

Patrol officers, who do the bulk of police work, complain universally that they are overworked, stressed, and burned out and that they are shunted without respite from one job to another, beaten down by paperwork, and harassed by unsympathetic supervisors. Calls for service, they say, are frequently backed up, waiting for a free unit.

At the same time, people from outside the police who study patrol operations frequently comment on how much time officers seem to have on their hands. The standing joke among observers is that patrol officers always seem to have been busier "last Wednesday." In fact, officers often apologize for the lack of "action" on a given night.

Unfortunately, there are very few hard data to resolve the conflict in testimony. Most police forces do not know the number of dispatched calls for service that are handled by the average patrol unit. Experienced sergeants supervising patrol shifts will talk at length about lack of personnel, dropped calls, and long delays in response, but when pressed, they are unable to come up with supporting figures. They may know how many units on average are deployed, but they do not know how many calls for service those units receive, let alone how many incidents patrol units become involved in. Communications personnel, however, often have statistics on aggregate calls for service per shift, but they do not know how many units are routinely available to handle them. The right hand of the police organization doesn't know what the left hand is doing, and senior officers, who should pay attention to both, do not appear to think that the calculation is important. In my experience, most police organizations are not able to demonstrate how much work their officers are doing. Quite literally, police organizations do not know what their workers are doing.

In an effort to determine just how busy patrol officers are, I searched in all 28 forces for hard statistical information about the number of incidents handled by motor-patrol units. When such information did exist, it was found in communications units and research/development offices. The people there were often delighted that someone thought such information was important and complained of being ignored by senior operational managers.

Calculating the number of incidents handled by patrol personnel is tricky. It cannot be done, for example, by dividing the total number of calls for service received by the number of police officers, which is what police forces often do. This is wrong for two reasons: A large proportion of telephone requests do not require a police response in the field, and not all police officers are deployed to handle radio dispatches. Furthermore, because patrol officers are often deployed in pairs, the calculation must be based on patrol units, which means vehicles rather than officers.[13] Finally, patrol officers may generate work on their own that does not show up in dispatch records. I have taken all these problems into account, except that I was rarely able to account for proactive, on-view work. Therefore, the figures reported understate the amount of work patrol officers do, although probably not by a great deal since the amount of proactive work is usually not great (see Chap. 2).

Among the nine U.S. forces studied, the highest number of radio dispatches per patrol vehicle in 1990 was 6.5 per eight-hour shift in New York City (New York Police Department 1991). The number ranged from 7.2 in Manhattan South to 4.2 in Staten Island.[14] Seattle was next with 5.6 runs per patrol-car shift (1991). Houston had 3.0 (1991); Suffolk County, Long Island, 2.2 (1991); and Rutland, Vermont, 2.0 (1991). Among the six largest city police forces in the United States in 1986, New York had the highest volume of dispatched calls for service per patrol unit at 8.2, and Houston the lowest at 2.1 (Pate and Hamilton 1991). The average for Chicago, Detroit, Houston, Los Angeles, New York, and Philadelphia was 5.0.[15]

In Canada the work load per patrol unit is considerably less. There are about 2–3 dispatched calls per unit, which puts Canadian forces at the lower end of the U.S. big-city range. Vancouver, for example, averaged 1.5 calls in 1990 (Vancouver Police 1990), one of Toronto's busiest downtown precincts had 1.5. (Toronto Police 1990), and Edmonton reported 3.1 (Hornick et al. 1989). In the early 1980s, Richard Ericson (1982) found 2.3 dispatched calls per unit in a suburban Toronto police department; Christopher Murphy (1986, pp. 263–264) 2.9 for small municipal forces and 2.3 for Royal Canadian Mounted Police detachments in small towns, all in Nova Scotia.

Great Britain has even fewer dispatched calls per unit, averaging 1.2 each day (Audit Commission 1990a). During 1991 the Kent Constabulary calculated that each deployed patrol officer responded to 0.65 incidents per shift (Kent Constabulary 1992). Newcastle West, a very busy police station in the north of England, was higher at 3.0 per patrol-car shift.

Australia was not able to provide information of this sort when I carried out my research there in 1989.

Granting that these figures are illustrative rather than definitive, it appears that patrol cars respond to an average of 2–3 dispatched calls for service during a standard shift, except in the largest cities in the United States, where they may handle two to three times as many. Generally, then, the testimony of skeptical observers about how busy patrol officers are appear to be more reliable than that of the police themselves. Most of the time patrol officers are not running from one incident to another.

An important qualification has to be made. Dispatched calls for service are only an approximate measure of the burden of work on patrol personnel because no allowance has been made for how long it takes to handle each incident. Some calls may be handled perfunctorily, whereas others may take hours. Furthermore, almost every event requires a written report. Police complain considerably about this, and with justification. The back rooms of police stations often resemble high school typing classes as young officers sit hunched over battered typewriters or, increasingly, computer work stations, pecking furiously with two fingers at long report forms, cursing the carbon paper and passing around the white-out.

The best way to determine how much activity police are involved in is through what are called work-load studies. In these, officers are asked to record whatever they do, along with the time the activity began and ended. They record not only incidents involving the public but administrative and housekeeping chores, such as eating, writing reports, attending meetings with supervisors, and delivering interoffice mail to headquarters. Work-load studies are relatively new, dating from the mid-1980s. Interest in them is uneven around the world. Most major Canadian forces have done them, at least for patrol units, as have a few Australian forces, notably New South Wales and South Australia. All British forces will soon be required to do them on a regular basis, according to a format laid down by the Home Office. Police forces in the United States are lagging in this regard and do not seem particularly interested. They generally argue that work-load studies are not worth the cost and are a bother to operational personnel.

At present, the most extensive picture of actual work performed on a national basis by patrol officers comes from Britain. According to a national survey taken in 1989–1990, British patrol officers spent 22% of their time patrolling, 11.7% responding to incidents, and 56.8% working inside police stations, half of that on administrative chores (Bennett and Lupton 1992, Tarling 1988). This picture has been confirmed by smaller-scale studies (Arkell and Knight 1975, Kent Constabulary 1992). Thus officers spend slightly less than one hour per shift responding to incidents, which confirms an early study by the Home Office that estimated the time devoted to "incident" work by patrol officers in British cities was 58 minutes per shift (Home Office 1975).

There is little hard evidence of this sort for the United States, and the studies that have been done have been by scholars rather than police departments. Studies before 1980 showed that patrol officers spent one third of their time on incidents and two thirds of their time on patrol, a small part of that involved in on-view encounters and on officers' personal business (Whitaker et al. 1981). New York City police estimate now that patrol officers are "out of service"—unavailable for dispatch—about 90% of the time, but they fail to specify whether they are involved in incidents or doing other sorts of things. Like many U.S. departments, New York wants its patrol officers to be available for mobilization about 40% of the time. This is the norm in Seattle and is one of the strategic goals of the Los Angeles police. Australian police forces follow a similar plan: 40% incident handling, 30% patrol, and 30% administration.

Are patrol officers today overworked? Are they so busy rushing from one incident to the next that they can't keep up with the public's requests or take more time with the calls they handle? I think not. There is certainly little hard evidence that would support this. In fact, rigorous studies of work loads tend to show that patrol officers have a considerable amount of uncommitted time. This does not mean they are never busy. Some past "Wednesdays" undoubtedly were frantic. At certain times, such as weekend evenings, and in certain places, such as high-density inner cities, patrol units are often in constant demand. But this is not the norm. As a senior officer said off the record, echoing many others, "They're bullshitting you, David."

But it's not the exaggeration that is worrisome. It is human nature to stress the exciting parts of one's work. Most jobs are boring in part, but few people define their work in terms of those periods. Police officers, who are active gung-ho people, naturally dwell on the purposful, adventuresome side of their job. They tend to magnify the time spent actually "fighting crime." It is hard for them to admit that they often simply drive around. Moreover, because their work is sometimes dangerous, it is easy for them to confuse the fatefulness of what they do with busyness.

What is worrisome about the posture of busyness is that police managers have not cared more to find out what is really going on. The subjective assessments of the workers at the coal face have been accepted as truth within the police. I have never been in a police force anywhere, over thirty years, whose officers, from top to bottom, did not say that front-line personnel are too busy to handle the demands placed upon them. It is an article of faith among police that external demands are overwhelming capacity. Consequently, blame for the ineffectiveness of the police is shifted from police managers to external circumstances. The police, according to the dogma, are helpless. The only solution, therefore, is to ask for more resources rather than examining whether existing resources might be used more effectively. Until police managers have the courage to look objectively at the work loads of their personnel, they cannot begin to fit resources rationally to the work that must be done.

Managing Work

In trying to determine whether police have enough resources to get the job done, it is critical to understand that the work they do is not a given. What the police do is not determined solely by social needs, public demands, and legal requirements. Police are not robots. Their work is shaped by decisions they make about priorities and procedures. Police work is a product of managerial decisions as well as social needs. In other words, how police manage what they are called upon to do determines to a large extent whether or not they are overburdened.

There are several examples of this. One is dispatch policy. New York City police say their patrol units are busy 90% of the time. However, New York sends patrol cars to 50% of the calls it receives, while Los Angeles sends cars to only 30%. Unless New York really has more genuinely urgent calls than Los Angeles, New York could develop the reserve capacity it says it wants just by changing its dispatch policy. In 1986, the proportion of calls for service to which the six largest police departments in the United States (Chicago, Detroit, Houston, Los Angeles, New York, and Philadelphia) sent police cars varied from 27% in Los Angeles to 65% in Chicago (Pate and Hamilton 1991). These differences exist today. Unless social conditions among these cities differ more than seems likely, the solution to the resource problems in several of these cities appears obvious—copy Los Angeles.

In the past few years Edmonton, Canada, sent police to 38% of telephone calls for service; Toronto 42.4% (Superintendent Chris Braiden private communication, Toronto Police Department 1990). The police in Britain tend to have much more liberal dispatch policies than North American police forces. The London police, for example, send a car whenever one is requested, a policy that in the United States is followed only in small towns. This undoubtedly helps to explain Peter Manning's (private communication 1992) observation that although American forces receive almost twice the number of calls per officer as British forces, the amount of work done on the street is about the same.

In 1979, Michael Cahn and James Tien showed that 18.9% of all calls in Wilmington, Delaware, could be handled by taking reports over the telephone or by scheduling later visits with complainants and that following this practice would reduce the demand for patrol cars by 21.1%.

Since then many departments have adopted telephone crime reporting, usually for larceny, malicious mischief, auto theft, and burglary.

Double or single crewing of patrol cars is another decision that affects the amount of work patrol officers do and the resulting impression that police are overworked. Some forces require two officers in police cars, others only one. In Canada and the United States two officers per car may be required by union contract, at least at certain times of the day. Since the personnel costs of deploying a patrol car on a year-round basis are far in excess of the physical cost of buying and maintaining the car, doubling the number of officers in police cars is a powerful disincentive to expand coverage. There are cases when the requirement that patrol cars be double crewed during certain shifts results in cars being unused. In the slang of one department, patrol cars are "put down" during the evening shift, when they are most needed, because officers are not allowed to work in them alone.

Calculations of work loads are misleading for another reason: There is no agreement within policing about the quality of response the police should make to different types of calls. Different officers and different departments may handle the same sort of situation quite differently. There is no standard for what is either needed or desirable. For example, officers in small departments may handle fewer calls than officers in large ones, but they may "work" them longer in the sense that they take more time to interact with the public. As departments become busier, they tend to tighten supervision of what officers do, in particular insisting that they take less time handling calls. In many big-city departments supervising sergeants keep track of the time officers are "out of service" and warn them against "unnecessary conversations." Some departments specify minimum times for the initial handling of calls for service. The onus is on each officer to justify taking longer in a particular case. The point is that one can talk meaningfully about being overworked only in relation to a standard of service. Since there is none in police patrolling, police departments cannot determine minimal staffing levels for given work loads. The time on-scene is a variable determined by police managers as well as by the patrol work group. Busyness, therefore, reflects operational judgments about how work should be handled.

The phrase "out of service" is revealing. The primary purpose of patrolling is not to handle requests from the public adequately, it is to be available. The worst thing that can happen to any police force, and to any commander within it, is not to have enough officers on hand when there is a dramatic need to assert authoritative control. Policing is geared to the big event. Patrol resources are not calculated on the basis of responding most attentively or helpfully. They are calculated so as to have enough capacity to deal with serious crimes in progress, such as bank robberies, hostage takings, or riots. Not being able to regain control is the worst nightmare of a police commander.

Patrol operations is a place, therefore, to store reserve capacity. This explains why senior commanders are always willing to assign officers temporarily out of patrol to other duties. They are not calculating that responses will be less adequate—they are gambling that the "big event" will not happen. Usually they are right. Even in the busiest cities, when an officer radios for help or a disturbance breaks out, many police cars swarm to the scene, what John Van Maanen (1988, p. 112) calls "bumblebee policing." Patrol is often looked upon as a reservoir of personnel that can be deployed to more pressing events, such as sports contests, parades and festivals, and intensive criminal investigations.

Despite what police say, the prime directive of patrolling is to be available rather than to respond adequately to the myriad calls for service. For police managers, therefore, patrol officers are "working" when they are simply cruising around. The implication of the prime directive is that no matter how many resources the police are given, they will always want to appear busier than they actually are. Police forces must store capacity, and they do so in patrol. For patrol officers as well as for commanders, claims of being busy are a way of disguising the invisible burden of always being ready. What appears to be underwork is not the result of laziness—it comes from the priorities of police organizations. Therefore, when police managers say patrol officers are too busy, they do not really mean that the officers are working all the time. They mean that the officers are so preoccupied with trivial business that they cannot be mobilized quickly enough and in sufficient numbers for more consequential events.

The pressure of police work is also affected by the way in which the work is organized and processed. Work-load studies in New York City (1990), Northhamptonshire, Britain (1984), and the Royal Canadian Mounted Police in British Columbia (1990) show that officers take 30 minutes on the scene to handle calls (New York Police Department 1991, Hobbs and Shapland 1989, Oostoek 1990). Report writing makes the total time taken by a call about 1 hour. The time involved depends on the nature of the event. For the Ontario Provincial Police and the police of Toronto and Vancouver (1989–1990), the initial handling of aggravated assaults, burglaries, thefts, and auto thefts takes roughly 1 to 1.5 hours. Homicide investigations take much longer, up to 10 and 11 hours. For more minor offenses the Toronto police work faster than the others, usually by about 30 minutes.

The processing of people arrested for drunken driving represents one of the best areas in which improved practices might save enormous amounts of police time. New York City police take from 3 to 4 hours to process such an arrest. The Suffolk County police on nearby Long Island, on the other hand, generally take less than 2 hours, while the New York State Police take from 1.5 to 2 hours. These time differences are substantial and cannot be explained by differences in legal codes or criminal justice processes. The Los Angeles police take 2 hours, but the Houston police require only 45 minutes because they dispatch a special drunk-driving investigation car that administers breathalyzer tests and transports arrested drivers to jail. Houston patrol officers only issue tickets and arrange for the drunk's car to be towed.

Recognizing that report writing takes a great deal of operational time, several British police forces have hired civilian typists to work with patrol officers. The same job is then done at less cost, freeing the officers to remain on the street and "in service." Chief Bob Holmes of Rutland, Vermont, estimates that he can get more time for criminal investigation by hiring a civilian typist to help the existing detectives than by hiring two additional detectives. Other forces are experimenting with mobile arrest-booking facilities so that patrol officers do not have to transport prisoners back to some remote central location. Still others are computerizing report writing and coordinating decisions about charging prisoners between arresting officers and prosecutors. In New York City in 1990–1991, changes in work practices reduced the time involved in processing suspects from arrest to arraignment from 40 hours to 26. That saved the police department $5 million in overtime, the equivalent of 56 police officers ("Better Crime Investment," *New York Times*, 2 October 1991).

These variations in processing time indicate opportunities for saving resources. Police departments need to search systematically for what the British call "best practices"—that is, ways of doing the same job more efficiently without losing quality. Small savings collected over repeated events can save lots of time. Given the pressures on government budgets in the foreseeable future, the police may be more successful in obtaining additional resources by improving internal management than by hiring more personnel.

The amount of work police do is affected by another critical management decision. There is an almost inexhaustible supply of offenses that police may choose to penalize. Mostly they involve traffic infractions; vice offenses, such as street walking, gambling, and drug dealing; and offenses against local ordinances, such as drinking in public, causing a disturbance, carrying an open container of an alcoholic beverage while driving, or violating a curfew. All of these actions generate "numbers" and "paper" that can make officers look busy and dedicated. It has been noted many times that special enforcement units can be sent into areas already covered by regular patrols and make arrests for numerous street offenses. In other words, the supply of occasions for enforcing the law is elastic in relation to the number of police officers deployed.

The amount of this sort of discretionary law enforcement that police do is determined by departmental policies and informal norms. Most departments insist that patrol officers do a certain amount of this work.[16] Although police commanders deny they have quotas, especially for traffic offenses, patrol and traffic officers know fairly exactly how much "activity" they must generate in order to satisfy their supervisors. On the other hand, they also know fairly exactly how much activity will be resented by their colleagues as "rate busting."

The general point, then, is that what police do and how busy they are are determined partly by the demand for their services and partly by the decisions they make concerning priorities, objectives, norms of activity, and organizational procedures. What the police do is the result of a perpetual and largely invisible negotiation between police and communities. Like any seller, police do not maximize the rate of return on the buyer's investment. They adjust what they do so as to provide a satisfactory return to the buyer at the least cost to themselves. While police capacity is not inexhaustible, it is always greater than it appears.

Moreover, as long as the public expects the police to provide authoritive intervention, especially with respect to physical confict, it is unfair to require the police always to be doing something apart from being available. The prime directive is a rational response on the part of police to the need to provide authoritative intervention. As a result, police will not and perhaps should not work at what is regarded as full capacity.

Indefensible Budgets

This section turns from the demands made on the police to how resources are allocated to meet those demands and how the police use resources. Police are not given money they can use as they deem necessary; they are given personnel and are told to use them as best they can. Policing is highly labor intensive. Eighty-five to 90% of the costs of policing are in personnel. In the United States in 1990, salaries made up 80.7% of the costs of state and local law enforcement.[17] Labor costs may be higher in large cities. In 1990, for example, in Seattle salaries and benefits represented 96% of the total police budget; in New York City the figure was 94%. In Britain the Audit Commission (1990b) estimated that 75% of police expenditures is for sworn officers. If civilian personnel, who now amount to 35% of total British police employees, are included, then the proportion of labor costs is substantially higher. In Canada in 1988, 82% of the costs of policing were for personnel (Engstad 1988). In 1990 they were 85% in Toronto, 90% in Vancouver, 95% in Montreal, and 85% in the Royal Canadian Mounted Police. Percentages are very similar in the eight Australian police forces (Hudzik 1989).[18]

Budget processes are dominated by formulas that determine the number of officers needed. These formulas invariably present needs as a function of population. A ratio of one officer for every 400 people is considered good, whereas one officer for every 600 people is thought to be bad. Crime rates are also considered, although not in a very explicit way:

High rates encourage greater expenditures and low rates less. The problems with these criteria for investing in the police are threefold. First, they measure community needs crudely and indirectly. It should be obvious that public safety is not a function of the number of people policed so much as of their nature. A town composed of 100,000 middle-income professional people is much safer than a town with the same number of unemployed manual laborers. Furthermore, population density is hardly ever considered. Surely it is easier to police 10,000 people in 10 square miles than 10,000 people in 1,000 square miles.

Second, there is no assurance that increasing the number of police will produce greater public safety. Not only has no connection been found between crime rates and the number of police, but adding police may actually raise crime rates, at least in the short run, because there will be more police to find criminal activity.

For these reasons, the Audit Commission (1990a) in Britain recommended strongly that neither crime rates nor crime clear-up rates be used as criteria for determining the need for police. A thorough and sensible British study of resourcing by a working group of the Home Office and the Treasury Department stated unequivocally that "No formula will ever answer the question 'how many police officers should there be?'" (Home Office–Treasury 1989). In other words, no one knows what the ideal number of police officers is.[19]

Third, basing resource formulas on numbers of police reduces managerial discretion. Since investments in policing are made primarily in terms of bodies rather than money, the means for solving public safety problems are largely predetermined. Policing is micromanaged from the outset. For example, police commanders on their own initiative usually cannot shift funds so as to replace police officers with lower-cost civilians, to adopt labor-saving technologies, to pay for civilians to assist the police in the field, or to ameliorate physical or social conditions, even on a limited scale, that might be criminogenic (Audit Commission 1990b, 1991). Some communities push micromanagement even farther, requiring official approval of any expenditure over a fixed amount.[20]

In recent years police forces have begun to find ways to increase their budgetary autonomy and to develop the kind of financial professionalism they don't currently have. One way is to sell services. If they have excess jail capacity, they may rent the space to often overburdened departments of correction. Or they may charge for escorting prisoners or for providing crowd and traffic control at commercially sponsored public events, such as rock concerts, retail fairs, and professional sports contests. Whether such sales increase the financial autonomy of the police depends, of course, on whether the proceeds go to the police or are put back into the general government budget. Much more important as a source of income are the recently enacted asset forfeiture statutes. These laws allow the police to confiscate and sell property that has been acquired from the "proceeds of crime." Once again, the money realized may or may not flow back to the police. Because very large sums of money are involved, this development bears careful watching. It may serve the cause of public safety by allowing police managers to escape from the rigidity of resourcing by body counts. On the other hand, it may be frittered away in self-serving, even dishonest, ways.

The problem with the budgets police are given is that they are not related to public safety needs. Police pretend to be producing public safety when, in fact, they are producing authoritative intervention and symbolic justice. Resources and outputs have not been connected. This sort of budgeting reduces police responsibility, undermining the search for programs that might enhance effectiveness with respect to crime prevention.

Managing Resources

By and large police managers do not use resources to achieve desired ends; instead, they supervise expenditures according to inflexible rules and traditions. Senior police officers have the mindsets of accountants rather than problem solvers.

Because police are given resources primarily to hire and support personnel, key resource decisions involve assignments. Allocations are made initially to functional commands (patrol, criminal investigation, traffic, and so forth) and later to geographical areas.

No police executive really knows the proper mix of personnel among the major functional commands. This is understandable because determining the relative cost effectiveness of different commands is difficult, especially with respect to the objective of crime prevention. Current allocations conform in a rough-and-ready way to the objectives of providing authoritative intervention and symbolic justice. Following the prime directive, patrol obviously comes first. The much smaller allocation to criminal investigation seems to reflect a tacit assessment, which is probably correct, that heavier investment will not substantially improve clearance rates.

When decisions must be made about the allocations of resources to the major commands, each unit fights fiercely for its historic proportion. Revealingly, different commands often cite exactly the same crime trends and crime problems to justify additional, or at least not reduced, personnel. Police resources are not used strategically to generate a mix of personnel that can be most effective given particular enforcement objectives. Rather, each command is given its customary proportion and told to address, in its own way, the general crime problems of the department. Police organizations operate very much like the military. Force structures and roles are fixed, so that whatever problem of defense arises each military branch gets a piece of the action. Because loyalties to commands in policing are strong, it is easier bureaucratically to allow each command to act independently on the same problem than to reshape the organization through funding decisions. So initial division of the resource pie changes little from year to year, hamstringing the ability of police organizations to match in a rational way capacities and needs. Organizational form in policing does not follow function, as rationality requires. Rather, function must adapt to relatively unchanging organizational forms.

Decisions about resources to territorial commands are made more objectively. Police forces often use formulas that take into consideration differences in population, calls for service, serious crime, miles of major roads, and distances to travel on the average radio dispatch. Some leeway is left for local judgments about special conditions, such as the presence of a large train terminal, a well-used park, a concentration of banks, or heavy nighttime use of entertainment facilities. Some commands have installations with special needs, such as courts or airports, to which a fixed number of personnel are assigned automatically, off the top.

The importance of such formulas in driving allocations varies from place to place. Los Angeles and San Diego police say 80% of most decisions about resource allocations to territorial commands are made on the basis of formulas. The value of allocation formulas is that they reduce the politics associated with decision making, protecting managers from charges of favoritism. Since existing allocations appear to be unrelated to effectiveness in crime prevention, however, the formulas put bureaucratic convenience ahead of institutional effectiveness. Rational in appearance, they tie the hands of managers. Although a popular slogan in policing during the last few years has been "let the managers manage," one must never forget that making decisions is risky, and most managers would prefer not to.

One result of this system is that local commanders play almost no part in determining the amount, nature, or uses of the resources for their commands. Despite a great deal of talk about the importance of allowing local commanders to manage according to local needs, they are given little opportunity to do so. Decisions about the number of personnel and their functional assignments are made at headquarters, as are decisions about vehicles, equipment, and operating expenses. Local commanders are not strategic problem solvers. At most they are lobbyists, competing with one another for scraps from the budget table.

Policing is riddled with regulations and tacit agreements that further reduce the ability of managers to use resources flexibly for strategic ends. Personnel, for example, must be assigned in groups, not discretely in ones and twos. An around-the-clock police station, for example, requires a certain minimum complement of officers distributed among various ranks. A patrol car requires as many as 5–6 officers to keep it functioning year round. Contracts negotiated with unions may specify whether patrol cars are to be single or double crewed, the ratio of vehicles to traffic officers, and even the number of vans for the canine unit. The size of a police station determines the rank of its commander, which in turn affects the number and ranks of support staff. All of these factors affect costs.

In short, because of the constraints on the use of personnel functionally, territorially, and organizationally, increasing or deceasing budgets has little effect on the way police work is done. The most fundamental resource of policing—people—is not being utilized flexibly according to strategic and community needs. Police forces are like balloons: They can be made bigger or smaller, but they are still balloons.

The Best-Kept Secret

The core strategy of policing is to provide a visible deterrent presence in public places. Police say again and again that the best way to prevent crime is to put police officers on the street. Politicians and the public seem to agree. What police officers do not say, and the public does not know, is that this strategy is no longer affordable. If visible presence is the key to preventing crime, then crime is going to continue to rise.

The reason crime will continue to rise is what I shall call the ten-for-one rule. In order to increase the street presence of the police by one additional officer, it is necessary to hire an extra ten officers. Let me demonstrate this.

To begin with, only 60% of police officers, on average, are assigned to patrol. The rest work various "inside" jobs or jobs in which they do not wear uniforms or move about in marked police cars. If one lumps traffic officers with patrol officers, since they too operate "visibly," then perhaps 70% of all police officers could be used to create a visible presence.

But not all officers who are assigned visibly to the streets are available all day every day. Because of restrictions on hours of work, they are organized into shifts, the usual number being four—three shifts on duty, each for eight hours, and one off duty.[21] So out of 70% of police officers who might be made visible, only 17.5% could be on the street at any given moment. Actually, some forces overlap shifts so as to produce heavier concentrations for short periods of time. But since these officers must come from some place out of the complement of 70%, the general principle about average coverage still holds.

Furthermore, all 17.5% of these officers do not work every day of the year. They must be allowed days off, sick leave, training time, and so forth. The New York City Police Department assumes for planning purposes that officers will work 206 days out of 365 ("How Best to Use 5,000 More Police," *New York Times*, 22 September 1990). Canadian police on average work 195 days a year (Donald J. Loree 1990 private communication). British police plan on the basis of 225 working days a year. Using figures like these, police forces can estimate the number of officers needed to maintain one officer on a shift year round. The New York City and Los Angeles police departments plan in terms of 1.9, Toronto 1.7, and New South Wales 1.86. Assuming an average of 1.5, which probably underestimates the requirement, shift strength is not 17.5% of total personnel but 11.7%. In other words, for every 100 officers employed, not more than 12 are deployed on the street at any given moment.

This calculation can also be made in a slightly different way. Rather than dividing the proportion of personnel assigned to visible street duties by four—the number of shifts—one can use the figure that most police use to plan the number of officers required to keep one officer on duty 24 hours a day, 365 days a year. Anthony Bouza, former chief of police in Minneapolis, says that the U.S. average is about 5.0 (Bouza 1990). The New York City Police Department estimates 5.73. Suffolk County, Long Island, however, uses 7.0. For all British forces except the London Metropolitan Police, the number is 5.6 (CIPFA 1992). In Canada, Montreal uses 7.0, Edmonton 5.1, and the Royal Canadian Mounted Police 5.0. The police of Western Australia say 5.8.

So, assuming it takes about 5.5 officers to keep one officer on duty at all times, again erring on the side of underestimation, out of 70% of police officers assigned to visible activities, 12.7% could reasonably be expected to be on duty.

But this still isn't the whole story. Further deductions are necessary. Although officers may be assigned to patrol or traffic, not all of them work on the street. Some proportion work in staff and supervisory positions. Moreover, even the remainder who do work on the street are not always visible. As work-load studies have shown, a considerable portion of a patrol officer's time is spent doing administrative tasks inside police buildings. Therefore, the proportion of police officers who constitute the famous visible presence is undoubtedly smaller even than 11.7% or 12.7%. A ten-for-one rule is generous to the police.

Police often publish figures on the ratio of police officers to population, as if these officers were always available to that population. The ratio of working police officers to population is very much lower. New York City, for example, with approximately 28,000 police officers, boasts a ratio of one officer for every 325 persons. The department says that 10,800 police constitute its "street enforcement strength" on any given day (in 1993), composed of uniformed patrol officers and plainclothes detectives assigned to street operations. Therefore, the average street enforcement strength, on any of the three daily shifts, would be 3,600 officers, and some of them are not visible because they are plainclothes detectives. Street enforcement personnel represent 7.8% of all police officers. This means that there is one street police officer for every 2,083 persons. In Los Angeles in 1990, I calculate that 8.3% of police were visibly on the streets, or one officer for every 4,972 persons; and in Seattle 8.1%, or one officer for every 5,059 persons.

With ratios like these, is it really so surprising that patrolling has little deterrent effect?

A recent authoritative study in Britain estimated that about 5% of all police officers actually do uniformed work on the street every day (Audit Commission 1990c). That would be a twenty-for-one rule. The Kent Constabulary calculates its effective street strength every day. On June 15, 1992, for example, 8.9% of the force was available for handling incidents. In 1984, the chief constable in Merseyside (Liverpool) did a similar study and was astonished to find that only 6.1% of his officers were on the streets (Loveday 1990).

The ratio of effective street strength to total personnel may not be so low in all forces. Studies have shown that smaller forces assign a larger proportion of personnel to visible patrolling (Ostrom et al. 1977, Langworthy 1986). But the principle is the same: A relatively small proportion of all police officers end up at the coal face. Ten-for-one is a good rule of thumb.

Since it costs at least $50,000 in salaries and fringe benefits to employ a police officer in Australia, Britain, Canada, and the United States, it would cost any community one-half a million dollars ($500,000) to increase the visible presence of the police *by one more person* at all times. If President Clinton's proposal for hiring 100,000 more police officers were adopted, the cost would be $5 billion. However, only 10,000 of them, at best, would be visible across the country at any given moment. That would be an increment of fewer than 200 per state if the officers were assigned equally to each state. It is hard to believe that this driblet of additional police officers would raise the crime prevention impact of the police. And it would certainly be hard to justify on cost-effectiveness grounds.

The costs of maintaining a single patrol car, which is arguably the most visible form of police presence, is also daunting. In the United States it is about $500,000 for a two-person car per year (Larson 1988); in Great Britain it is about £250,000, or about $500,000 at current exchange rates (CIPFA private communication 1992, Audit Commission 1990a).

The implication of the ten-for-one rule is that it is unrealistic to expect that public safety is going to improve or crime is going to fall if the most effective measure the police can take is to increase uniformed presence on the street. At costs like these, substantial strengthening of the core strategy of policing is exceedingly unlikely. It is fair to say that policing is bankrupt intellectually if funding its core strategy would bankrupt financially the communities police have been created to protect. Police officers are too expensive and too thin on the ground to deter crime by their sheer presence.

Conclusion

Police budgeting represents the triumph of organizational process over rational decision making (Allison 1969).[22] Police resources—which are mostly people—are allocated by police managers according to formulas, institutional traditions, tacit understandings, and contract rules, all of which have little to do with public safety. Indeed, it is fair to say that the major determinants of police allocations are not considerations of community safety at all but organizational convenience and worker morale.

The first major reason the police do not prevent crime, as we saw in Chapter 2, is that they do not consider crime prevention their primary work, despite rhetoric to the contrary. The second major reason is that police resources are not being used rationally—that is, according to the requirements of public safety (Goldstein 1990, Smith and Gray 1983, Ahern 1972, Reiss 1992, Bennett and Lupton 1992). This is why the Audit Commission (1991, p. 12) in Britain concluded that "the terms of public debate need to move off the assumption that more police officers and more police expenditure leads to a commensurate increase in the quantity and quality of police outputs."

A beautiful illustration of the lack of connection between the effectiveness of crime prevention and the resourcing of the police occurred in June 1992 in Britain, according to an article in *The Guardian*, 25 June 1992. Her Majesty's Inspectorate of Constabulary (HMIC), which is responsible for keeping British forces up to the mark, decided that it would not certify that the Derbyshire police force was worthy of financial support by the central government. HMIC charged that the county council had failed to support schemes that would have brought Derbyshire into compliance with HMIC's parameters for sound management. This was the first time HMIC had ever taken such drastic action. It would have been reasonable to conclude, therefore, that public safety in Derbyshire must have been in a parlous state. But this was not the case at all. Out of 42 regional police forces in Britain, 27 had *worse* crime rates. Derbyshire was among the 15 safest police-force areas in the country. Moreover, despite having a ratio of police to population that was 19% below the national average, the worst in the country, its crime rate was 20% better than the national average.

4

The View from Inside

The basic resource of the police is its people. If police are to be more successful in preventing crime, then police personnel will have to operate in new ways. This is easy to say but difficult to achieve. Large organizations develop customary ways of organizing activities, making decisions, and managing people. These habits constitute what is called the organizational culture of an institution. Organizational culture is like the water that fish swim in—it affects all that police do even though they are not aware of it. The organizational culture of the police is distinctive in four ways that powerfully shape what they are capable of doing. These are (1) the privileges of detectives, (2) the character of management, (3) the ethos of the occupation, and (4) the status of the police officer.

This chapter explains how each of these features of police organization affects the way police personnel think and work. It is important to note that police officials themselves have begun to question whether these elements of the traditional organizational culture are best suited to meet the challenges of the future. Whether or not the mission of the police is reformulated to embrace a more effective crime prevention role, it seems likely that these features of police organization will be the subjects of reform in the years to come.

Privileges of Detectives

Criminal investigation is the epitome of policing. It represents the crime-fighting function of the police at its purest. As countless novels, television shows, and movies illustrate, the detective is the hero of the police drama. Dirty Harry and Kojak are household names; Renko and Lucy of "Hill Street Blues" are largely forgotten. Within police organizations as well, detectives enjoy higher standing than other officers, and their unique status is reinforced by special privileges.

In all police forces, criminal investigation is a specialization for which only experienced officers are selected. Unlike patrol work, criminal investigation is not for beginners. Moreover, in most forces in Australia, Canada, and the United States, criminal investigation is more than a particular kind of job; it is a rank. This means that detectives are usually paid more than police officers. In New York City and Los Angeles, for example, detectives rank above police officers and below sergeants. This is not true everywhere. In Britain and Japan, criminal investigators have the same rank as officers in patrol and traffic. In Britain there are detective constables, detective sergeants, and so forth.

Besides selection, promotion, and pay increases, detectives receive other privileges. They usually work in civilian clothes rather than in uniform, thus removing the burden of being marked at all times as police officers. Detectives are managed more like professionals than are line officers. For example, they are given more control over their work hours, setting them in accordance with the needs of particular cases. Supervision tends to be looser, and it focuses on results rather than on sheer volume of work processed.

Selection as a detective also confers several intangible benefits. There is the satisfaction of being elevated above one's peers to a job that is considered demanding and to require particular skills. Selection also represents the first large step up the promotion ladder, positioning detectives above the majority of police officers for further advancement. More subtly, criminal investigation is regarded, both inside and outside policing, as being police work par excellence. Detectives escape from the ambivalent regard that attaches to patrol officers, who must simultaneously be crime fighters, mediators, domestic counselors, social workers, traffic cops, and medical attendants. Finally, becoming a detective is like joining an elite club. Detectives hang around together, develop their own argot, and even establish rituals of membership, usually involving drinking.

Because of the special status of criminal investigation, detectives develop a powerful interest in the status quo. They tend to resist attempts to reshape the mission of the police, especially if it involves elevating the importance of patrol work or searching for new ways of preventing crime. Their special position may be more than a matter of custom, but of legal contract, as is the case in the United States where detectives often have their own union. The net result of these entrenched privileges is that the two primary functions of modern police—authoritative intervention and symbolic justice—are not given equal weight within police organizations.

Some police agencies have tried to reduce the power and status of criminal investigators. The chief constable of Northumbria, Great

Britain, did away with the designation detective, calling everybody by rank regardless of specialty. So did Chief of Police Joseph McNamara in San Jose, California. In both cases, the title crept back. Some forces have tried to decouple rank and function by treating criminal investigation as a job that can be performed by designated officers of every rank. That is, the job is specialized but not limited to particular ranks. This is the situation now in Houston, Englewood, Colorado, and Rutland, Vermont.

Underlying the superior standing of detectives is the presumption that successful criminal investigation requires specialization, that it is not a job any police officer can do. Curiously, although this presumption is almost sacred in policing, it is frequently fudged in practice. There are wide differences among police forces with respect to the role they allow nonspecialized patrol officers to play in criminal investigations. The division of labor between detectives and patrol officers in criminal investigation is rough and ready in practice.

At one extreme some forces require investigations to be turned over to detectives automatically. In Los Angeles and Montreal, for example, patrol officers simply make out an initial report on a criminal occurrence and then hand the case over to detectives. Toronto and Seattle police do the same thing, although patrol officers may investigate minor crimes that can be wrapped up in less than an hour. At the other extreme patrol officers are instructed to investigate as many crimes as they have the time and ability to handle, relying on detectives for advice and technical support. They even investigate very serious crimes of the "smoking gun" variety—that is, solvable on arrival. Police in small towns in the United States and in remote outback stations in Australia operate in this fashion. So, too, do Canada's famed "Mounties." All officers of the Royal Canadian Mounted Police are trained as criminal investigators. The RCMP is discovering, however, that as Canada becomes more urbanized, it is becoming more difficult for its patrol officers to find time to follow through on criminal investigations. The demands of authoritative intervention and symbolic justice may be difficult for one person to handle.

The practices of most police forces fit somewhere in between. Sometimes the division of labor between patrol officers and detectives is fixed by rules that specify the sorts of crimes that each should investigate. In Australia, for example, patrol officers are generally instructed to investigate only minor crimes that can be closed immediately either because an arrest can be made or because the case is unsolvable. All serious crimes, as well as those that require ongoing investigation, are turned over to detectives. In Britain, patrol officers investigate "beat crimes," such as minor assaults, criminal damage, and auto thefts. Certain categories of serious crime are automatically turned over to detectives, such as rape, murder, and burglary when the value of the property stolen is very high. Finally, the division of labor may be regulated by process rather than by classification. Every case, regardless of its nature, is referred to a supervisor, who determines whether it should be investigated by patrol officers or detectives. In Edmonton, Canada, and Newcastle, Great Britain the decision is made by a patrol sergeant. In London, however, the decision has been made since 1988 by a detective sergeant who directs the "crime desk" of each divisional (precinct) police station.

The variety of practices with respect to this crucial division of labor shows that the status of detectives owes more to expediency than science. There is no clear evidence that specializing the criminal investigation function results in a larger proportion of crime clearances. The organizational customs of police departments with respect to the role of detectives vis-à-vis patrol officers in criminal investigations seems to depend on the relative importance given to four requirements for successful crime clearances—skills, immediacy, demand, and teamwork.

First, some crimes require unusual skills in order to be solved, such as computer crime, commercial fraud, and money laundering. Not all police, indeed not all detectives, can be trained in the full range of skills that may be needed at one time or another. Moreover, people with specialized skills that would be valued outside policing would generally not be willing to serve as patrol officers. Therefore some specialists have to be hired by police forces to serve exclusively as detectives.

Second, for the crimes that most concern the public—murders, rapes, robberies, assaults—actions taken by patrol officers who get to the scene first are often the crucial ingredient in an eventual solution. They need quickly to determine what happened, who is the likely suspect, and which people can provide reliable testimony. Several studies have shown that identification of suspects by the public accounts for 90% of the crimes that are solved (see Chap. 1). For example, a study conducted in New York City and Los Angeles showed that arrested suspects were more likely to be convicted when patrol officers took time to find witnesses, take informative testimony, and collect physical evidence (Forst et al. 1982). This kind of careful follow-up distinguished the activity of the 7.9% of officers in New York and 19.9% in Los Angeles who were making 50% of all the arrests that resulted in convictions. The lesson is that immediacy of investigation can be more important than specialized skill, depending on the nature of the offense and the circumstances of the crime.

Third, the volume of calls for service from the public may be so great that patrol officers cannot be spared to conduct more than cursory follow-up investigations. There are trade-offs between providing authoritative intervention and symbolic justice. The same people may not be able to handle both. Therefore, a division of labor may be necessary. The New York City and Los Angeles police officers just described made high-quality arrests because they took time to find possible witnesses among onlookers and to pinpoint critical physical evidence. Most patrol officers, especially in large cities, are prodded by their supervisors to respond quickly, disperse onlookers, take initial statements, and get back "in service" as quickly as possible. The priorities of patrol and of criminal investigation may conflict.

Fourth, the specialization of criminal investigation may create harmful rivalry among police that may undermine the teamwork necessary for successful criminal investigation. Specialization implicitly belittles the competence of patrol officers, creating an invidious blue-collar versus white-collar division, when what is really needed is greater cooperation. Research in the United States in the 1960s and 1970s found that having patrol officers work with detectives in investigating crimes produced higher clearance rates than when detectives worked alone (Robinson et al. 1988). This experience shaped the Integrated Criminal Apprehension Program (ICAP) of the Law Enforcement Assistance Administration, which involved having patrol officers screen cases for their solvability and play a larger role during the initial stages of investigation. The London Metropolitan Police have recently begun assigning uniformed constables as "trainee investigators" so that they can share more directly the crime-fighting job of the police and, in the process, develop an appreciation for what patrol officers need to do in order to contribute usefully to criminal investigations. All police officers in Santa Ana, California, do a two-month internship as criminal investigators. In Big Spring and Abilene, Texas, all rookie patrol officers do a 90-day internship as plainclothes investigators assigned to the clearance of minor felonies.

In sum, there is a growing realization in policing that the status of detectives cannot be justified by considerations of efficacy. Successful criminal investigation does sometimes require special skills and sometimes the ability to concentrate on a case for substantial periods of time, but it also requires immediacy and teamwork. Therefore, patrol officers may often be as important as detectives, especially in the investigation of ordinary crimes. Nonetheless, most attempts to use personnel more flexibly and to share responsibilities are resisted by detectives, who are concerned with preserving their status and its attendant privileges. Detectives are a powerful group with a vested interest in the status quo.

Character of Management

Above all things, police organizations want to avoid making mistakes for which they can be blamed. They seek to achieve this through an elaborate hierarchy of command, an insistence on compliance, and punitive supervision based on detailed rules covering almost everything that a police officer might do. Decisions are traditionally made at the top and passed down what is referred to as "the chain of command." Decision making is rarely participative or collegial across rank lines. Senior ranks hesitate to delegate responsibility to subordinates, and subordinates are reluctant to accept it.

Police are a uniformed service in which authority is distributed according to rank. The most elaborate system is in Australia, with 11 and sometimes 12 levels of ranks (Bayley 1992b; see Table 4.1). Forces in the United States have the simplest hierarchy, generally 6 ranks. In between, Canada has 7 and Japan and Great Britain 8. In every country larger forces have more ranks. Thus city forces have more ranks than suburban or rural forces. London, for example, has 11 ranks and New York City 12. This fact probably explains why Australia has so many ranks, since each of its eight police forces is very large by world standards, averaging about 5,000 police officers.

The distribution of police personnel among the ranks is far from regular. In all countries except Japan, about 75% of police are at the lowest rank. In Japan, by contrast, only 44% are at the lowest rank (Bayley 1991b). The proportion in the United States can only be estimated because national figures are not available. In large U.S. cities, however, the proportion is the same as abroad, about 75%, declining as the size of forces becomes smaller. Since about 91% of all U.S. police are employed in forces with 25 or fewer officers, the distribution of personnel by rank is probably more like that in Japan than those in the other countries (*Sourcebook* 1991, Table 1.23).

In effect, the personnel pyramid in policing, except for small police forces, has a very flat, extended base and quickly tapers to an elongated top. This means that the chances of promotion are severely limited in most places, although less so in Japan and the United States.

Another implication of these figures is that Japanese sergeants supervise many fewer police officers than is the case in Australia, Britain, and Canada. The ratio of sergeants to police officers is 1 to 4.5 in Australia, 1 to 5 in Britain, 1 to 4 in Canada, and 1 to 1.3 in Japan.[1] Among my sample of large U.S. forces, the ratio is 1 to 6.4. I suspect, again, that it is much less in most U.S. departments.

The flat-based pyramid also means that supervisory responsibility falls primarily on one rank—sergeants. Sergeants and police officers constitute 94.5% of police strength in Australia, 91% in Britain, and 80.4% in Japan.[2] In the Royal Canadian Mounted Police sergeants and lower ranks constitute 96.5% of all personnel, in the Ontario Provincial Police 94%, and in Montreal and Toronto 98% plus. Except in Japan, senior ranks have hardly anyone to supervise except one another. In the jargon of management, their span of control is very narrow. Despite the emphasis in policing on personal qualities of leadership, most senior officers lead only two or three subordinates in any direct and immediate way (Audit Commission 1991, Smith and Gray 1983).

TABLE 4.1
International Rank Structures

Countries

Australia	Great Britain	Japan	Canada	United States
Commissioner	Chief constable	Chief	Chief	Chief
Deputy commissioner	Deputy chief constable	Deputy chief	Deputy chief	Deputy/Assistant chief
Assistant commissioner	Chief superintendent	Chief superintendent	Superintendent	Superintendent
Commander (three states)	Superintendent	Superintendent	Inspector	Lieutenant
Superintendent	Chief inspector	Inspector	Staff sergeant	Sergeant
Chief inspector	Inspector	Assistant Inspector	Sergeant	Detective
Inspector	Sergeant	Sergeant	Constable	Police officer
Sergeant first class	Constable	Police officer		
Sergeant second class				
Sergeant third class				
Senior constable				
Constable				

Selected Forces

Royal Canadian Mounted Police	London	New York City	Tokyo	Edmonton
Commissioner	Commissioner	Commissioner	Superintendent-general	Chief
Deputy commissioner	Deputy commissioner	Deputy commissioner	Superintendent-supervisor	Deputy chief
Assistant commissioner	Assistant commissioner	Chief of department	Senior superintendent	Superintendent
Chief superintendent	Deputy assistant Commissioner	Chief	Superintendent	Inspector
Superintendent	Commander	Assistant chief	Inspector	Staff sergeant
Inspector	Chief superintendent	Deputy chief	Assistant inspector	Sergeant
Staff sergeant	Superintendent	Inspector	Sergeant	Constable
Sergeant	Chief inspector	Deputy inspector	Senior police officer	
Corporal	Inspector	Captain	Police officer	
Constable	Sergeant	Lieutenant		
	Constable	Sergeant		
		Police officer		

Not only do rank structures duplicate and attenuate supervision, they hinder the appointment of the right people to the right job. All police jobs are rank graded—that is, reserved for officers of particular ranks. This means that for any position only a limited number of people may be considered, regardless of whether more competent people are available at other ranks. Moreover, because promotion to higher rank is permanent, barring serious violations of law or department regulations, positions at an appropriate level must be found for all officers of each rank whether there is work to be done in those positions or not. Generally, police promote officers and then train them for their jobs, rather than training and then promoting them because they possess the skills needed. The Peter Principle of complex organizations states that people will be promoted one level beyond their demonstrated competence (Klein and Ritti 1982). Rank structures ensure that people will be appointed to jobs regardless of their demonstrated competence.

Ranks hamper communication by underscoring the importance of chains of command. Deference to authority is mandatory. Higher ranks give orders to lower ranks; lower ranks obey. Lower-ranking officers commonly address superiors by "sir" or their titles. Superior officers address subordinates by their first names. Communication flows downward; junior officers need permission to speak. In the police, rank is more important than knowledge. In one British force, for example, officers at headquarters refused to discuss plans for closed-circuit video surveillance of a downtown mall directly with the constable who had done the research and formulated the plan. They insisted that all communication pass through an intermediary superintendent and his subordinates.

Daniel Guido, formerly chief of police in several U.S. departments, tells a revealing story about the deforming effect of rank. On the first day of his appointment as chief, he drove to headquarters and found that twelve parking places had been allotted to senior officers, in descending rank order. Following the habit of a lifetime, he reversed his car and backed into the chief's slot. The other eleven cars were parked front end in. The third day, he noticed that the second car was now parked backward in its slot. The fourth day, two more were parked backward. At the end of two weeks, all cars in the line had backed into their parking spaces.

Finally, rank structures are costly. According to the Audit Commission (1990b), the cost of all ranks above that of constable (police officer) in Britain was 43% of the total cost for personnel. It calculated that if the cost of senior ranks could be lowered by just 2%, 1,000 more police officers could be hired (Weatheritt 1992). Whether savings as dramatic as these could be achieved in other countries depends on respective salary differentials. Given the similarity in rank pyramids, especially among large forces, one would expect that they could.

For all these reasons police are beginning to talk about "rank flattening," which means abolishing some of the supernumerary supervisory
grades. Robert Lunney (1989), Chief of the Peel Regional Police Force,
Canada, has proposed that only four ranks are needed—executives,
managers, supervisors, and workers. However, even modest proposals
for rank flattening generate enormous resistance, especially from the
senior ranks. These officers often argue in a seemingly selfless way that
promotion is necessary to provide incentives to work hard and well.
This is ironic since most police officers will never be promoted at all.

Management in policing is not only highly stratified, it is command
oriented. Police organizations have volumes of regulations, orders,
directives, and rules covering every aspect of activity. Some are important, such as those dealing with the use of deadly force or the handling
of confiscated drugs, whereas others are minor, such as those dealing
with hair length and how far shirtsleeves may be rolled up in the sum-
mertime. Management in policing is by exception, stressing adherence
to formal regulations rather than achievement of general organizational
objectives such as preventing crime or satisfying security needs. Senior
officers function primarily as auditors who monitor conformity to rules
rather than as problem solvers who use resources to accomplish organizational goals.

Because police officers are almost always at risk of violating some
stricture, management is perceived by police officers as oppressive and
quixotic. Officers learn to be cautious about displaying initiative or taking responsibility for actions. At all ranks officers are uncomfortable
making decisions on their own, continually checking upward with their
superiors about what should be done. The watchword in every police
force is "cover your ass"—meaning follow the book and, when in
doubt, ask for orders. Police tell the story of a commander who met a
young patrol officer on the street late at night and asked him what he
was doing. "Nothing, sir, nothing," replied the officer anxiously.[3] Police
organizations treat their personnel like children—ordering them about
without explanation, requiring them to ask permission when exercising
the slightest initiative, and punishing them for petty infractions by way
of setting an example.

The command-and-control system of police management is para-
doxical: It seeks to regulate in minute ways the behavior of individuals
who are required by the nature of their work to make instant and complex decisions in unpredictable circumstances. Police organizations
allow enormous discretion in practice while at the same time maintaining a top-down command system. The formal and informal structures
of authority in policing are not congruent.

The inescapable fact of policing is that police officers at the bottom
of the rank structure who respond to citizen calls for service and investigate crime constantly act in highly judgmental and discretionary

ways. Thrust into the hurly-burly of life, they must "sort out" what has happened and what needs to be done. This involves judging whether offenses have been committed, who might be guilty, whether arrest and prosecution would really be helpful, how enforcement should be handled, and what other remedies might be tried. Two young officers saw a man in a car drive away from the rear door of a school late in the evening. "Your basic pillar?" asked one officer."Yup," replied the other, "Your basic pillar," and they did not stop the car to find out what was going on. Policing at the coal face is case centered, like law, medicine, and social work. It involves particular people at certain times in highly specific situations. It is not subject to generic decisions by remote commanders.

The only way police organizations can reconcile the requirements of this work with the traditional management structure is to turn a blind eye. Since the organization cannot control front-line decisions in a practical way, it must ignore the wide latitude of action taken by working officers *as long as things go well.* In other words, it pretends to a degree of control it doesn't have, which has several unsettling effects.

First, the working officer feels unprotected when performing as circumstances seem to require. The officer's best work is done in the shadows of the discipline system.

Second, front-line supervisors, primarily sergeants, are put in the untenable position of being responsible for encouraging subordinates to act effectively but at the same time of being responsible for maintaining the appearance of control. They cannot supervise every decision their officers make, nor do they want to discourage what amounts to necessary initiative. So they too pretend to be in charge, feeling as much at risk as the people they supervise.

Third, since the discipline system is supposed to prevent mistakes, police organizations repress knowledge of mistakes rather than learning from them. Mistakes prompt a single response: Tighten discipline, punish individuals (Bayley 1993). If things go wrong, it is never the organization's fault—it is the fault of the working officer who failed to follow the rules. Police forces do not deal with the possibility of mistakes in the way that truly professional groups do—namely, by admitting the impossibility of controlling everything, encouraging peers to accept responsibility for supervision, forming supportive work groups that diagnose potential shortcomings in performance, and providing corrective training and advice.

In sum, the traditional discipline-centered management system, given the highly discretionary nature of police work, is a fig leaf that not only conceals but poisons.

The establishment of this discipline-centered management system is not really the fault of the police. In democratic societies police power is regarded with enormous suspicion. Its exercise must be justified by and carried out in accordance with law. Police have no choice but to pay close attention to constitutions, statutes, and judicial opinions. For good reason the police become wary of doing anything not covered by written rules and sanctioned by law. Responsible for applying law to others, it is not surprising that they use that model to manage their own affairs. Indeed, in recent years the demands for accountability to law and public opinion have intensified in democratic countries (Bayley forthcoming-b). The public becomes highly incensed, even violent, when police stray "beyond the law" (Skolnick and Fyfe 1993). It is not surprising, then, if the police conclude that being wrong is much worse than being ineffective.

Rules, ranks, supervision, and punishment are the response of the police to the demand for democratic accountability. It is their way of demonstrating commitment to the rule of law.

Occupational Ethos

Police speak of themselves repeatedly as being professionals, and there may be some senses in which the police are professional. But the workaday atmosphere of policing is decidedly unprofessional. Two aspects are particularly striking.

First, police officers do not voluntarily accept responsibility for seeing that the objectives of the institution are achieved. Policing is a directed occupation in which workers are continually monitored to determine if they are doing what they are supposed to be doing. They are regulated by time clocks, shift rosters, hourly wage rates, and benefits schedules. Like hourly blue-collar workers, they work grudgingly, always calculating how they can maximize the benefits of the job with the least personal effort. This is not to say that police do not work hard, but it is enforced hard work. As an Australian police inspector said, "Professionals are managed, ditchdiggers are supervised." Police officers are supervised.

Also like blue-collar workers, relations between police officers and the organization that employs them is invariably adversarial. Discipline is not accepted pridefully as a mark of accomplishment in a demanding line of work, as it commonly is in medicine, law, and teaching. Discipline is not considered a part of being effective. Instead, it is resented as a humiliation that the organization inflicts on its workers. As two U.S. scholars have argued, there are two cultures in policing—that of the workers, who continually search for space within its authoritarian system, and that of the managers, who seek to achieve organizational objectives through command-and-control discipline (Reuss-Ianni and Ianni 1983). Rather than being caught up in a common enterprise, police officers feel beleaguered and harassed by the organization. They are truly workers on the shop floor or at the coal face. They are the "troops," whose role is "not to reason why."

The gap in objectives between workers and organization is seen dramatically in the unwillingness of officers to regulate the behavior of peers. Police officers protect their own, not only against the general public but against their own organization. Attempts to uncover violations of organization rules are inevitably frustrated by the "code of silence" (Chevigny 1969, Maas 1973, Goldsmith 1991). The responsibility for maintaining high standards of performance is not shared between working officers and the organization. Discipline is not associated with skilled performance—it is a weapon used by "bosses."

Second, police officers are preoccupied with monetary rewards. Although they are salaried workers, they do not work to get a job done; they work to maximize returns in relation to hours worked. They never lose track of what the organization owes them for their effort in terms of days off, vacations, meal breaks, and sick leave. Police officers continually scheme to make the system work for them financially. For example, British officers have developed what is called the "Spanish practice," whereby they work a public holiday at double-time rates and then take two days of sick leave, which earns them an extra vacation day at no monetary loss.

Police officers hardly ever work for free. Any extra hour of duty must be compensated. Overtime payments have become a large portion of most police budgets, and officers regard them as an entitlement. In Seattle, for example, which is not unique in the United States, one third of all officers earned 10% of their yearly income in 1990 from overtime payments. At least 200 earned $8,000 in overtime, above an average base salary of $40,000 (*Seattle Times*, 16 November 1991). Police departments try to monitor overtime practices to prevent exploitation. A common practice is to make an arrest at the end of shift that might have been overlooked earlier, thus earning overtime. In one large U.S. city, the state and city police departments formed a joint task force to investigate drug dealing. Cooperation became strained because the state police, who were not allowed to claim overtime, wanted to make the raids early in the shift, while the city police, who could earn overtime, wanted to make them late in the shift.

The importance of material rewards is especially obvious in Canada and the United States where a large proportion of police officers work extra jobs. Moonlighting is not permitted in Australia, Britain, or Japan, but it has been estimated that 20–30% of U.S. officers are engaged in "off-duty security employment" (Cunningham and Taylor 1985). For example, a seasoned U.S. patrol officer worked the day shift for a city police department and the evening shift for a private security company. He juggled the slightly overlapping hours by showing up late for the private job or sneaking out early on the public one.

Even more impressive was the amazing Andy. A crisply dressed officer in his early thirties, Andy took me to briefings at his police station at 10 A.M., two hours before the noon to 8 P.M. shift that I was to spend with him. For this he earned two hours of overtime. As the day progressed, I learned that Andy had just come off a private security job at a high-rise condominium, which lasted from 11 P.M. to 5 A.M. that morning. Andy had taken a three- to four-hour nap prior to meeting me. However, the night work came after serving *two* back-to-back shifts for the police department the previous day, from 8 A.M. to 10 P.M., with some overlap in the shifts. He had managed to take another short nap between 10 P.M. and the private security job. Finally, he earned another hour of overtime at the end of our patrol shift because of an unusual suicide that had to be wrapped up before going off duty. Altogether, Andy had been policing for someone, public and private, 31 out of 37 hours, with not more than 5 hours of scattered sleep. Andy also had his own "Spanish practice": he would "burn" some of his overtime by taking an extra day off on the weekend and then work two out of the three days as a private security guard.

Although this is undoubtedly an extreme case, officers in Canada and the United States brag continually about exploits like these. For many of them, two and sometimes three jobs are a way of life. The salience of material rewards is not, as one might think, the result of low pay. Policing used to be a "poor man's" job, but it no longer is. Police officers and constables start at salaries of from $35,000 to $40,000; supervisors in large forces earn from $50,000 to $100,000, depending on rank. Despite the fact, then, that police salaries equal those of white-collar professionals, the ethos of the organization remains solidly blue collar.

At the same time, however, not all police officers are motivated solely by money. Although shy to articulate their softer sensibilities, police officers say things like, "In policing you can really make a difference to society" or, "You can really help people as a police officer." Beneath the uniforms, the cynicism, and the swagger, there is often a profound commitment to public service, to community, and to people.

Policing is shot through with contradictions—rigidity with discretion, hierarchy with responsibility, servicing with enforcement, and professional ideals with blue-collar rewards.

Status of the Police Officer

People think a police officer is anybody who works for a police organization and is authorized to carry a gun and make arrests. For police themselves, however, a police officer is the bottom rank, and most of those who hold that rank do patrol work. The police officer is truly the front line of policing, responsible for the vast majority of contacts between police and citizens, responding to almost all calls for service, and making most of the arrests in any force. As senior officers never tire of saying, policing is only as good as the performance of these officers. The disturbing fact is, however, that this critical assignment has the lowest status in policing.

Police officer is a job for beginners, the rank to which all rookies are appointed, and patrol is the job to which all are initially assigned. Moreover, three quarters of all officers, except in Japan, stay at that rank, many in that very assignment. Police officers constitute the pool from which ambitious and skilled personnel are selected for promotion as well as specialized assignment. Therefore, police officers are inevitably regarded as leftovers. This view is accentuated by the practice in many forces of punishing officers by returning them to police officer rank and patrol duty. Police officers are the buck privates of policing (Bradley et al. 1986).

The bulk of police officers are young, 20–35 years old; the few gray heads among them always feel obliged to explain why they are still doing patrol work and, by implication, why they are still at that rank. A typical group of patrol officers resembles an army platoon or a college sports team. Although people think of police officers as being older and vastly experienced, this is an aura cast by the uniform. The fact is that our communities are policed by kids. They are wonderful kids—bright, poised, educated beyond the average, and caring. Communities take these inexperienced young men and women, equip them with guns, high-speed cars, and the latest communications technology and thrust them into the street with the authority to deprive people of liberty, to make life-and-death decisions on the spur of the moment, and to pry into the deepest secrets of personal lives. The wonder isn't, then, that things occasionally go wrong. The wonder is that they don't go wrong more often. Considering what modern police face, they generally do a fine job.

The fact that police officer (or constable) is the lowest rank is a reflection of the nature of the work police do. Three characteristics in particular contribute to this: physicality, danger, and sleaze.

First, a police officer does a grubby, physical job that involves coming into close hands-on contact with people who are dirty and foul smelling, often covered in vomit, urine, and blood. People think that police use their guns and clubs often; they don't. But they frequently have to wrestle with people, struggle with them on the ground, push them up against walls, restrain them in the back seats of patrol cars, twist their arms behind their backs, or hold them tight to prevent violence. The work of police officers is also physically grueling. They have to work all hours of the day and night, in many departments rotating from day to evening to night shifts every week or ten days. Bone tired and often perpetually jet lagged because they "swing" through different shifts, they also have to work outdoors in rain, snow, or blistering heat as they respond to calls for assistance.

Second, police officers live with danger. The central fact of a police officer's life is that she or he must be prepared to step forward to protect the rest of us from life-threatening danger. They never forget this. Memorials to fallen officers are found in all police headquarters; pictures of officers killed in the line of duty hang on the walls; and police funerals are conducted with great pomp and solemnity. Police officers are expected to be brave. The ultimate disgrace in policing is cowardice.

Although police in all countries must be prepared to fight, the centrality of force, especially the prominence of firearms, differs from place to place. Police in the United States are the most anxious, with good reason, and rely more on firearms than the police of Australia, Britain, Canada, or Japan. British officers do not regularly carry firearms, although firearms may be issued on request in certain situations. The frontier image of Australia is belied by the fact that its police were not routinely equipped with visible firearms until the 1980s. In the Northern Territory, arguably the most outback of Australian states, police are still not armed. Japanese police carry .38-caliber revolvers, but they are almost never used. Instead, Japanese police must master a martial art. In order to be appointed a police officer (*junsa*), every recruit must earn a black belt in either judo or kendo (sword fighting with sticks) (Bayley 1991a). Canadian police are more like those in the United States, but tighter control of handgun ownership makes the use of firearms less common.

Police officers in the United States especially go to work as if they were going to war. They strap on guns, wear bulletproof vests under their shirts, insert clubs into metal rings on their heavy leather belts or down hidden pockets along the trouser seams, pick up cans of aerosol mace, feel for the pouch containing their handcuffs, and test personal radios to make sure help can be summoned if needed. They may practice inserting and ejecting shells from shotguns that they lock into stanchions in their patrol vehicles. In many cities they pick up a bag containing a visored helmet and special riot gear. Finally, they make sure they have a stout flashlight, sometimes six cells long, that can double as a club.

The paradox is that though police officers must prepare for war, they spend most of their time making peace in nonforceful ways (Skolnick and Bayley 1986). Studies consistently show that not more than 5% of the encounters between police and the public involve the use of physical force (Bayley and Garofalo 1989, Reiss 1971, Worden 1993). Among the 28 forces I studied, 12 could provide information on police deaths and injuries. From these data and other sources, I estimate that each year one police officer is killed on duty, both feloniously and accidentially, for each 2,480 officers in Australia, 4,385 in the United States, 18,000 in Canada, and 27,000 in Japan.[4]

In the United States, policing has actually become safer in the past few years. In 1990, 65 officers were killed feloniously, down from an average of 80 a year during the 1980s (*Sourcebook* 1991, Table 3.161). The felonious death rate among U.S. police was 1 for every 10,000 officers. That is only slightly higher than the homicide rate for the general population, which was 1 for every 10,638 persons (*Sourcebook* 1991, Table 3.127). Nonfatal assaults, on the other hand, were much more common for police officers than for the general population. There were 71,794 in 1990, or 1 for every 10 officers (*Sourcebook* 1991, Table 3.169).

In Canada, too, policing has become safer. During the 1980s, 3 police officers on average were killed on duty each year, which is approximately 1 death for every 18,500 officers.[5] The felonious death rate has fallen in Canada from 10.9 per 100,000 police in the 1960s to 8.3 in the 1970s and 5.6 in the 1980s.

Contrary to expectation, policing is not the most dangerous occupation. In the United States that dubious distinction belongs to farming, followed by construction, and mining/quarrying. The death rate in policing is the same as for transportation/utilities.[6] What makes danger so central to the police experience, then, is not its objective incidence but its character. The risks that police face stem from the deliberate acts of other human beings. They are not accidents. Police, like the military, must deliberately put themselves in harm's way for the sake of others. Braving danger in a human jungle is part of the police job description.

The third element that gives the work of police officers an unglamorous, nonprofessional cast is its sleaziness. Police constantly deal with the seamy side of life—with lust, perversion, greed, rage, and malice. The people they deal with daily are not the sort they would choose to associate with. Their involvement with these people, moreover, is intimate, tawdry, and shaming.

Furthermore, unlike most other professionals, police officers do not work in surroundings they control. They work where the rest of us would not want to go: dark back alleys, rubbish-strewn streets, vandalized housing projects with elevators stinking of urine, badly lit skid rows, decrepit bars, dirty restaurants, and the shacks of the homeless.

Finally, police facilities are rarely bright, cheerful, and clean but tend to be crowded, old, noisy, and shabby. A police station is a locker room, storage area, office, and canteen. It is also a factory for processing the motley, ill-assorted human beings that police officers sweep off the streets.

The status of the police officer is low, therefore, because physicality, danger, and sleaze contaminate the standing of the work itself. Policing taints those who do it. The only escape for police officers is promotion off the street and into other lines of work.

Physicality, danger, and sleaze also explain why policing has not been considered a suitable job for a woman.[7] It is the kind of life women have customarily been shielded from. Nevertheless, the number of women in policing has increased rapidly during the last decade. About 10% of police officers today in Australia, Britain, and the United States are female; in Canada the proportion is 7%. There were hardly any women twenty years ago. For example, only 1% of U.S. officers were women in 1975, the first year such data were available (*Sourcebook* 1975, Table 1.25).[8] The position of women has not improved in Japan. Today 2% of officers are female, the same proportion as twenty years ago.

Police forces are still not welcoming to women. Sometimes discrimination is deliberate, as in Japan. Many people continue to think it is improper for women to be exposed to the physicality, danger, and sleaze of policing. More often, police simply don't care to make the job congenial to women. For example, the atmosphere in police stations is often coarse and lowbrow. A police station is often like a high school boys' locker room or an army barracks, where raunchy jokes are told loudly and with pride, pinup pictures adorn the walls, sexual innuendo is the essence of humor, and physical prowess is revered.

The employment of women as police officers is also subtly demeaning to the pride of male police officers. The work that police do is often not pretty, but at least it has been manly. If women can do it as well as men, what is there left to be proud about? Again and again I have heard the story of the rookie female police officer who went with her partner to a bar fight, then locked herself in the patrol car, weeping, and refused to come out. The story sounded plausible the first time I heard it but not the twentieth. It is a standard story in Australia, Britain, Canada, and the United States. Such stories reveal a great deal more about police organizations than they do about the performance of women.

Policing is beset with a fundamental paradox. The status of police officers, whatever their gender, is inversely proportional to their responsibilities. They exercise most of the discretionary authority police possess, working alone and making decisions hastily, which are then reviewed unsystematically. Senior officers, however, who enjoy considerably more status, make relatively fewer decisions, are assisted by subordinates and colleagues, work under relaxed deadlines, and routinely have their decisions reviewed and revised. Police officers have the same sort of authority and de facto autonomy as other human-service professionals, but the organization that employs them refuses to accord them commensurate respect. This situation is different from those in hospitals, law offices, and universities, where the people who possess the greatest practical responsibility—healing, litigating, teaching—have recognized professional status and high social standing (Reiss 1971, Fyfe 1988, Shapland and Hobbs 1989, Bittner 1990).

The inverse relationship between the power and status of a police officer within the organization also applies to the status of policing generally within the criminal justice system. Police have lower status than prosecutors, who in turn have less standing than judges. Yet the decisions police make determine to a far greater degree criminal justice outcomes than those made by prosecutors or judges. Police decide whether the system will be invoked at all and, generally, what the outcome is likely to be (President's Commission on Law Enforcement and the Administration of Justice 1967). Moreover, police are much more independent and less accountable than prosecutors and judges. Police work alone, out of the public eye, and their decisions are reviewed unsystematically, if at all. Prosecutors and judges, on the other hand, work cooperatively, must create a public record, and are subject to full oversight. To round out the picture, corrections officials, who preside over the final stages of criminal justice processing, are also low-status functionaries, but they exercise much less discretionary authority than police.

The criminal justice system stands on its head. Those with the greatest responsibility have the least education, the lowest pay, and the least social status. Those who are better educated, higher paid, and enjoy unqualified professional standing have less autonomy, discretion, and power.

Conclusion

The success police have in carrying out their mission of reducing crime and enhancing public order is affected to a large extent by four aspects of organizational culture: the privileges of detectives, the character of management, the occupational ethos, and the status of police officers. Efforts to raise police effectiveness must take into account these conditions of organizational life. Chapters 2 and 3 explored two reasons for the inability of the police to prevent crime—a preoccupation with other tasks and an inflexible, unresponsive use of resources. The third reason the police are not effective in preventing crime is that their organizational culture does not value and reward initiative, responsibility, problem solving, and hands-on servicing of the public. In short, policing lacks many of the professional characteristics that are needed for creative adaptation to the shifting circumstances of modern life. Its organizational culture is inimical to the mobilization of the best that is available in its personnel in terms of intelligence and commitment.

But perhaps this is too much to expect. Perhaps police organizations have to have the kind of organizational culture described here. I think not. The four elements just discussed are neither inevitable nor necessary. They are the result of decisions that have been made in the past about how police organizations should be run. Tradition makes them seem sacred, but, in fact, they are artifacts. The best evidence for this proposition comes from Japan (Bayley 1991a). The organizational culture of Japanese policing differs in almost every way from that of Australia, Britain, Canada, and the United States, despite some formal similarities.

Although the Japanese police are uniformed and ranked, responsibility is more freely delegated and readily accepted. Subordinates are expected to understand basic policies and carry them out without detailed instruction. Mistakes may be punished but are more likely to be treated by reeducation, counseling, training, and informal supervision. Japanese police work cooperatively in groups, with strong bonds of mutual support between subordinates and supervisors. Adherence to high standards is obtained through the pride taken in belonging to an elite organization. Failure to behave properly is seen not only to harm the individual but to detract from the reputation of the institution. Personal self-esteem and the standing of the institution are intertwined. The maintenance of discipline is not the exclusive responsibility of supervisors but is shared by peers at all levels, who pay close attention to performance and instruct one another quietly when necessary.

Policing in Japan is a vocation that demands total commitment to an exemplary standard of behavior both on and off the job. It is not just a job undertaken primarily for material benefits. Japanese police do not work two jobs; instead, they are prepared to work extra hours without compensation. And they do not count the days until retirement.

The chances of promotion for police officers are greater in Japan than elsewhere, with only 46% remaining at entry-level rank. Pay rises automatically with length of service. Experienced police officers (*junsa*) may earn more than newly promoted sergeants or inspectors. Though police officers are at the bottom of the rank ladder, their sense of self-worth is heightened by their pride in their organization. In exchange for their dedication to the institution's ideals of conduct, the organization supports them well with material benefits, but, more important, makes them feel valued and special.

The Japanese case shows that there is more than one way to organize a police department and that similar, formal authority structures can operate in significantly different ways. Can police organizations in Australia, Britain, Canada, and the United States operate similarly? I believe they can. Although in Japan organizational life is affected by broader cultural habits, it is not entirely dependent upon them. Judging from the success with which Japanese management practices in business have been transferred internationally, and vice versa, it does not seem necessary for U.S., Australian, British, or Canadian police officers to become

Japanese in order to change their organizational culture. The great inhibitor of change in police organizations is not culture but lack of vision—the inability to recognize that organizational practices are a means to an end rather than an end in themselves.

The challenge, then, is to determine which aspects of organizational culture need to be changed in order more successfully to prevent crime and maintain social order. It is easy enough to criticize the police, as one might any complex institution. In order to formulate a reform plan, one must determine, first, what strategies and policies might reasonably prevent crime, and, second, whether these strategies and policies will require changes in the occupational culture. These questions are explored in the next two chapters.

II

POSSIBILITIES

5

Agendas for Change

Police are in a bind. They are costly without being clearly effective. The usefulness of their core strategies—mobile patrolling, visible presence, and deterrent criminal investigations—is doubtful. Understandably, therefore, during the 1980s, as crime and the costs of policing both rose inexorably, the police came under acute political pressure to demonstrate that they were giving value for money. Their legitimacy was no longer guaranteed by their mission and their authority under law. The question naturally arises, then, What should the police be held responsible for doing? Both the public and the police seem to agree in general terms. The performance of the police should be judged in terms of three criteria: effectiveness, efficiency, and rectitude.

Effectiveness is judged in terms of whether the police are achieving the objectives for which they were created. The general public would say this means the enhancement of public safety and good order. Simply put, the criterion of police effectiveness requires a reduction in crime.

Efficiency deals with the costs of what the police do in relation to what they achieve. The question is not what the police accomplish but whether the costs of what they do are minimized. Efficiency and effectiveness represent, respectively, the costs and benefits of police activity. Although both must be considered in judging performance, greater attention may be given to one or the other at particular times by different police forces.

Rectitude cuts across the first two categories and is probably the most sensitive issue for the general public. Here attention focuses on whether the police are treating people properly, legally, and morally, regardless of their effectiveness in preventing crime or their efficiency in reducing costs.

Altogether these three criteria create different agendas for improving police performance. Effectiveness is concerned with doing the right

79

things; efficiency with doing things right; and rectitude with treating citizens right.

This chapter first examines what the police are doing to achieve effectiveness, efficiency, and rectitude. It surveys what can be considered current and choice in police innovation. Then, in the section "The Growth of Evalution," I discuss the ways in which performance is being measured so that effectiveness, efficiency, and rectitude can be demonstrated to an increasingly skeptical public. This exercise is fundamental to creating an accountable police force. The public cannot judge the police, as democracy requires, if their performance is invisible. Moreover, the choice of performance indicators, as well as of the processes for studying them, affect the direction in which police forces are likely to move. Although it may not seem obvious, measurement affects policy as well as purposes. The dynamics of this relationship are explored in the final section, "Principles of Meaningful Assessment."

Effectiveness

Building on research conducted mostly in the 1970s showing that the primary strategies of policing were not protecting communities and reducing crime, police in the 1980s experimented with new approaches on a broad front. The best-known innovation is undoubtedly community policing, now a worldwide movement in developed democratic countries. Because this development is so important, as well as complex, I discuss it in a separate chapter (Chap. 6). But community policing does not exhaust the inventiveness of the police. Following are five other broad strategies that have been tried in the last few years.

Crackdowns

Police have known for a long time that crime is not distributed evenly across communities. For generations maps on the walls of police stations have indicated with colored pins the patterns of crime occurrence. The statistical analysis of emergency calls for service that pinpoints hot spots of criminal activity is merely a more sophisticated version of this time-honored practice (Sherman, Gartin, and Buerger 1989). Acting on this kind of information, police then try to monitor these locations closely, waiting for precisely the right moment when law enforcement can produce the most significant results. This strategy has been a primary tactic against drug dealing (Bynum, Worden, and Frank in press), as well as prostitution, gambling, street robbery, illegal parking, and the use of unsafe bicycles (Sherman 1987). Crackdowns can be effective in reducing criminal activity, although their effect decays over time. After reviewing many studies, Sherman (1987) concluded that "it is hard to sustain persistent deterrent effects over a long-term crackdown, but that even short-term crackdowns can produce residual effects," sometimes for as long as two years. In other words, short but intense and focused law enforcement can be sweet. Sherman also recommends random— meaning unpredictable—crackdowns at troublesome locations so that would-be criminals are kept anxious and off-balance (Sherman 1986). This is the tactic police have been using for years when they "crack down" on dangerous driving or randomly administer breath tests to drivers in particular locations.

Market Disruption

Traditionally, crime has been viewed as a problem stemming from a few antisocial individuals who prey upon their naive and helpless neighbors. The best approach to its suppression, the thinking has been, is for the police to arrest such people and put them in prison, where they cannot harm the innocent public. More recently, police have adopted a new technique, based on the observation that some forms of street crime are market driven and commercially motivated. The key to suppressing this form of crime is to make it unprofitable. If "market criminals" are only arrested, then others may spring up to take their place, the chances of arrest being viewed as an acceptable cost of operation (Greenberg 1989). Obviously this model does not apply to murder or rape, but it does to "victimless" crimes, such as prostitution, drug dealing, pornography, and gambling. It may also apply to robbery and burglary.

Acting on this insight, police are doing more than raiding and arresting known dealers and purveyors; they are trying to eliminate the profitability of crime. In cases of drug dealing and prostitution, police combine enforcement crackdowns with very visible surveillance that makes both buyers and sellers uncomfortable. Uniformed officers may be stationed up and down known market locations, strictly enforcing minor laws against littering, loitering, jay-walking, or impeding traffic. They may take pictures of dealers and their customers and of the license plates of the buyers. In Britain, for example, Leicestershire police patrol with hand-held video cameras, photographing the "curb crawlers" looking for drugs or sex.

This strategy shifts the focus of police action from enforcement to disruption, from people to situations. It may also dictate the timing of police action because police concentrate on times of the day or week when business is most brisk, thus maximizing the impact on profits. Los Angeles police used the market-disruption strategy when they erected metal gates to create cul-de-sacs, as did Houston police when they built "speed bumps" in the streets of Link Valley and mobilized the community to monitor and photograph street drug dealing (Sparrow, Moore, and Kennedy 1990).

Asset Forfeiture

Another way to reduce the economic incentive to commit crime is to confiscate the profits of crime. In most jurisdictions in Australia, Britain, Canada, and the United States laws allow the confiscation of assets purchased with the proceeds of crime. Japan enacted a law in 1992 allowing the confiscation of proceeds from drug trades. It is considering a wider measure, especially one that might apply to the assets of organized crime, similar to the U.S. Racketeer Influenced Corrupt Organizations (RICO) law. Assets frequently include not only personal property, such as houses and cars, but equipment that facilitates criminal activity. Police in South Carolina have taken the beds and furniture used by prostitutes in motels whose owners condoned the illegal activity; police in Portland, Oregon, have seized the cars of men cruising for prostitutes. As a result of this policy, governments now possess vast inventories of goods and property worth a great deal of money. This can have its amusing side. Through forfeiture the FBI became the owner of a topless bar in Washington a short walk from its headquarters. Although it eliminated the sex, the FBI continued to run the bar, ostensibly as a training facility in undercover tactics.

Money realized from the sale of confiscated assets, as well as cash seized outright, is becoming a substantial increment to many police budgets, which can be used for discretionary off-budget purchases. Police agencies with a concurrent jurisdiction sometimes get into bitter wrangles over the division of these spoils. So too do police and the governments they serve. Police argue that the money should come to them, whereas governors and mayors want the proceeds to go into the general budget. The uses to which forfeited assets, which are a kind of free money, are put should be watched closely by communities. Asset forfeiture puts the police in the position of the "thief takers" in eighteenth-century London, who were awarded a portion of the property recovered from thieves. Although one can argue that the police always have a vested interest in crime, asset forfeiture allows the police to profit directly from crime.

Stings

"Sting" is the slang name for an operation in which police pose as willing or naive participants in criminal activity in order to arrest suspected participants. The normal police procedure is to try to get to crimes before they happen. But this is difficult to do—most of the time the police arrive too late. Stings solve this problem by bringing crime to the police. Rare before the late 1970s, stings became a favorite tactic during the 1980s (Marx 1988, Marx and Reichman 1984). In the most common kinds of stings police pose as purchasers of stolen goods or illegal drugs, customers of prostitutes, "marks" for street robbery, and bribers of civil servants. The tactic is sometimes used against the police themselves. Since the Knapp Commission investigation of corruption in the New York City Police Department in 1972, undercover police officers have posed as victims of crime carrying sizable quantities of cash in order to discover whether investigating officers would turn in the seized evidence according to procedures (Henry 1990). The FBI's famous ABSCAM investigation into bribery among federal politicians in the late 1970s was a sting operation, as was the arrest of Washington, DC, Mayor Marion Barry for drug use. Stings are an extension of market disruption because they undermine criminals' confidence in the profitability of their illegal activity. Stings are particularly useful against victimless crimes, where none of the participants are willing to complain or testify.

Tracking Career Criminals

Studies indicate that a large proportion of street crime—burglary, robbery, drug dealing, aggravated assault—is committed by repeat offenders. In one of the most influential studies, Marvin Wolfgang and colleagues (Wolfgang et al. 1972) concluded that a small proportion of known offenders commit a disproportionate amount of crime. They estimated that the 6% of a birth cohort who were chronic offenders, or 18% of the known juvenile delinquents in the sample, accounted for 52% of all arrests. A decade later Peter Greenwood (1982) estimated that sentencing practices which properly target chronic offenders could reduce robbery by 15% and reduce the prison population by 5%. The conclusion was that if the criminal justice system would "selectively incapacitate" habitual or "career" criminals, a disproportionate dent could be made in the incidence of crime (Walker 1989).

Police have pursued this tactic in several ways. The Repeat Offender Project in Washington, DC, in 1982–1984, shadowed habitual felons after they were released from prison in an effort to catch them in the act of committing new crimes. Offenders would then be prosecuted and convicted with very long sentences. During the late 1970s and 1980s the Special Crime Attack Team (SCAT) in Denver operated in the same way. Unfortunately, these operations tend to be expensive in relation to results because it is difficult to maintain close enough surveillance to detect people in the act of committing crimes (Martin and Sherman 1986).

In a variation on the surveillance strategy, police track habitual offenders overtly rather than clandestinely. Police want offenders to know that they are being watched, so that they will be deterred from their customary activity. Officers in the Targeting Repeat Aggressive Predators (TRAP) program in Los Angeles visit released career criminals when they return to their normal haunts, wish them well, encourage them to get a job, but also warn them about reoffending. The Target 8 Project in Minneapolis tried to "harass"—as critics charged—career felons into going straight by watching them closely and then arresting or citing them for violations of any law or ordinance, no matter how minor. The purpose of this surveillance was to dramatize to repeat offenders that they were marked.

Technological Surveillance

The most obvious example of technological surveillance is the installation of video cameras in places where serious street crimes take place, such as banks, convenience stores, shopping malls, railway and bus terminals, warehouses, and selected street corners and parks. Less intrusively, police are becoming skilled at using computers to study the lifestyles, especially the purchasing patterns, of likely offenders to determine if they are violating rules associated with government entitlements, probation conditions, or commercial codes (Marx and Reichman 1984). Auditory surveillance—in the form of wiretaps, bugs, and long-range listening devices—is another form of technological surveillance that is growing in sophistication.

Crackdowns, market disruption, asset forfeiture, stings, career-criminal tracking, and technological surveillance are all areas that are being explored and developed to enhance the effectiveness of law enforcement as a tool of crime control. The police in the United States lead the world in developing such strategies. This is not just because the United States has more police agencies and more police: Strategic innovation is a distinctive emphasis in contemporary U.S. policing. Police in the United States are still looking for "silver bullets"—perhaps because they feel more desperate than police in other countries.

Efficiency

Police efficiency, meaning lowering costs for each unit of activity, can be improved in many ways: installing personal computers, reducing the number of reporting forms, purchasing longer-lasting equipment, reorganizing chains of command, reducing the number of ranks, and replacing police officers with lower-paid civilians. Three changes, however, are especially important because they require broad organizational rather than narrow technical innovations. These innovations, which challenge the customary organization of police organizations, are (1) the development of managerial expertise, (2) the improvement of planning and research, and (3) the decentralization of command. A fourth change that is being undertaken in the name of efficiency is the shortening of chains of command by eliminating redundant supervisory ranks (see Chap. 4).

Development of Managerial Expertise

For years police organizations have been criticized for years for failing to develop skilled managers—that is, people who can manage complex organizations as opposed to commanding field operations. Senior police officers have been called "reluctant managers" who do not anticipate needs and reshape their organizations to accomplish new objectives (Elliot 1973). Instead, the stock solution of police managers to any problem is to get the "right man" for the job. Police organizations manage by personality, in the sense that mistakes and inefficiency are always attributed to the personal inadequacies of individuals, never to organizational systems, processes, and mindsets. The President's Commission on Law Enforcement and the Administration of Justice characterized police management as "unarticulated improvisation" (1967, p. 18). Judging from current criticism, the description is still apt.

Police are trying to improve their management policies in several ways. Because senior managers in all countries except Japan are "promoted constables," educational requirements for recruitment are being raised, and bachelor's and postgraduate degrees are prerequisites for promotion to managerial positions. Probably half of all senior managers in the British police now have university degrees. In the United States, the average education of police officers rose from a high school diploma in 1969 to two years of college in 1990 (*Sourcebook* 1990, Table 1.36). In Los Angeles, most officers of the rank of captain and above hold an advanced degree, often in public administration or business administration. By contractual obligation, several officers are sent each year from the New York State Police and the New York City police for postgraduate degrees at local universities. The National Institute of Justice awards two Pickett Fellowships each year for management training at the Kennedy School of Government, Harvard University. And the Police Executive Research Forum runs an annual workshop on management. Australia, Britain, and Canada send senior officers for advanced courses in management to their national command colleges. Some forces are beginning to provide management training through in-house workshops, retreats, and mentoring by senior officers of newly promoted junior officers.

Another way of obtaining skilled managers is by lateral entry at senior levels. The Japanese do this through a system of stratified recruitment whereby highly qualified people are hired directly to middle rank (inspectors) to be trained for promotion to senior managerial positions (Bayley 1991a). These "elite course" individuals are appointed from the brightest graduates of Japan's best universities. They are trained for a year at the national police college and then posted throughout the country as middle-echelon managers.

Australia, Britain, Canada, and the United States have discussed stratified recruitment but have always rejected it as being inegalitarian. This thinking is curious because the military, on whom police departments are partially modeled, has long accepted the distinction between commissioned and noncommissioned officers. In some police forces a handful of senior administrative posts may be filled by civilians who are recruited directly. Generally they handle budgeting, accounting, finance, and personnel. New York City, for example, has a civilian deputy commissioner for management and budget, Montreal a civilian director of administration, Toronto a deputy chief for administration, and Leicestershire an administration officer. Usually these appointments are made from other public services, although there is a trend toward recruitment from the private sector. Increasingly, too, police are obtaining advice from commercial management consultants as well as from private business executives who come "on loan" for short periods.

Planning and Research

If resources are to be managed efficiently, police need to anticipate problems, devise strategies for solving problems, reshape organizational practices, and evaluate the quality of implementation. Managers need to be organizational problem solvers who find new ways of getting work done. Management is more than supervision—more than monitoring compliance with customary norms. Outsiders who study policing are surprised at how rarely genuine management occurs, especially compared with business (Goldstein 1990, Sheehy Commission 1993). Management in policing, as one officer said, is "reacting and scheduling." It is repetitive troubleshooting and crisis management, all within short time frames.

Although most medium- to large-sized police agencies have research and development offices, few do research on either the effectiveness or the efficiency of police operations (Weatheritt 1986). By and large designated research offices have not been given responsibility for identifying the best practices, nor have they developed the capacity to do so. For the most part, they do not make plans or work out strategies. Instead, they take care of administrative housekeeping chores for the chief. They write speeches, organize visits of dignitaries, collect statistics, write annual reports, devise administrative forms and procedures, draft regulations, and advise about the impact of new laws on police practices. Sometimes they supervise the planning of building projects or the purchase of equipment (Sparrow, Moore, and Kennedy 1990).

In the United States, police devote less than half of 1% of their budgets to research and development, compared to 10–15% by the Department of Defense (Reiss 1992). This is proportionally about the same percentage as that of the furniture industry. Research, Reiss concludes, is not a "core technology" of policing.

Police are beginning to see the importance of planning and research. Many forces now regularly formulate "strategic plans," where information about future conditions is collected and operational units are asked to formulate plans to meet these conditions and to estimate the costs of and the time required for implementation. These exercises are sometimes undertaken in an ad hoc fashion, often after the appointment of a new chief officer, to put the new leader's stamp on the organization. In only a few forces has strategic planning become institutionalized, with senior commanders regularly planning several years ahead.

Strategic planning frequently involves reorganization. With a delightful irony, a strategic planning group in Victoria State, Australia, named its effort Project Arbiter after Petronius Arbiter, c. 50 A.D., who is supposed to have said: "We trained very hard—but it seems that every time we were beginning to form up into teams we would be reorganized. I was to learn later in life that we tend to meet any new situation by reorganizing: and a wonderful method it can be for creating the illusion of progress while producing confusion, inefficiency, and demoralization."

The capacity of the police to undertake useful planning is about to undergo a revolution. Up to now it has been difficult for managers to keep track of personnel deployed in different specialties, of the incidence of different sorts of crime, of the actions being taken by officers, of the volume and nature of the public's calls for service, and of changes in the circumstances of communities. Not only was tracking difficult for forces as a whole, it was even more difficult for operational command units, such as police stations and precincts. Computers, however, are about to change all that. Building on computer-assisted dispatch systems (CADs), several forces now have on-line systems for tracking the availability of personnel at all operational levels, for monitoring work loads by unit and even by individuals, and for reporting the actions taken by officers in the field. This capability is then combined with CAD information on calls for service, crime-reporting information by occurrence, and, finally, census data on extant and projected social conditions. Being able to combine data in this way depends on the coincidence between police and census-collection boundaries, as well as the boundaries of other government agencies with relevant information. It can now be done in New South Wales, Australia. Britain is close. The United States and Japan do not yet have this capability. So, for the first time, the potential exists for police managers to match and project resources, work loads, demands, and socioeconomic conditions, and to do this for manageable command units.

Decentralization of Command

A common criticism of the police is that they are too centralized. Resources are allocated, as we saw in Chapter 3, according to generic plans drawn up at headquarters. The officers who are in closest touch with operational problems have little opportunity to shape policy. Centralized command puts a premium on compliance rather than on initiative. The solution, many people believe, is to shift the locus of planning and budgeting from headquarters and the senior ranks to constituent territorial commands and the middle ranks. Under this system field commanders would determine needs, strategies, resource levels, and allocations. Headquarters would provide appropriate resources to field operations as needed. Intervening supervisory layers, such as areas, regions, and burroughs, would be eliminated.

Decentralization is such a popular idea that forces of all sizes now say they are doing it. The reality, however, falls short of the rhetoric. Most precinct or police station commanders display little initiative. Since they have no control over the assignments of the personnel they are given—patrol, criminal investigation, traffic—their tactical flexibility is severely limited. Most can shift uniformed personnel to plainclothes undercover work for short periods of time, but they never—or certainly only rarely—try to use detectives to create a uniformed, visible presence. Commanders may set up task forces to address particular problems. In Britain, for instance, officers in charge of some subdivisions decide how many patrol officers should be assigned to radio cars as opposed to community-policing beats and whether patrol vehicles should be single or double crewed. By and large, however, field commanders supervise more than they lead and audit more than they direct. Elliot's (1973, p. 62) description of U.S. field commanders in the early 1970s is still true today throughout Australia, Britain, Canada, Japan, and the United States:

> Field commanders never plan or if they do it is a hasty last-minute affair. It is the rare [precinct] commander who can tell you how many people he will have available a week from today, what special problems he will face, what he will do if he doesn't have sufficient manpower, or how he plans to use any extra personnel.

This is not the fault of the local commanders: The system neither expects nor allows more. Their performance is judged narrowly and perfunctorily. Three criteria are crucial: changes in crime rates, overspending the overtime budget, and an incident of serious misconduct by a police officer. In other words, commanders have done well if crime remains steady, overtime expenditures are closely monitored, and "shit doesn't hit the fan." These performance criteria, while limited, are not unintelligent. They correspond quite neatly to effectiveness, efficiency, and rectitude. The problem is that there is very little that local commanders can do about two of them—crime rates and police misbehavior. The best that commanders can do, therefore, is monitor the overtime budget and give the appearance of being "leaders." They become fatalistic accountants, albeit with some swagger. Japanese precinct commanders are in a somewhat stronger position because their police culture requires senior officers to display moral leadership and to create interactive and supportive working groups (Bayley 1991a). They play a larger role with respect to both efficiency and rectitude than Western commanders.

Budgetary devolution, too, which almost every large force says is occurring in dramatic ways, is largely a fiction. The main reason, as we saw in Chapter 3, is that personnel costs dominate budgets, but personnel levels and allocations are set by headquarters. Local commanders are given peanuts to play with. For example, the Leicestershire police, in Britain, proudly say they have devolved budgets to subdivisions. In fact, only 2.6% of subdivisional expenditures can be touched by local commanders, and these involve laundry services, travel expenses, cleaning supplies and equipment, copying costs, postage, and fuel for vehicles—hardly areas of great strategic moment. In New South Wales, Australia, only 6% of a subdivisional budget may be spent as the local commander directs. An officer in charge of a major metropolitan precinct in Canada spoke for many when he said that the biggest budgetary decision he had made the previous year was whether to purchase a bulletin board for the squad room.

The most radical proposal for real decentralization has been put forward by the British Audit Commission (1991). It recommends that decisions about security needs, strategies, and resources be made by the commanders of "Basic Police Units" (BPUs). These functions, which are now monopolized by the headquarters of Britain's 45 police forces, should be given to the country's approximately 500 subdivisions (precincts).[1] All specialized units not based on subdivisions, along with all administrative services, should be considered to be in "support" of local operational commanders. Under this system, budgets would be built up from the projected requirements of subdivisions. Subdivisions would be charged for the services of specialized units, such as dog squads or firearms-response teams. Eventually, subdivisions would bear the costs of training, auditing, and recruiting. This process has begun in the Thames Valley police, where each subdivision has negotiated contracts with force-wide specialists, such as the air service and the dog squad. This requires, of course, that the subdivisions accurately anticipate their needs for these services, and that if they overspend, they make it up elsewhere.

The British proposal seems radical and risky until one stops to think about how U.S. police departments are structured. The United States has precisely the kind of decentralized command, planning, and budgeting system that other countries are only thinking about. According to the Bureau of Justice Statistics, the United States has 12,228 local police departments, 3,093 sheriffs' offices, and 48 state police departments (*Sourcebook* 1990, Tables 1.23, 1.24, 1.27). This compares with 8 police forces in Australia, 45 in Britain, 461 in Canada, and 47 in Japan (Bayley 1992b). The average number of officers in a U.S. police department is 30 (*Sourcebook* 1990, Table 1.28), and the average number of people served is 16,139 (Bayley 1992). Not all U.S. forces, of course, are so small. One fifth of U.S. police officers are employed in 25 large departments with an average of approximately 4,800 officers. The United States, then, has mostly small departments responsible for few people, but it also has more large departments than Australia or Canada.

If decentralization is the wave of the future, whether to make policing more efficient or more effective in dealing with local conditions, then the United States knows more about it than any other country. Big-city police chiefs in the United States frequently disparage small-town chiefs for being sergeants with inflated titles. But this misses the point in two ways. First, although big-city sergeants may supervise more officers than small-town chiefs, they are given considerably less managerial authority. Second, a complicated hierarchy of command may not be necessary to make appropriate decisions about policing. Big-city sergeants and other middle-rank officers might well perform satisfactorily as operational commanders and administrators if they were given the opportunity.

In addition to developing management skills, enhancing planning and research, and decentralizing operations, many forces are trying to increase efficiency through cost cutting. Four ideas for accomplishing this objective seem particularly popular at the moment.

1. *Use of civilians.* In most countries civilians can replace police officers for nonenforcement work at about half the cost. At the present time, over 30% of Britain's police employees, omitting cleaners and maintenance staffs, are civilians, as are 27% in the United States, 20% in Australia, just under 20% in Canada's largest forces, and 12% in Japan.

2. *Administrative support.* This involves creating specialized units, often composed of civilians, to take over administrative chores, especially report writing and data entering, from operational police officers. In Britain, for example, when the Northampton police created an Administrative Support Unit in one subdivision, largely to assist detectives, the time detective constables devoted to paperwork fell to 27.6% compared with 54.3% in a comparable subdivision. The saving allowed detective constables to triple the time devoted to making inquiries and to raise by one third the time given to conducting interviews.

3. *Elimination of ancillary work not directly related to policing.* The prime candidates here are police officers serving as guards in jails, transporting prisoners among jail facilities, conducting certain kinds of public-safety inspections, and attending deaths outside medical premises.

4. *The charging of fees for police services.* Normally, the services of the

police are regarded as a public good—something that is provided by government for the good of all. Everyone is equally entitled to the safety police provide. However, sometimes police activity bestows particular advantages on small groups of people who profit financially from it, at a cost to the rest of society in terms of diminished police capacity. Examples are police coverage at rock concerts and professional sporting events and the monitoring of burglar alarms. Many police forces are actively discussing how they might balance their general obligations against narrower commmercial ones. Excepting Japan, the countries of my study do not have national policies concerning the charging of fees for police services. A hodgepodge of practices exists among forces that may operate right next to one another.

Rectitude

The 1980s represented a watershed period with respect to the moral dimension of policing. During those years, police in jurisdiction after jurisdiction were forced to share responsibility for maintaining appropriate levels of discipline with newly created civilian review bodies. In effect, police lost their monopoly on determining whether police officers were treating citizens right.

The handling of allegations of police misconduct involves two stages—investigation of the charges and determination of the punishment. Traditionally, police departments have handled both stages. Increasingly over the past decade, however, civilian-review bodies have moved into investigations and more recently into determinations of disciplinary action. In each area there are gradations of civilian involvement. In the investigation of complaints, civilian boards may be allowed to review police investigations, to supervise and direct them, or to conduct their own investigations. In the determination of disciplinary action, civilians may be allowed to recommend action or to take action on their own (see Table 5.1). There is a progression to the growth of civilian oversight, usually beginning with reviewing investigations, then supervising them, and finally undertaking investigations independently. The taking of disciplinary action against police officers represents the most extensive civilian involvement, with review boards allowed first to recommend and later to supplant police authority. Although this progression has characterized developments in several jurisdictions, there is nothing historically necessary about it. No step is taken without bitter political conflict between the police and their communities.

In most of the United States and in all of Japan police continue to monopolize investigations and disciplinary determinations. One might argue that the national and prefectural Public Safety Commissions in Japan have authority at both stages, but, in fact, they rarely exert it

TABLE 5.1
Disciplinary Responsibilities

	Police	Nonpolice
Investigation	Japan United States	*Review:* New Zealand
		Supervision: Victoria State, Australia Australian Federal Police RCMP
		Independent: Britain Quebec, Canada
Disciplinary action	Japan United States	*Recommendation:* Britain
		Independent: Ontario and Quebec provinces, Canada Queensland, Australia

(Bayley 1991a). Some large U.S. forces have accepted civilian review of investigations—for example, New York City, Houston, Detroit—and a few allow recommendations concerning punishment (Walker and Bumpus 1991). None permit civilians to impose disciplinary punishments on the police (Petterson 1991).

Australia, Britain, and Canada have gone much farther in empowering civilian review boards. In Australia complaints about police misconduct are lodged with both the police and a civilian tribunal, sometimes an ombudsman. These bodies may review and direct police investigations. If allegations are made against very senior officers—who have no really independent superior—then the civilian panels are required to investigate. They may also do so when an investigation is in the "public interest"—for example, when a charge is particularly grievous or public opinion is especially aroused. In most cases the police determine the appropriate punishment on the basis of evidence. These decisions may be appealed to the Police Ministers of each state, who are civilians, or to specially created boards or tribunals. Tribunals are usually made up of judges and lawyers, with some lay representation.

In Canada the pace has been set by the provinces of Ontario and Quebec, which have established, respectively, a Provincial Complaints Commission and a Police Ethics Commission, which have authority over all police in the province. Each commission may review any police investigation and conduct its own if it deems it necessary. The standard used by the Ontario and Quebec commissions to determine guilt is less stringent than that employed in Australia. It is the civil court principle of "clear and convincing evidence" rather than the criminal one of "beyond a reasonable doubt." The Ontario and Quebec commissions also review disciplinary decisions made by police and may refer such decisions to specially appointed civilian boards.

In Britain the review process is country-wide but it is not as intrusive as the two Canadian examples. The Police Complaints Authority (PCA), established in 1985, may review and supervise the investigation of any allegation of police misconduct. In cases of death, serious injury, or whenever its members "deem it proper," this board is required to make its own investigation (Police Criminal Evidence Act of 1984). Unlike in the Canadian provinces of Ontario and Quebec, findings against an officer must be supported by evidence that is "beyond a reasonable doubt." If the PCA disagrees with the disciplinary decisions of the police, it can refer the decisions to a tribunal consisting of the chief constable of the force involved and two PCA members who have not been associated with the investigation (Maguire and Corbett 1989).

In practice, a three-tiered system has evolved to handle charges of wrongdoing by the police. Minor complaints, which represent most cases, are handled through informal conciliation between the police and the aggrieved citizens. Cases of moderate importance are reviewed by the PCA, usually without additional directions being given. For a handful of very serious allegations, especially when public interest is high, the PCA manages the case from investigation through the determination of punishment (Reiner 1990).

Partly in response to the growing assault on their disciplinary prerogatives, police themselves have developed a variety of programs designed to improve the rectitude of performance:

1. Enactment of new internal regulations for processing complaints and conducting investigations (Tasmania, Britain).
2. Creation of larger, more visible units for the investigation of misconduct, and making service in these units a condition for promotion to senior ranks (Victoria State and New South Wales).
3. Diversified recruitment (everywhere).
4. Training in cultural sensitivity (Quebec, London, Houston).
5. Training in nonforceful methods for resolving conflict between citizens (London, Northern Territory).
6. Encouragement of the filing of complaints (Japan).
7. Creation of policy guidelines for different sorts of especially controversial police actions, such as the use of firearms and armed raids on premises (Australia, Britain, the United States).
8. Disbanding or reorganizing units with records of abuse or illegality, such as armed-offender and career-criminal surveillance squads (New South Wales, Los Angeles).

The Growth of Evaluation

Because the credibility of the police has declined in most democratic countries during the last twenty years, police are being asked to demonstrate that they make communities safer, manage their affairs efficiently, and treat citizens fairly. In Canada, for example, the Treasury Board has required the Royal Canadian Mounted Police to develop performance indicators for each of its lines of work, so that government can determine whether benefits justify costs. In the United States, the Police Executive Research Forum published a booklet entitled *How to Rate Your Local Police* (Couper 1983). Local governments are increasingly calling in management consultants to evaluate the quality of police service. And the police themselves, as we saw earlier, are vigorously exploring new ways of preventing and suppressing crime.

In Britain the Audit Commission recommended a short list of performance criteria to assist local governments in assessing the quality of police service. These criteria included crime clearances, seriousness of crimes solved, crime rates, the match between patrol resources and emergency calls for service at different times, speed of dispatch responses, changes in the incidence of motor-vehicle accidents, public satisfaction with the police, and public complaints and commendations. Starting in 1993, the Audit Commission began collecting information about these criteria for all forces in Britain except the London Metropolitan Police. This information will be published by the Audit Commission in 1994 and yearly thereafter.

Largely in response to the Audit Commission, the Association of Chief Police Officers (ACPO) in Britain, in effect the "union" for the very senior ranks, has appointed a working committee to develop its own list of performance indicators. Its "Quality of Service Initiative" will evaluate police in the areas of crime, traffic, management of calls for service, public order, and community relations. At the same time, Her Majesty's Inspectorate of Constabulary, which is responsible for overseeing police performance throughout Britain, has developed a computerized database of information about the capabilities and activities of all regional forces in England and Wales.[2]

In addition, successive British Conservative governments have pushed the idea of citizens' charters, which require all government agencies to stipulate the levels of service for which they should be held responsible. Agencies would have to monitor performance according to these criteria and make the results public.

The Kent Constabulary was the first British police force to become accountable through a citizens' charter. Beginning in March 1992, the Kent Constabulary began public monitoring of its performance in nine areas: (1) public satisfaction with police service, (2) adequacy of patrol coverage for the volume of calls for service, (3) satisfaction of crime victims with the handling of their cases, (4) ratios of crimes detected to crimes committed, (5) promptness in answering telephone calls, (6) caller satisfaction with actions taken, (7) speed of emergency responses, (8) satisfaction of all people having contact with the police, and (9) criticism of the police. In support of this self-evaluation effort, the Kent police make 4,000 telephone calls each month to crime victims, to people who have requested police service, and to people who have called for information. For this work the force has created a special unit. In addition, each police station must make ten follow-up calls each month to people who have asked for assistance. A private company has been hired to make two annual county-wide public opinion surveys, supplemented by smaller surveys as needed, of what people believe are special problems in particular locations. Periodically, the police themselves mail out questionnaires designed to elicit citizens' perceptions of police service. The results of these evaluations of each of the nine indicators is updated and published every three months.

Much less attention has been given in Australia and Japan to the explicit evaluation of police service. National data on police and crime are not collected by the Australian government, largely because the states have jurisdiction and resist being compared with one another. Until very recently state governments were reluctant to provide even crime data, let alone information about police activities. The Japanese police, who are enormously proud of their accomplishments, make use of very crude performance indicators, mostly crime rates, arrest rates, and one or two items in a yearly national public opinion survey. In all fairness, there is little reason for the police in Japan to provide data on crime. Crime rates are remarkably low, although police costs are the same as in other affluent democratic countries (Bayley 1991a). The Japanese can afford to be complacent.

The interest on the part of scholars and university-based researchers in measuring police performance has mushroomed in the last two decades, although interest varies considerably from country to country. Among the five countries studied here, the United States is by far the leader in research. Scholars and bona-fide consultants can get permission from almost any police force in the country—especially local ones—to undertake evaluations, as long as they do not disrupt operations or violate the privacy of either citizens or police officers. In the United States police routinely allow people with a serious reason to ride in police cars that are on duty. Police departments submit to endless surveys and interviews. Contrary to popular impression, therefore, police operations in the United States are not supersecret and hidden. Indeed, next to public schools, police may be the most open government bureaucracy. Britain and Canada follow the United States in the amount of collaborative evaluation between police and academics. Australia lags, while in Japan police and scholars distrust each other actively and do almost no joint research.

Principles of Meaningful Assessment

Demonstrating performance is a fateful exercise. The legitimacy of the police is at stake, as well as the rationality of public expenditures for policing. Is it possible to collect information that will show accurately and unambiguously that the police are performing as communities might wish? Many countries believe so and, as we have just seen, are exploring ways of systematically collecting and publishing information about what are called performance indicators (PIs). The choice of PIs is crucial. The public naturally wants the PIs to reflect its abiding concerns—security and fair treatment; police want the PIs to be realistic, what they might reasonably achieve; and governments want the police to eliminate waste and use resources wisely. Because of the divergent aims of interested parties, the value-for-money discussion can be bewildering. The lists of PIs seem to contain apples, oranges, grapefruit, and all manner of other fruits and vegetables. In order to make sense of the various measures that have been suggested, it is helpful to recognize that qualitatively different standards are involved, and each has comparative advantages and disadvantages. Fortunately, there are only two crucial differences between the various kinds of PIs. When they are understood, the choices open to evaluators of police performance become clear.

The first distinction is between direct and indirect measures of police performance[3] (see Table 5.2). Measures of performance are direct when they indicate what police activity has accomplished in a community. Measures are indirect when they indicate what the police have done but not whether their activities have had an effect on the quality of community life. Indirect measures indicate what police do; direct measures indicate what police have achieved. Some commentators have referred to this difference as the difference between police *outputs* and police *outcomes* (Ostrom et al. 1978). One might also think of this difference as the difference between means and ends.

Indirect performance indicators are presumptive. Improving the rating of a police force with respect to them does not improve what the public experiences. For example, if the police make more arrests, one cannot assume that communities will be safer. The arrests might be largely for trivial or nuisance offenses, such as drinking in public or defacing public property, so that a community might still be terrorized by drug dealing or household burglaries. Not surprisingly, police would rather be judged indirectly than directly. They can control what they do

TABLE 5.2
Performance Indicators

Measures		Results
I. Direct		
	A. Hard	Crime rates
		Criminal victimizations
		Real estate values
		Public utilization of common space
		Commercial activity
		Number of disorder situations pacified
		Number of community problems solved
		Substantiated complaints about police behavior
	B. Soft	Fear of crime
		Public confidence in police
		Commitment of people to neighborhoods
		Satisfaction with police action
		Complaints about police service
		Willingness to assist police
		Perceptions of police rectitude
II. Indirect		
	A. Hard	Number of police
		Number of patrol officers
		Ratio of administrators to police officers
		Response times
		Arrests
		Clearance rates
		Number of community crime-prevention meetings
		Number of Neighborhood Watch meetings
		Speed in answering telephones
		Number of follow-up contacts with crime victims
		Value of drugs seized
		Strength of internal affairs units
		Written policies in problematic areas
		Departmental value statements
		Recruitment diversity
	B. Soft	Morale
		Officer self-esteem
		Police perceptions of their public reputation
		Police knowledge of communities

more easily than they can control the effects of what they do. Further-more, because indirect measures use information that is readily available within police organizations, indirect measures are less costly to assess than direct ones. For all these reasons, indirect measures tend to dominate the performance assessments by police departments themselves, by management consultants, by accreditation agencies, and by professional police associations.

The second distinction is between "hard" and "soft" indicators, meaning those that measure objective changes and those that measure subjective perceptions of change. This distinction may be made for both direct and indirect PIs. However, choices between hard and soft measures are more often made when making direct evaluations of police performance than when making indirect ones. The great advantage of soft measures is that they are easier to study. In the jargon of social science, the validity of hard measures is high, but their reliability is problematic. That is, they are indisputably relevant to measuring what the police are achieving or doing, but the quality of information is apt to be questionable unless strenuous and costly effort has been expended in gathering the data.

Soft measures, on the other hand, rely on well-accepted techniques of opinion surveying. Reliability can be estimated, although their relevance to measuring what police do or accomplish is more questionable. Public opinion is fickle, not closely related to objective conditions. It is well known, for example, that elderly people are most frightened by crime, even though they are least likely to be victimized. Conversely, young men consider themselves invulnerable even though they have the highest rate of victimization. Similarly, police almost always think they are less well respected by the public than they really are.

The value of measuring police performance subjectively, through soft direct indicators, increased during the 1980s when researchers discovered that the public's perceptions had behavioral consequences that affect quality of life. For example, fear of crime can produce sickness and cause absenteeism and truancy; suspicion of the police reduces the willingness of people to provide essential information to the police, thereby decreasing the chances that crimes will be solved; fear of victimization can raise distrust among neighbors, undermining the ability of communities to undertake cooperative crime-prevention action; and the fear of crime may contribute to the decline of neighborhoods as people stop maintaining their property, avoid local businesses and places of recreation, and move to safer, more desirable communities (Wilson and Kelling 1982, Skogan 1990). In short, during the last decade subjective phenomena have taken on an objective importance in evaluating the contribution of policing to community security.

The soft direct measures of performance tend to be popular with the police for a number of reasons (Butler 1992). Police are aware that direct measures, even soft ones, are more persuasive to outsiders than indirect ones. Some police may also believe, more cynically, that subjective impressions are more manipulable than objective measures, so that police have a better chance of winning the perception game with them than with hard measures. It is also considerably easier to collect information about soft direct measures. Finally, the subjective approach allows police to avoid vexatious questions about the purpose of policing. Rather than having to stipulate clearly what the police should be responsible for achieving in terms of community impact, the soft-measures approach reduces the matter to impressions. As some senior officers are beginning to say, a police force is as good as the public thinks it is. If the public is satisfied, then the police are delivering value for money, regardless of what they are doing. Soft direct measures, then, are the fallback position for the police when they are challenged for relying too heavily on indirect performance measures.

Understanding the differences between direct and indirect and hard and soft performance measures is not an academic matter. Police operations and management can be profoundly affected by the indicators chosen. The greater the emphasis police place on maximizing indirect PIs, the less attention will be given to maximizing the effects of policing. It is easier for hard-pressed commanders to do what they want to do than to figure out what should be done in order to make communities safer. It is easier, in other words, for police to do things right than to do the right things.

Concentrating on indirect PIs discourages organizational experimentation with respect to new ways of achieving public safety. Police organizations often say they want innovation and adaptation, but at the same time they may demand that telephone calls be answered within fifteen seconds, that citizens be greeted courteously at the reception desks, that rudeness be avoided in public contacts, and that response times be quickened. From the point of view of middle-rank commanders, headquarters are sending conflicting signals. They seem to want commanders to take charge, but not too much. They want innovation, but within new sets of work norms. Thus, at the very moment that contemporary police are concluding that force-wide strategies are cramping effectiveness, attempts to raise the quality of service through the application of indirect PIs creates what seems like a new generic program.

Unless police are carefully watched, a kind of Gresham's law may affect police management as it embarks on the value-for-money enterprise. Rather than bad money driving out good, in this case indirect evaluation drives out direct. Pressured to demonstrate their worth, police collect the information most readily at hand. These are always indirect measures. Paradoxically, then, the evaluation of police performance may not encourage programmatic innovation, but rather may inhibit creativity by encouraging more of the same, albeit more cheaply and perhaps more fairly. So I suggest Bayley's corollary to Gresham's law: The greater the pressure on the police to become efficient, the less the likelihood that they will become effective.

Bayley's corollary may explain why the reform agendas in Britain and the United States at the present time seem to be diverging. Pushed by the British Audit Commission to become demonstrably more efficient in management, the PIs emerging under the citizens' charters tend to be indirect. In the United States, on the other hand, police are giving more attention to becoming demonstrably more effective. Pressed by academic evaluators, they are still searching for new ways of using police resources to protect communities. The only major studies of police efficiency in the United States in the last twenty years are the Greenwood, Petersilia and Chaiken (1977) analysis of criminal investigation and Eck's (1982) study of the investigation of burglary. Police in the United States continue to emphasize the development of new strategies, whereas the British police emphasize the more efficient management of existing resources.

If the public's interest is to be served, then both sets of performance measures must be used. In order to achieve effectiveness, efficiency, and rectitude, the police cannot be allowed to substitute the more convenient indirect measures for direct measures. The utilization of indirect PIs reinforces the traditional compliance-oriented style of police management. Utilization of direct PIs encourages managerial risk taking and the search for strategic innovations. Indirect measures shift attention from community problems to organizational activity. It must never be forgotten that the institution of the police was created, like all public agencies, for the community's sake rather than for its own. The rational use of public resources requires that police contribute directly to public safety, as opposed to being demonstrably energetic but to no purpose beyond looking good.

The public should also be distrustful of an over-reliance on soft measures. The benefits of policing are not only in people's minds, even if people's impressions and evaluations can influence safety and the quality of life. The image of the police in the public mind is important to the success police have in providing security, but a satisfied public is not necessarily a well-protected public—any more than a dissatisfied public is necessarily poorly protected. Police must not be allowed to make performance a "con game" of appearance management.

Finally, assessments of police performance need to be made at appropriate levels of police organization. Generalizations made over large, force-wide jurisdictions often obscure great differences in the quality of service from neighborhood to neighborhood and among individuals. The police and the public can be seriously misled by a finding that 80% of a population think the police are doing a good job if, in fact, subgroups are paralyzed by their fear of crime or believe the police discriminate against them. Moreover, force-wide evaluations do not provide operational feedback about what is working and what is not when programs vary across jurisdictions in content as well as in vigor of implementation. The value of performance measurement for policy making decreases as the geographic area of the survey expands. More feedback is obtained for policy making from small studies and surveys in particular locations than from large ones that cover several commands.

This suggests a relationship between the nature of performance measures and the scale of evaluation. Assessments of efficiency, which utilize indirect measures, can usefully be applied to a police force as a whole. Assessments of effectiveness, however, which use hard direct and soft direct measures, are best employed for small-scale commands. Police rectitude, however, transcends organizational levels and can be evaluated informatively both force-wide and in particular commands.

Conclusion

The quickening search for demonstrability with respect to police performance points to the fourth major reason that the police have not been more effective in preventing crime. Their attempts at evaluation have been presumptive, self-serving, and too generic. Police, as well as civilian policy makers for the police, must insist that performance be separated into distinct qualitative elements—(for example, effectiveness, efficiency, and rectitude)—be measured as directly as possible, and be targeted on the people or units that are responsible for what is being assessed. Until these practices are followed, the police will be playing pin the tail on the donkey with crime prevention.

There is a general impression—for many good reasons—that the police as an institution are rigid, conservative, defensive, militaristic, secretive, and suspicious. At the same time, the police have slowly but surely begun to criticize and reevaluate almost everything they do: purpose and mission, core strategies, scale of police forces, organizational structure, management practices, occupational culture, police autonomy, and democratic accountability. Few sacred cows remain; major changes are looming. Because of the extent and intensity of this soul searching, the last decade of the twentieth century may be the most creative period in policing since the modern police officer was put onto the streets of London in 1829.

6

Taking Crime Prevention Seriously

The police are supposed to prevent crime, but they are not demonstrably doing so. This is not because they think crime prevention is not their mission. Police do judge themselves by the standards of crime containment and crime reduction. The problem is that their strategies—deterrence through a visible patrol presence and through prompt apprehension and punishment of criminals—are not working. During the 1980s police began to recognize the limitations of these strategies. The result was an intensive, widespread effort to devise more effective approaches.

This chapter examines three questions: (1) What do progressive police now think are better approaches to crime prevention? (2) What forms are these approaches taking in practice? (3) How successful have these practices been in preventing crime?

Rethinking the Basics

The development of new crime-prevention strategies was shaped by three insights: first, that the police cannot prevent crime without community help; second, that the police must do more than react to criminal incidents; and, third, that patrolling is too passive. Let's look at the rationale behind each.

First, the police cannot solve society's crime problems alone. They need the assistance of the public in warning off would-be criminals, in notifying them of crimes and potential crimes, and in providing information that leads to the arrest and punishment of criminals. Crime prevention is not a service people are given; it is an activity people must engage in. The public must become co-producers of public safety (Ostrom et al. 1978).

Second, police resources need to be deployed proactively against crime, which means addressing the circumstances that generate crime. The police spend almost all their time reacting to crime and very little in genuinely preventing it. They have been shutting the barn door after the horse has escaped.

A more proactive approach is practical because crime and disorder are not randomly distributed. Studies show that crimes can be antici- pated, especially as to place of occurrence. Calls for service, both crime and noncrime related, tend to be concentrated geographically. It is now generally agreed that fewer than 10% of addresses in cities produce over 60% of total calls for service (Sherman, Gartin, and Bruerger 1989, Pierce, Sparr, and Briggs 1984, Kelling 1988). Police are called again and again to the same places. Over half the locations in cities never generate any police action at all. In fact, over 95% of the space in cities is altogether free from predatory crime. Moreover, the predatory crimes that people fear most, such as robbery, rape, and burglary, are generally concen- trated even more than calls for service. Robbery is the most concentrated of all (Sherman, Gartin, and Bruerger 1989). Furthermore, crimes com- mitted inside buildings, such as most rapes, assaults, and murders, are concentrated more than crimes that take place outdoors.

In other words, police would be justified in focusing their resources in particular places if they could figure out what they might do there to prevent crime.

Third, police patrolling is too passive. Police presence, which is sup- posed to deter crime, is not visible enough. Mobile patrols, accounting for the bulk of patrolling, do not reassure the public, nor do they warn off criminals. What the police need to do instead is actively and visibly assist in creating a climate of order, security, and trust in public places, especially in locations in which crime is concentrated. They can do this, when they are not responding to calls for service, by regulating public behavior that is not criminal but that is unsettling, fear inducing, and disturbing (Wilson and Kelling 1982). These activities include public intoxication, playing loud music, panhandling, "hanging out," danger- ous skateboarding and cycling, using obscene language, and gambling. The police should also take an active part in helping communities reduce the physical "signs of crime," such as uncollected trash, aban- doned buildings, graffiti, junked cars, and broken street lights, that make areas appear unsafe, neglected, and unsupervised.

Although the police can do little to prevent particular instances of crime, they can reduce the "disorder" that, as research shows, encour- ages and facilitates crime (Skogan 1990, Reith 1948, Jacobs 1962, Sykes 1986, Kelling 1987). As an experienced police captain said, "If you see garbage all around, you begin to act like garbage." The purpose of patrolling, then, is to assist in creating a palpable moral order with respect to public appearances and behavior that fits the standards of local communities.

These three insights have formed the basis for the strategic rethinking that has become known as community policing.[1] The intellectual reassessment of policing in the 1980s has generated so much sustained activity that it is fair to refer to community policing as a movement. A dauntingly large number of books and articles have been written; conferences, seminars, and workshops abound; and consultants, both police and nonpolice, advise police departments about it. The National Institute of Justice, the research arm of the U.S. Department of Justice, has funded pilot projects and research on community policing. Professional organizations such as the International Association of Chiefs of Police, the Police Foundation, and the Police Executive Research Forum encourage it. There is even a National Center for Community Policing at Michigan State University. Interest in community policing is not restricted to the United States. It is discussed widely in Australia, Britain, Canada, and Japan, as well as in other countries not studied in this book. Experiments, pilot projects, and examples of full-scale implementation occur in all of them. Community policing represents the most serious and sustained attempt to reformulate the purpose and practices of policing since the development of the "professional" model in the early twentieth century (Kelling and Moore 1988, Walker 1977, Richardson 1970, Fogelson 1977).

What lessons can be derived from this energetic attempt to take crime prevention seriously? What must police do in order to prevent crime more effectively? There are two ways to proceed in answering these questions.

The first is to examine instances of community policing and pinpoint the differences between them and current practice. The problem with this approach, however, is that the lessons will depend on where one looks, which in turn depends on what one means by community policing. The conclusions are preordained: The lessons will be determined by what the observer thinks community policing is supposed to be. Since there is tremendous disagreement in professional circles about the meaning of community policing, lessons discovered in this way might be very idiosyncratic, based on a particular person's views. I have heard police describe community policing as being foot patrol, aggressive enforcement of minor ordinances, electronic surveillance of shopping malls, enhanced traffic enforcement, and any police action that instills public confidence. Because the phrase has so often been used imprecisely, it has been cheapened. A chief of detectives said, "Criminal investigation is the epitome of community policing." One police chief thought that any contact between the police and the public was community policing. No wonder a British comedian thought it was necessary to help define it. "I'll tell you how you know when you've got community policing. It's when you are walking along a street and a police van pulls up, several coppers leap out, pin you to the ground, and tell you what time it is" (Alexi Sayle n.d.).[2]

The second way to uncover the new lessons of crime prevention is to make an inventory of what is new whenever police departments make a determined effort to change their traditional practices in an effort to prevent crime. When it comes to crime prevention, all that glitters is not necessarily called community policing. This approach allows one to discover what community policing is from the substantive efforts of committed departments. Commmunity policing is defined operationally, in terms of real activities. This is the approach I take.

When police departments take the challenge of crime prevention seriously enough that they break with the practices of the past, four elements recur again and again: *consultation, adaptation, mobilization,* and *problem solving.* Since nothing can be discussed in policing without using an acronym, I shall refer to the new crime-prevention strategies as CAMPS. Consultation, adaptation, mobilization, and problem solving are what I shall be referring to from now on when I use the phrase "community policing."

Elements of Improved Crime Prevention

Consultation

Police forces that are trying determinedly to improve their crime-prevention performance have made a point of establishing new mechanisms for discussing priorities and strategies with their communities. Sometimes this means deepening contacts and meeting regularly with existing groups. More dramatically, it means creating entirely new councils and committees. For example, since 1984 Britain has established over two hundred community consultative committees at the precinct level. The Royal Canadian Mounted Police has set up citizens' advisory councils in all its detachments; in New South Wales all police stations have created community consultative committees; and the Seattle police have set up a police department advisory panel as well as grassroots community advisory councils in each precinct (Feden and Klinger 1992). Japan has begun to do the same for its neighborhood police posts (*koban*) and the Ontario Provincial Police in its newly created beats.

These consultative committees serve four functions. First, they advise police about local problems and needs. The security concerns of communities are often very different from what the police think they are. Police tend to focus on serious crimes—murder, rape, robbery, and burglary—the sorts of events dramatized in the media. When police meet with the public in small groups, they quickly discover that although people say they want the police to fight crime, they are as much concerned about more prevalent and low-key troubles (Cordner 1985, Eck et al. 1987). In Portland, Oregon, for example, the most frequently cited problems that communities wanted police help in solving were drug dealing and burglaries, as expected, but in addition, abandoned buildings, chronic theft/vandalism, gangs, loitering youth, unsafe parks, and liquor retailers who sell to minors (Portland Police Department 1991). A community council on the south side of Chicago in June 1991 complained about the following problems: cars playing stereo sound systems loud at night, chronic double parking at a nearby pizzeria, teenagers hanging around on street corners blocking sidewalks, drunks urinating in public, and loud cursing and foul language. When people in Victoria State, Australia, were asked what the major problems were for the police in their neighborhoods, they cited vandalism (24.4%), unsupervised juveniles congregating in groups (22.1%), stealing/housebreaking (12.9%), access by juveniles to alcohol (9.9%), and illegal riding of unmuffled motorbikes (8.6%) (Victoria Police 1983). In rural areas of the United States one of the most common complaints police hear is about teenagers who deliberately knock over rows of mailboxes with their cars at night.

Second, community meetings help police educate people about crime and disorder and enlist the cooperation of the public in dealing with them. Such meetings are the tip of interest networks that police use to encourage people to become co-producers of public safety.

Third, community meetings allow people to ventilate grievances against the police face to face, unimpeded by bureaucracy. Such sessions help people let off steam, providing the psychological satisfaction of speaking one's mind to the police directly. Although hearing these grievances makes the police uncomfortable, they too have an opportunity to present their point of view, whether it is about their frustrations in stopping certain sorts of crime or about what really happened in incidents of alleged police misconduct.

Fourth, community meetings provide information to the police about the success of their efforts. They are readymade evaluation panels whose information can be used by the police to refine their operations.

There is a natural progression in these functions by newly established community forums. At first, meetings tend to be dominated by complaints. Since this is embarrassing for the police, some forces draw back at this point. When police are patient, however, discussion soon shifts to security concerns. At this stage police can begin to use meetings to explain the limitations of police action and to draw people into planning coordinated responses to perceived problems. Finally, when trust has been established, community meetings can be used to help evaluate the impact of crime-prevention initiatives. The life cycle of consultation moves from highly specific grievances to cooperative evaluation of shared programs.

Consultation may occur on a geographical basis, as in the examples just cited, or according to interests. When police solicit input from groups with special needs, they tend to call it liaison. In New York City the police department makes a special effort to remain in close contact with new immigrants, in Vancouver with Orientals, in Britain with Asians, in Ontario, Canada, with First Nations, in Australia with Aboriginals, and in Los Angeles with gays and lesbians. Perhaps the most unique liaison effort is in Victoria State, Australia—with lawyers.

Adaptation

Recognizing that crime and order needs vary from place to place, police have sought to reshape command structures so that local commanders can use resources more flexibly. This involves decentralizing commands geographically as well as placing decision-making responsibility farther down the rank hierarchy. Rather than relying on generic strategies formulated at headquarters and applied force-wide by subordinate commanders, the new initiatives call upon local commanders to device plans and adapt resources to local needs.

The first step toward adaptation has usually been to create manageable territorial commands. Houston, Texas, for example, recently created four command stations and Santa Ana, California, several neighborhood police stations. To police forces that already have precincts or subdivisional stations, this change hardly seems creative. Eastern cities in the United States have had decentralized command structures for more than a century, but precincts have not made the police noticeably more effective in preventing crime. A related change involves redrawing command boundaries to conform to the boundaries of self-identified communities. Adelaide, South Australia, for instance, replaced 4 patrol bases with 16 subdivisional police stations, each one coinciding with the jurisdiction of a local government council. The London Metropolitan Police are considering a similar move, which would actually increase the size of each subcommand, since there are now 69 stations and only 38 borough councils.

Because large police forces usually have subdivisional commands, a more meaningful development in terms of adaptation is to shift responsibility for devising programs and coverages to teams of officers assigned to specific areas and beats within a station's jurisdiction. Inaugurating the community police program of Commissioner Lee Brown in New York City, the 72nd precinct was organized into three zones, each composed of five standard beats. Each zone is commanded by a sergeant, who determines how personnel should be used to meet local needs. The sergeants make use of radio cars, community police officers, and two detectives who are permanently assigned to the zone. If the program works, the model precinct will become three mini-police departments, each with its own sergeant commander supported by a network of community contacts.

Sector policing in London, started in 1991, is similar. Divisions (precincts) are divided into two or three sectors, each commanded by an inspector. The inspector and the four sergeants commanding the different shifts assess the needs of each sector and plan appropriate responses. The inspector is required to establish a sector working group for community consultation. Its members represent government agencies, civic associations, residents' and block groups, and local politicians.

Edmonton, Canada, has adapted its organizational structure in a somewhat different way. After analyzing the geographical pattern of calls for service, the police designated 21 high-volume areas as beats and assigned one or sometimes two community police officers to each. Backed by patrol cars, the community police officers assess local needs and formulate plans to meet recurring problems. Working mostly on foot, the officers set their own hours and establish local offices where they can be reached or messages can be left. The objective is to fix responsibility for policing on an officer who has daily operational contact with a community. In the traditional system, different shifts of officers rotate through an area without anyone taking responsibility for the area. In an analogy used by Superintendent Chris Braiden, who devised the Edmonton program, this was like expecting people who rent a house to repaint it on their own. What is lacking in both cases is ownership. The beats belong to the community police officers. What happens in these areas is their responsibility; it can't be fobbed off on the next shift or on a remote supervisor.

Mobilization

Rather than relying on their own efforts exclusively to prevent crime, police have developed programs that enlist the active assistance of the public. In the words of the Lincoln, Nebraska, Police Department (1991): "The fundamental mission . . . is to provide the leadership and professional support to sustain and improve the community's efforts to develop a balanced and cooperative police-community program against lawless and disorderly behavior."

The best-known community crime-prevention programs, sometimes called the Big Three, are Neighborhood Watch, Operation ID, and security surveys. Familiar to Americans since the early 1970s, the programs involve neighborhood meetings in which information about local crimes is shared and people are encouraged to watch for and report to the police any suspicious behavior. They also promote the marking of personal property with personal identification numbers and the inspection of residential and commercial premises with an eye to improving security. The principles of watching, marking, and securing have spread internationally, so that the distinctive Neighborhood Watch signs have become as common as billboards. Neighborhood Watch has become Vertical Watch for high-rise apartments, Business Watch for shopowners and retailers, which focuses on shoplifting and passing bad checks; Apartment Watch, where landlords are trained to screen and regulate disruptive tenants; Marine Watch for private boat owners; Vehicle Watch, where identification numbers are etched onto car windows and headlights; Rural Watch for farming communities; and even, in Britain, Pub Watch, where owners notify one another about disorderly drinkers on the prowl and bouncers are trained to spot drug dealers, defuse conflict, and eject troublesome customers with a minimum of fuss.

These programs are only the beginning of a mind-boggling array of mobilization schemes devised or encouraged by the police (Grabosky 1990). Whereas the Big Three are passive programs that emphasize physical security and vigilance, civilians are also actively involved in spotting and interrupting criminal behavior. The drivers of radio-equipped taxis, delivery vans, and telephone-repair vehicles are sometimes trained to spot criminal activity and notify the police. Police support and train mobile patrols of ordinary citizens who are linked to police control rooms through their own civilian-band (CB) radios. In many inner-city neighborhoods walking patrols of volunteers, wearing distinctive caps, armbands, or jackets, deliberately appear at places where criminal activity is likely. Although these patrols are discouraged from taking enforcement action, some have carried signs warning off drug dealers or have photographed men soliciting prostitutes.

Along Hindley Street in Adelaide, South Australia, and 53rd Street in Hyde Park, Chicago, civilian youth workers patrol in the evenings to advise and caution youths who might get into trouble with the police. Young people are drawn to these streets, accessible by public transportation, because of the concentration of fast-food restaurants, cinemas, record shops, stores, and arcades. Acting like familiar, nonthreatening older brothers and sisters, the patrols warn kids about behavior that alarms or inconveniences older people and that might require a response by the police. When individual youths do commit minor offenses, the police often turn them over to the youth workers for counseling and follow-up discussions with families and schools. This alternative to arrest reduces law-enforcement costs as well as the kind of aggravation that leads to charges of police harassment.

Police have learned to ask the permission of communities to do things that might otherwise be impossible under the protection of law. For example, store owners along Union Avenue in Seattle agreed to allow police to come into their entryways to evict drug dealers, as did the owners of private parking lots. When parents in rural Ontario Province, Canada, leave teenage children at home alone for a weekend, they may give the Ontario Provincial Police permission to enter and inspect the home if circumstances warrant. Police also persuade people to take precautions to lessen opportunities for crime and disorder. For example, convenience stores may be asked to hire more than one clerk during evening hours or to put up signs barring loitering in their parking lots. Fast-food restaurants and other businesses that draw teenagers have signed agreements to close if the crowds become large and unruly.

It is not just the general public that police try to mobilize. Other government agencies can play a critical role in crime prevention if their actions are focused properly and coordinated with police and community action. To remove the signs of crime, sanitation departments haul away abandoned cars and clean up trash-strewn vacant lots; parks and recreation agencies open facilities at night or develop programs for young people; fire and building inspectors condemn abandoned buildings that are being used as drug houses; health and safety departments find legal pretexts for closing bars and nightclubs that draw a criminal trade; schools provide remedial tutoring for underachieving students; and social service agencies intervene with chronically troubled families to prevent recurrences of domestic violence and child abuse or neglect. In Los Angeles the police have developed a program called Police-Assisted Community Enforcement (PACE), through which community police officers take the lead in formulating multiagency plans to alleviate conditions that facilitate crime, especially drug dealing. Britain's Multi-Agency Crime Prevention Initiative (MACPI), started in 1985, has the same objective, as does the Thames Valley Safer Community Partnership, begun in 1992.

Whereas police mobilization of other government agencies focuses mostly on conditions that encourage crime, communities with high crime rates often ask police to address a host of unmet needs. This puts police in an awkward position: Either they offend other agencies by politicking for the community or they alienate the public by refusing to lend their support. A noncontentious example of the sorts of issues police become involved in arose in the outback town of Menindee, Australia. An old woman complained at the police-community meeting that for two years she had been asking the shire council to trim the trees in her yard, which had become a favorite roost for cockatoos. Her backyard had become unusable because it was covered with cockatoo droppings. The police-community consultative committee heard her desperate plea and sent a letter to the council on her behalf. The problem was immediately taken care of, and the woman sent a letter of heartfelt thanks to the police.

Following the lead of fire departments in their attempts to provide protection from fires, some police forces have begun to advise governments and private builders about their development plans in terms of crime prevention. Specialists in the Seattle and Ontario Provincial police departments participate in hearings on development, suggesting design changes aimed at preventing crime. Builders in Leicestershire, Britain, who incorporate police suggestions into their plans, are allowed to post a "secured by design" sign and in Edmonton, Canada, a "shield of confidence" sign, which allows homeowners to qualify for lower insurance rates.

New mobilization efforts support victims and witnesses in an effort to encourage them to testify in criminal proceedings. In Canada and the United States, victims'-assistance programs, about half of which are run by the police, provide the crime victim with emotional support, offer advice about filing insurance claims, and help collect government benefits to which the victims might be entitled. These programs often support victims through the legal proceedings that follow, educating them about procedures, providing transportation to courts, accompanying them through trials, and providing lounges in court buildings where they can rest and have a cup of coffee. Australia's Witness Watch does the same for witnesses to crimes, who, like victims, are often frightened and inconvenienced by the legal aftermath of crimes.

Mobilizing communities for their own defense against crime is not new for the police. Most police departments have had crime-prevention offices for many years, although they usually have been small and marginal to police operations. These offices have traditionally been responsible for special programs, such as Police Athletic Leagues, "Crime Stoppers" radio and television programs, anonymous crime-tip telephone systems, and the Safety Houses/Safe Havens/Helping Hands refuges for children who seek to avoid danger on the streets. Crime prevention is, therefore, tricky to talk about in police circles. Most police think they already do it. What is new about mobilization is that community-based crime prevention becomes a central strategy of policing, a mainline function that is the responsibility of every officer.

Considering the pressures on government budgets at all levels and the enormous costs associated with increasing the visible presence of the police, mobilization of communities is probably the most practical way of increasing crime-focused resources. At today's prices, an ounce of community prevention may be worth a pound of police cure (see Chap. 3).

Problem Solving

Instead of responding to crimes and other emergencies after they have occurred, police have begun to study the conditions that lead to calls for their services, to draw up plans to correct these conditions, and to take the lead in evaluating and implementing remedial actions. In other words, police are learning to view crime and disorder as problems that need to be dealt with rather than as isolated events to which they apply law or emergency services (Goldstein 1979, 1987, 1990, Eck et al. 1987). The problem-solving approach supplements authoritative intervention and symbolic justice with activities that have an impact on conditions that generate crime and insecurity. It extends the time frame of police action and broadens the range of possible police responses. Problem solving stresses the need to analyze and assess the full range of activities that police and communities might undertake to prevent crime. It leads to focused and specific programs for crime prevention rather than diffuse and generic ones.[3]

Here are five examples of police problem solving. Merchants in Madison, Wisconsin, complained that a new downtown mall was attracting deinstitutionalized mental patients who behaved in bizarre ways, frightened shoppers, and gave the mall a bad name. The police received hundreds of phone calls about particular incidents. When they studied the situation, the police discovered that there weren't "hundreds" of "emotionally disturbed people" but only 13. Moreover, the 13 were supposed to have been taking prescription drugs that should have prevented their disruptive behavior. The problem, the police concluded, was that the people were not taking their medications. So they worked out a plan with local mental health and social service agencies to supervise the administration of the medications. Once this happened the problem disappeared (Goldstein and Susmilch 1982).

In most communities the police are repeatedly called to a certain bar or nightclub to deal with fights, drug dealing, noise, harassment of neighbors, and violation of liquor laws. A community police officer in Edmonton, Canada, solved this problem by doing research. He obtained copies of the applications a nightclub owner had made for the various licenses required to sell alcohol, allow dancing, and provide live entertainment. One application, the officer discovered, contained false information: The owner had lied about the amount of off-street parking available, which was less than that required by zoning ordinances. Armed with this information, the officer petitioned the appropriate municipal board. The result was that the nightclub was closed until the owner could provide additional parking—which was physically impossible in the circumstances. The surrounding neighborhood was delighted, and the police were pleased that a chronic troublespot had been eliminated (Edmonton Police Department 1989b).

Again in Edmonton, the police received calls almost every weekend about Native American youths who were breaking into cars, stealing, and generally making mischief late at night after their recreation hall closed. Up in arms, the neighborhood demanded that the recreational facility be closed. The local community police officer recognized that the majority of the youths were not really criminals but tended to get into mischief when they had to wait around to be taken home after the recreation hall closed. So he discussed the problem with the Native bands (councils) that ran the recreation center. Together they agreed that the bands would send elders as chaperones and would provide vans to take the youths home when the center closed. As a result, the troubles in the neighborhood vanished overnight. The crime "problem" turned out to be a lack of supervision and of transportation (Edmonton Police Department 1989b).

A neighborhood park in Baltimore County, Maryland, attracted so many disruptive paint-sniffing teenagers that people in the surrounding area were afraid to use it. The police tried patrolling the park and hassling and arresting the teenagers, but both approaches were expensive and and ineffective. Then the Citizen-Oriented Police Enforcement (COPE) squad studied the situation, talked to residents and paint sniffers, and formulated a new plan. The police continued to arrest the sniffers, but got prosecutors to agree to treat such arrests seriously and to prosecute sniffers to the extent of the law. Police circulated a list of the names of chronic abusers to local merchants, requesting that paint not be sold to them. They persuaded merchants not to display the colors that sniffers believe give the best "high." By these coordinated actions the park was "liberated" and the police could turn their attention to other matters (Cordner 1985).

Finally, the Newton Street area in south-central Los Angeles (70% Hispanic and 30% African-American) was terrorized in the late 1980s by street drug dealing and its associated violence, including a rash of drive-by shootings. Residents huddled in their homes at night, often sleeping in back rooms so they would not be hit by stray bullets. After much study, discussion, and door-to-door canvassing, the police proposed—if the community agreed—that metal gates be erected at the ends of nine streets to create a network of cul-de-sacs, making the area difficult to drive through for people who weren't familiar with it. At the same time, police stepped up drug enforcement, assigning 40 full-time officers to the fifteen square block area. During the day, some of these officers patrolled on bicycles, so that their presence would be noticeable and they could move about freely. With state money, two youth workers were hired to tutor schoolchildren and to organize athletic programs. The results of these coordinated efforts were dramatic. Shootings fell almost immediately by 80%, without displacement to adjacent areas. The drug markets evaporated, even though over a period of time police patrols were reduced to only six officers. Most surprising, attendance at the local high school doubled. The school's crippling truancy rates appear to have been caused by fear, not by lack of motivation on the part of the students (Sparrow, Moore, and Kennedy 1990; personal communication, Robert Vernon, Chief of Operations, July 1, 1991).

The art of this approach to crime prevention is to locate within the myriad calls for police service "problems" that generate a disproportionate number of calls but that, at the same time, can be remedied relatively quickly with the resources police and communities have available. Problem solving cannot work against every sort of crime or source of insecurity. Many of these are rooted in conditions that cannot be changed locally, such as chronic unemployment or dysfunctional families. Problem solving is not social restructuring. But it represents more than the traditional police responses of authoritative intervention and symbolic justice. Problem solving requires the police to develop the capability to diagnose the causes of recurring calls for police service, to explore practical remedies, to collect and focus resources, to participate in cooperative solutions, and to evaluate results.

In practice, pinpointing problems appears not to be difficult. Police can relatively easily find the middle ground between separate complaints and structural social reform (Goldstein 1990). The most common problems dealt with are disorderly youths at convenience stores and malls, street prostitution in residential areas, thefts from cars in parking lots, burglaries, sick elderly people who live alone, families that habitually threaten and harass neighbors, and frequent robberies in particular locations (Goldstein 1990, Chap. 6). The methods police use to alleviate these problems vary. They include focused law enforcement; mediation; enhanced social control through parents, teachers, friends, and employers; the improvement or the redesigning of physical environments; and petitioning for enactment of new ordinances or statutes, the institution of civil processes, and the provision of new government services (Goldstein 1990, Chap. 8).

Problem solving by police is not entirely new. For many years police have given special attention to several sorts of "problems" without being conscious that they are employing a distinctive approach. Juvenile delinquency is one such problem; another is the closely related phenomenon of youth gangs. Officers who are assigned to units that deal with these problems have customarily used an approach that blends enforcement and consultation and mobilization. Perhaps the best example of traditional problem solving is traffic management. Here specialists study accident patterns and devise multifaceted solutions that encompass physical engineering, enhanced law enforcement, revised traffic regulations, and community education. Traffic specialists routinely assess the impact of their actions, both in the aggregate and as a consequence of addressing problems in particular locations.

It must be emphasized that neither problem solving nor the entire CAMPS approach involves foregoing law enforcement. Effective problem solving often requires more law enforcement, not less. Within a problem framework, however, enforcement is used instrumentally to achieve change in a particular situation. Problem solving may also lead to magnified enforcement as other forms of civil, social, and regulatory authority are brought to bear. With problem solving, however, enforcement becomes truly preventive rather than being an end in itself.

A Many-Splendored Thing

The new approach to crime prevention, involving CAMPS, can be implemented in different ways. It cannot be reduced to a single program. As community policing, in the sense outlined here, has developed in many different places, several variations recur. They involve nine elements.

1. *Personnel.* Community policing may be practiced by all officers in a department or may be assigned to a specialist unit. In Newport News, Virginia, and Denton, Texas, police departments have insisted that all personnel, regardless of their functional assignment, use the community policing approach. On the other hand, community policing in New York City and New South Wales, Australia, has been delegated, respectively, to community police officers and beat officers. In Britain patrol personnel are separated into beat duty officers (BDOs) for community policing and general duty officers (GDOs) for traditional patrolling. London's sector-policing scheme is intended to transform all patrol personnel into community policing officers. New York City's "model precinct" was created for the same purpose, so that the department can explore how best to involve an entire geographical command in community policing.

2. *Organization.* Responsibility for community policing may be given to existing commands, such as patrol or criminal investigation, or to a specially created new command. Detroit's ministations are a separate command that reports directly to the chief of police, as are the programs in Edmonton, Canada, and Madison, Wisconsin. The community police officer program (CPOP) in New York City, on the other hand, reports to the patrol commander. (McElroy, Cosgrove, and Sadd 1992).

3. *Deployment.* If community police functions are given to specialized personnel, where are these officers based? They may be dispersed into beats, as in Edmonton, Leicestershire, New South Wales, or New York City. Or they may be formed into squads to operate over wider areas, such as a precinct in the case of San Diego's STOP (Selected Tactics of Policing) program or force-wide as with Baltimore County's COPE (Citizen Oriented Police Enforcement). Or community police officers may be based at headquarters, as is the case with units that specialize in calls for service analysis or, more traditionally, juvenile delinquency and youth gangs.

4. *Mode of Deployment.* Do specialist community police officers work on foot, as in New South Wales and New York City; on bicycles, as in Boston; out of offices, as in Japan and Edmonton; from mobile

ministations, as in Fort Worth, Texas, and Toronto, Canada; or from cars and vans, as in San Diego and Baltimore County?

5. *Functions.* What should community police officers be required to do? What activities are to distinguish them from conventional patrol officers? In Edmonton and Ontario Province, community police officers respond to emergency calls. Detroit's ministation officers do not, except when they are nearby, nor do the community squads in Seattle or the neighborhood police officers in Singapore (Feden and Klinger 1992, Bayley 1989).[4] Community police officers in New York City are required to patrol on foot; ministation officers in Detroit are not. Problem solving is emphasized in Edmonton and Newport News, Virginia, but not among Japan's *koban* or Britain's beat officers (Bennett forthcoming). Some community police officers are responsible for liaison with community bodies, as in Edmonton; others are not, as in Japan.

6. *Scope.* Community policing may be practiced throughout a force's jurisdiction, as with CPOP in New York City, or in selective areas, as in Edmonton.

7. *Consultation.* Consultation may be explicitly organized or done in an ad hoc fashion. Police in New South Wales have created special community consultative committees for each police station. Community police officers of the Ontario Provincial Police are told either to create police communities or to interact with existing groups. Community police in New York City, London, and Japan are told only to "get to know" their neighborhoods, which means interacting with people they happen across while patrolling or developing contacts with community organizations that already exist. They take advantage of what is already there rather than establishing new forums for consultation.

8. *Coordination.* Do police obtain assistance from other government agencies through formal mechanisms set up for that purpose, as in Thames Valley, Britain, or do they solicit help on a case-by-case basis through normal bureaucratic channels?

9. *Public Participation.* Police departments may encourage citizens to join them in their work or keep them at arm's length. For example, Detroit and Houston have supported civilian-band (CB) radio patrols and use civilians to staff neighborhood police stations. CPOP officers in New York City and beat officers in New South Wales work for the most part on their own.

These nine dimensions of community policing represent choices police departments make when they explore ways to improve crime-prevention performance. Judging from international experience, departments that are interested in community policing need to think through the advantages and disadvantages of these choices before they become deeply involved. If they do not, officers will be confused, frustrations will mount, and the programs will lack credibility.

Given the confusion about what community policing means, and the ways in which it is practiced, one sees that community policing is not one-dimensional. Community policing, like love, is a many-splendored thing. The important question for contemporary policing is not, "What is community policing?" That discussion can be left to academics. For police the important question is, "How can we become more effective in preventing crime?" The answers—as the police themselves have been discovering—are found in CAMPS. These activities, whether or not they are called community policing, are what seem to be required to make the police truly effective as crime-prevention agents.[5]

Does Community Policing Work?

The honest answer to the question of whether community policing works is we do not know. There has certainly been no general test of the crime-prevention efficacy of community policing in the sense of CAMPS (Kennedy 1991, Weatheritt 1989). The best candidates for such an evaluation are Singapore and Japan, where community policing is the operating paradigm for the entire police system.

At the same time, there have been many attempts to evaluate specific elements of community policing in particular places. This is a sensible approach because it recognizes that community policing, as I have argued, is not a single program but involves a multitude of changes and innovations. These focused evaluations have generally shown that community policing has had a small effect or has produced contradictory results. In addition, the studies have been challenged on methodological grounds (Police Foundation 1986, McElroy, Cosgrove, and Sadd 1992, Toronto Police Department 1989, Eck et al. 1987, Sherman 1991).

Two problems are inherent in many of these studies. First, they are often not genuine evaluations of police effectiveness but are descriptions of processes of implementation (Feden and Klinger 1992, Hornick et al. 1989). They consider only whether a police activity was meaningful or was worth evaluating. Second, they tend to be impressionistic and anecdotal (Sherman 1991, Koller 1990). From these studies it is difficult to determine whether the effects of community policing are long lasting, displace problems elsewhere, are due mainly to the community policing initiative, or are as substantial as the police and citizens involved with them perceive them to be. As Mollie Weatheritt (1986) has said, "The incidence of policing successes tends to be in inverse proportion to the rigour with which policing schemes are evaluated."

The best evidence about the crime-prevention efficacy of community policing comes from particular problem-solving exercises. Parks have been "liberated" from drug dealers; Link Valley in Houston stopped being a drug bazaar; the incidence of emotionally disturbed behavior on the mall in Madison, Wisconsin, was reduced; and burglaries and thefts have decreased at certain locations.

Doubts are also growing about the usefulness of one of the core elements of community policing—namely, community-based crime prevention (mobilization). A key assumption of community policing has been that ordinary citizens can take effective action, if properly directed and organized, to reduce the incidence of crime. Sadly, research to date has not supported this assumption. The Big Three of community crime prevention—Neighborhood Watch, Operation ID, and security surveys—have not been shown to produce clear or lasting reductions in thefts and burglaries, their primary objectives. This has been the case in Britain as well as the United States (Bennett forthcoming, Rosenbaum 1987, 1988). Evidence is also weak or lacking altogether for the efficacy of self-protection measures by homeowners, the physical redesign of buildings, community programs to get at the root causes of crime, fix-up, clean-up campaigns, ministations, and neighborhood crime-prevention newsletters (Skogan 1990, Rosenbaum 1987, 1988, Rosenbaum and Heath 1990, Weatheritt 1989).

After a thorough review of the evaluations of community crime prevention, Westley Skogan (1990, p. 9) came to the disheartening conclusion that "Rigorous evaluations of community crime prevention initiatives have by and large failed to find clear cut evidence of success." He noted that community crime prevention was least likely to occur and to work least well in high-crime neighborhoods—in other words, in exactly the places that need it the most. If this is true, then a pillar of community policing has been destroyed.

I say "if" because it is unclear at the moment whether the lack of evidence is the fault of the theory, half-hearted implementation by police, or defects in the research. In other words, the promise of community policing cannot be fairly determined because of flawed implementation and flawed research.

Police departments have to struggle to enlist the full and enthusiastic cooperation of their own members in community policing programs. Community policing goes against the grain of police organizations. Departments are also often preoccupied with other matters and do not believe they can devote the resources that might make community police programs succeed.

On the other hand, the fault may lie with the evaluations themselves. Police and social scientists are beginning to wonder whether rigorous tests of effectiveness may be too demanding. The best efforts at evaluation keep coming to the same conclusion—nothing works. This possibility is especially threatening to community policing. The search for improved strategies for crime prevention was based on the lack of evidence for the usefulness of traditional police practices (Chap. 1). If social science cannot show that the new approaches are succeeding either, then perhaps it has not shown that the old ones failed.

The consistent inability of scientific evaluations to demonstrate the preventive effect of community policing as well as the deterrent effect of authoritative intervention and symbolic justice has two important implications for policy makers. First, police departments that conscientiously want to explore ways of improving crime-prevention performance will have to rely more on theory, logic, and gut instinct than scientific evidence. Under these circumstances, it is very much to the credit of the police that they have been as willing to explore community policing as broadly as they have. Second, the public must be told that there are no magic solutions or "silver bullets" when it comes to preventing crime—not from the police, not from communities. This does not mean that the search for improved strategies should be called off. But it does mean that police-based crime-prevention programs should not be oversold. The temptation to do so is very great for politicians who are anxious to be elected, for police concerned to get resources for traditional as well as new programs, and for policy advocates who want to move the police in favored directions.

Conclusion

Police in the United States and around the world are conscientiously searching for new ways to prevent crime and disorder. The reform efforts that have grown out of the intellectual ferment of the last decade are generally described as community policing. Examined operationally, community policing involves consultation, adaptation, mobilization, and problem solving (CAMPS). Although these elements appear to represent the strategic future of policing, it is premature to say that their adoption is assured. Commitment is uncertain and programmatic implementation uneven. Many forces have yet to do anything more substantial than talk about community policing. Some that have tried it have pulled back, and most remain skeptical. Only in Japan and Singapore has community policing in the full sense become institutionalized—that is, become the operating tradition of a department. In most forces implementation of community policing depends almost entirely on a few senior leaders; when they change, its future becomes uncertain.

The 1990s are a watershed period in policing because very different paradigms are competing for the hearts and minds of police officers: on the one hand, the authoritative intervention–symbolic justice model; on the other, the CAMPS model (Kelling and Moore 1988). The current debate represents a great deal more than a choice among strategies and tactics, important as these are. Community policing represents a potentially momentous shift in the location of authority over the police.

Modern police were initially created by states to protect the interests of government. They preserved order for the elites who were in control of the newly developing centers of state power. This occurred in Western Europe roughly from the late seventeenth through the nineteenth centuries (Bayley 1985). As a result, the primary functions of the police were the suppression of collective unrest and the regulation of populations, what might be called state-directed policing (Bayley 1985).

Early in the twentieth century a great change occurred in the policing of democratic countries. Impelled by an expansion in political participation, police became responsive to the security needs of the general public. Their ability to do this was facilitated by changes in technology, especially the invention of the telephone and the automobile. The demand for police services no longer emanated solely from the state but was distributed across a multitude of individuals. Demand was disaggregated, and the police developed a new set of masters. The police became democratically responsible in terms of their day-to-day operations. This was a revolutionary development that has yet to occur in many countries. Although it is easy to criticize the reactiveness of today's police in free societies, the political significance of police forces that respond instantly to the needs of individuals should not be downplayed. The change from earlier policing represents the domestication of the coercive authority of the state. It is a qualitative advance in political evolution.

Community policing creates yet another source of authority over police activities. It does so by creating a new level of demand that is inserted between the state and the disaggregate public. Through CAMPS the police are required to respond to interests and needs collected and articulated at a new place, namely, small communities or neighborhoods. Community policing is not simply a change in tactics; it is a change in the source of the demands that are made on the police.

Until now, the police were politically accountable to states but operationally accountable to individuals. Community policing challenges again the customary distribution of authority over the coercive power of the state. If communities can define police work, a new center of political power has been established. Community policing represents a renegotiation of the social contract between the police and society.

III

SOLUTIONS

7

Options for Policing

The most critical decision modern societies must make concerning the police is whether they should be held responsible for preventing crime. For most people the answer is obvious: of course, what else? But the issue is not as simple as it seems. There are two reasons why making crime prevention central to the mission of the police may not be a good idea.

First, the police may not be able to prevent crime. This is a matter of capability. Is it reasonable to expect that crime can be prevented by the actions of a single government agency whose main activity, at least until now, has been law enforcement? The answer depends on what is required to prevent crime. Furthermore, even if crime could be prevented through the focused effort of the police, can the police, as police departments are currently constituted, adapt enough to do it? The customary practices of the police have great institutional momentum, which will not be easy to change. Like aircraft carriers, police organizations may be capable of only wide and slow turns.

Second, do we want the police to do what they might have to do in order to prevent crime? This is a matter of political values. Order is not the only objective of government, especially not in democratic societies. Freedom is also important. Putting police in charge of crime prevention would surely tilt public policy in the direction of constraint rather than amelioration. The police stand at the fulcrum between liberty and order, but they lean to the right.

Taking both organizational capacity and political values into consideration, democratic societies have five options with respect to the role of the police in preventing crime. They are (1) *dishonest law enforcement*, (2) *determined crime prevention*, (3) *honest law enforcement*, (4) *efficient law enforcement*, and (5) *stratified crime prevention*. These options are not theoretical but are reflected in practices that exist or are being considered in contemporary policing. This chapter explores these options.

Option One: Dishonest Law Enforcement

Dishonest law enforcement, the first option, is by and large what we have now. It occurs when the police promise to prevent crime but actually provide something else—namely, authoritative intervention and symbolic justice. Both functions are valuable, and both must be provided. The dishonesty arises from the pretense that law enforcement in this form is an adequate solution to the problem of crime. Dishonest law enforcement exploits the public's fear of crime. It oversells law enforcement, a fact that is known quite well by the police themselves. This state of affairs is acceptable only if there are no alternatives. There are, in fact, four: determined crime prevention, honest law enforcement, efficient law enforcement, and stratified crime prevention.

Option Two: Determined Crime Prevention

Determined crime prevention occurs when the police dedicate themselves to taking demonstrably effective action to reduce crime. It means facing up to the dishonesty of the current role. If crime prevention is what the police have been created to do, then they should take the lead in doing that.

What would the police have to do if they redirected their efforts so as to prevent crime? The answer is fairly clear and emerges out of the experimentation associated with community policing during the last decade (Chap. 6). A police force that seriously tried to prevent crime, rather than simply responding to its occurrence, would have to do the following.

1. *Assess Needs.* Prevention requires anticipation, so the police would need continually to assess the changing security needs of communities. They would have to monitor trends in crime and disorder, including qualitative changes in people's daily lives. They would also need to appraise the fears of citizens with respect to security because subjective perceptions affect objective behavior. The police would be responsible for framing the agenda of public safety.

2. *Diagnose Causes.* In order to take effective action, the police would have to analyze the circumstances that give rise to crime and disorder. They would become society's official criminologists, seeking to determine the causes of disorder. These might be macrosocial conditions, such as income inequalities and unemployment among youth; local circumstances, such as disruptive families; dilapidation and physical signs of crime; ethnic hostility; inadequate laws; demographic changes; and so forth (Goldstein 1990, Banton 1978, Tremblay and Rochon 1991).

3. *Develop Strategies.* Having diagnosed the causes of crime and disorder, the police would have to take the lead in developing corrective

action. As we saw in Chapter 6, solutions to crime and disorder involve a good deal more than law enforcement. They include ameliorating conditions of neglect, overseeing the design of buildings, making residential streets less accessible to strangers, building pedestrian overpasses, removing self-service stores from the vicinity of schools, requiring residential caretakers at recreation facilities, timing the arrival of buses carrying fans to soccer matches, forming collaborative partnerships among public and private agencies, and campaigning to keep schools small (Reiss 1982, Frisbie et al. 1978, Felson 1987).

4. *Advocate Courses of Action.* Since the police cannot carry out these multifaceted plans themselves, they must mobilize others, drawing together all of the resources of a community. They need to persuade communities to adopt long-range courses of action (Bayley 1991a). Currently their advocacy does not extend beyond the needs of their traditional functions. For effective crime prevention, it must include any community need that affects crime (Goldstein 1990, Skolnick and Bayley 1986). David Couper, a former police chief in Madison, Wisconsin, and a leading spokesman for community policing, said that police need to become the "conscience of the community," calling attention to the social problems that underlie crime and disorder (Executive Session on Police 1991).

5. *Implement New Approaches.* Law enforcement would undoubtedly continue to be an ingredient in crime prevention, for which the police would be responsible. But determined crime prevention would require the police to integrate law enforcement into other sorts of activities and, perhaps, to undertake some of those themselves if other agencies were unwilling or unable to do so.

6. *Coordinate Actions.* Having taken the lead in diagnosing and planning, police would need to coordinate, or at least supervise the coordination of, actions from a variety of public and private sources.

7. *Evaluate Results.* Police would have to collect information, developed either by themselves or others, to determine whether plans achieved objectives. This would need to be done over a short term in order to provide feedback to processes of implementation; it would also need to be done over the long term to measure the effectiveness of crime-prevention strategies.

Obviously, undertaking meaningful crime prevention transforms the role of the police. Their attention shifts from crime to conditions and from people to circumstances. The range of their activity expands beyond the narrow bounds of law enforcement as they become publicly engaged in advocating solutions to social problems at several levels of government. Crime is a product of complex biological and social conditions, and its prevention must involve rigorous analysis of and intervention into those conditions. This creates a profound dilemma for democratic societies.

Maximal or Minimal Policing

In the United States, Australia, Britain, and Canada the police have been viewed historically as a necessary evil. They represent the power of government at its most naked and fearful. Police can deprive people of their liberty and, on occasion, their life. In order to restrain the police, Anglo-Saxon countries have confined their activity to the enforcement of laws enacted by legislatures and supervised by judiciaries (Bayley 1985). Crime prevention changes that. When police assume responsibility for preventing crime, they can no longer be specialists in law enforcement exclusively. Instead, they become all-purpose agents for assessing, planning, mobilizing, implementing, and evaluating. They assume many of the functions that in Anglo-Saxon tradition have been assigned to other government agencies. An effective crime-prevention police begins to look like police in the continental tradition, where policing was indistinguishable from the power to govern (Cramer 1964, Fosdick 1915).

Determined crime prevention leads to a maximalist view of the function of the police, as opposed to the circumscribed minimalist view of liberal democratic tradition. "The police officer," said Herman Goldstein (1990, p. 106), a leading proponent of community policing, "is to government as the general practitioner is to the entire medical establishment." John Alderson (1979, p. 195), a British spokesman for community policing, comes to the same approving conclusion: "With the accent on preventive policing, the future role of the police in a free, permissive society is seen as primarily one of caring, informing, persuading and generally enforcing their way towards a semblance of 'orderly disorder.'"

Full-fledged crime prevention harnesses social control to social amelioration. It leads to the blending of force and welfare under the same auspices. Successful crime prevention justifies, indeed obliges, the police to collect information about all aspects of community life, not simply about circumstances surrounding specific crimes. Under the banner of crime prevention, police will penetrate into the private space of individuals and communities, watching, prodding, guiding, taking with them the paraphernalia of coercion. Successful crime prevention also blurs the executive and legislative functions of government. Police would not merely enforce laws, they would advocate policies that would be enacted into law. They would become political actors.

Finally, the efforts of the police in mobilizing communities in the interests of crime prevention might seem more than subtly coercive. People might feel they cannot afford to refuse. Conversely, mobilization would make the police a gatekeeper of community participation; they would have a powerful voice in determining who deserves to become associated with efforts at community regeneration (Morgan 1989).

Determined crime prevention by the police, according to the lore being developed through experiments in community policing, fractures the traditional division of labor within government between those who formulate and those who execute and, more sinisterly, between those who coerce and those who minister. Putting the police in charge of crime prevention is like putting the Department of Defense in charge of foreign policy. An ounce of prevention may be worth a pound of cure, but a pound of determined crime prevention may not be worth a pound of cure (Bayley 1988).

The popularity of determined crime prevention, reflected in the community policing movement, is curious and perhaps sad. People who used to be suspicious of the police now look upon them as agents for all sorts of community good works. Progressive voices in the 1960s, alarmed by the unregulated discretion possessed by the police, wanted the police to be made more accountable to law and popular opinion. Today "liberals" want the police to lead social reform and to revitalize inner-city communities. The coercive arm of the state is viewed as a promising instrument for social reconstruction.

Relying on the police may show acute political insight. During the 1970s and 1980s governments in Australia, Britain, Canada, Japan, and the United States showed little stomach for social engineering (Glazer 1987, Skogan 1990). An activist role for government was not popular. In an era when Margaret Thatcher and Ronald Reagan were preaching that governments were best that governed least, the only agents of government who could legitimately address conditions of neglect were the police. The crisis of crime presented an opportunity for enlisting the police to do from the bottom up what leaders at the top refused to do.

Geoffrey Pearson (1983, p. 239) has noted dishearteningly, "Too often matters of vital public importance—jobs, homes, schools—are swallowed up in the maw of 'law and order' discourse, and publicly addressed as if the only important consideration was whether these social deficiencies might lead to crime, vandalism and hooliganism." This is exactly the connection that makes determined crime prevention attractive to social reformers. It is also true that the police, for all their talk about law and order, seem to be the only ones who realize the limitations of law enforcement, who recognize that community-wide solutions are essential if crime is to be prevented. So the police, once regarded as reactionary defenders of the status quo, have become the last best hope for those who want progressive, ameliorative, grassroots social change.[1]

There are other, more instrumental reasons the police are being chosen to lead a concerted effort to prevent crime. They are strong in terms of resources, powerful in communities, and on the spot. No other government agency, the military excluded, can deploy resources whenever they are needed around the clock, 365 days a year. When the police decide to do something, they can deliver. Police also have a vast fund of useful information about people, social circumstances, and institutions. Moreover, having seen what it is like to be poor, marginal, and dispirited in modern communities, they are apt to have considerable sympathy for the plight of at least the "respectable poor." Police also command a great deal of respect, with both the public and other government agencies. They are authoritative—what they say matters (Sparrow, Moore, and Kennedy 1990). Finally, the police alone can ensure the minimal security that is necessary for crime prevention. Although safety in the long run depends on the alleviation of distressed social conditions, in the short run, alleviation depends on the creation of safety. Social reform cannot take place in chaos.

For all these reasons, the police are central to any effort to prevent crime and reduce disorder. The dilemma is whether they can play a leading role without creating an unwanted authoritarianism. Determined crime prevention entails serious political risks.

Option Three: Honest Law Enforcement

The simplest course of action for the police in the future is to concentrate on what they are already doing well and to give up the pretense of preventing crime. Under this option, they would provide authoritative intervention and symbolic justice, with a special focus on traffic regulation. These functions conform to the minimalist tradition of Anglo-Saxon law enforcement. But the police would be honest about it. They would take credit only for what they actually accomplish. They would admit also that they are not the solution to crime, that effective crime prevention requires a much broader program of action, under leadership that is not monopolized by themselves (Elliot 1973, Morris and Heal 1981, Murphy 1992, Kinsey and Lea 1986).

Disavowing a crime-prevention role will seem politically risky to the police. It will undermine their carefully crafted public image. Police have been very successful in obtaining public funds by claiming to prevent crime. Honest law enforcement puts an end to that.

Disconnecting the police from crime prevention makes sense for a number of reasons. First, authoritative intervention, symbolic justice, and traffic regulation are valuable services that must be provided (Giner 1987). In fact, authoritative intervention and symbolic justice may be, arguably, what the public really values in the police. Although the public may like the idea of crime prevention, they may not choose it if it must be achieved, as the police repeatedly say, at the expense of authoritative intervention and symbolic justice. The police continually argue that the quickest way to anger the public is to neglect calls for service. If this is true, then the public may be more concerned that incidents that should not be taking place are stopped right now rather than that crime is prevented in the future. The great service the police provide at the present time is a competent, often courageous, and, in developed countries, noncorrupt response to violence in all its forms, man-made as well as acts of God. Having a police officer available when someone needs one may be the most important service policing can provide.

Second, crime prevention goes against the grain of contemporary police organizations. To carry it out, they would have to change their mission, structure, management, and organizational culture. For example, the police are deployed now to deal with the effects of crime. To be effective as agents of crime prevention, they would have to be deployed against the causes of crime. Reaction and anticipation might not fit together easily within a single organization (Parker 1954, Reiss 1982, Bittner 1990).

Third, honest law enforcement saves the police from promising something they cannot deliver. Police often say—correctly—that they should not be blamed for increases in crime because the causes of crime are beyond their control. Honest law enforcement solves this public relations dilemma by narrowing the police mission to a set of actions they can demonstrably perform well. As Peter Manning (1977, p. 18) has insightfully pointed out, the police "have tied themselves to a socially determined process [that is, crime] over which they have no control. They have thus achieved success in focusing public attention upon an activity which can be seen as explosive and self-defeating." Honest law enforcement cuts this Gordian knot.

These arguments for honest law enforcement are defensive, in the sense that they say the police are valuable even if the police do not prevent crime. In fact, honest law enforcement might be the best thing that could happen to *crime prevention*. The fundamental problem with dishonest law enforcement, beyond its potential for embarrassing the police, is that it prevents communities from facing what really needs to be done. As long as people believe police can prevent crime, communities will not insist that something else be done (Shearing 1991). The police know—or are rapidly discovering—that successful crime prevention requires multifaceted programs involving all agents, informal as well as formal, of social control and social amelioration (Clinard 1978, Alderson 1979). Crime prevention requires a kind of scanning, assessment, and diagnosis that police cannot realistically be expected to provide. It also requires coordination among private police, citizens, volunteers, commercial interests, welfare agencies, architects and builders, politicians and legislatures, and a host of other government departments (Shearing 1991, Stenning 1989).

What modern societies lack is an institution apart from the police with responsibility for formulating and implementing crime-prevention programs (Shearing 1992). The police will always be an important part of crime prevention, but they should stop monopolizing it. Once communities recognize the ineffectiveness of the police in crime prevention, as well as their unwillingness to engage in it wholeheartedly, they can create alternative forums for this work. The police are like the proverbial banyan tree, whose shade is so dense it prevents anything else from growing (Home Office 1991). If the police cannot prevent crime because of their own institutional limitations and should not do it because of the threat to liberty, then honest law enforcement clears the deck for creative and long overdue thinking about better and safer auspices for doing it (Ashbury 1990, Hoogenboom 1991).

Choosing among dishonest law enforcement, determined crime prevention, and honest law enforcement may not be determined according to the usual political divisions in democratic countries. Police policy may strain existing alignments in novel ways. Conservatives tend to believe that law enforcement is the solution to crime (Walker 1989). Therefore, they will prefer dishonest law enforcement and will reject determined crime prevention. At the same time, there are attractions for them in honest law enforcement. On the one hand, it can be viewed as "keep the lid on" policing. It is old-fashioned policing without the "community" frills. On the other, conservatives more familiar with Edmund Burke will find honest law enforcement attractive because it minimizes the police role in social reform. They prefer to keep the government out of social engineering. For liberals, or Laborites in Australia and Britain, the choice will be equally unclear. They will disavow dishonest law enforcement, but are likely to split between determined crime prevention and honest law enforcement. Some liberals will press for a reformed police that embraces crime prevention as its primary objective. They will do this out of concern for the social damage that is inflicted by crime, especially among the poor, and also because the "conservative" political temper of the times leaves no other choice. Other liberals, however, will find determined crime prevention both threatening and ineffectual. They would, as a result, join with conservatives to keep the police within their current ambit but, at the same time, seek to create new institutions for harnessing the energies of communities for crime prevention. Their policy option will be to use honest law enforcement as a springboard into the reconstruction of policing in the generic sense.

Dishonest law enforcement, determined crime prevention, and honest law enforcement do not exhaust the options available in democratic countries. There are two hybrids, both of which impel the police into crime prevention but in ways that take into account organizational capacity and the danger to political freedom. I call them efficient law enforcement and stratified crime prevention.

Option Four: Efficient Law Enforcement

If contemporary police forces cannot prevent crime because they are too busy doing other things, the obvious solution is to change their priorities. Not only would this free resources but it would help to change an occupational culture that is preoccupied with enforcement. Efficient law enforcement has the police give up, reduce, or civilianize activities that do not contribute to preventing crime, using the savings achieved for CAMPS (Chap. 6). Efficient law enforcement is a piecemeal solution to the problem of reordering priorities. It takes resources as a given and tries to accommodate crime prevention. Whether streamlining in favor of crime prevention helps to mitigate the political danger of combining enforcement with amelioration is less clear. This beneficial result would occur only if the functions that were deemphasized are primarily coercive.

Several conventional activities might be considered as candidates for deemphasis in police forces that focus on crime prevention: responding to calls for service, routine mobile patrolling, criminal investigation, crowd control, and traffic regulation. Let's examine each.

Since most calls for service are not crime related and are not genuine emergencies (Chaps. 2 and 3), why must high-priced law-enforcement specialists respond to them? Does it make sense to send two $50,000 police officers, as many cities do, when one $30,000 civilian would serve as well? As Elliot (1973, p. 13) said more than twenty years ago:

> A significant proportion of police work could be handled by a Boy Scout. Such service tasks as traffic control, providing emergency first aid, investigating minor automobile accidents or crowd control require a trivial amount of training, imagination, education, and persistence. A Boy Scout with a little muscle could also take care of such police tasks as handling drunks, settling barroom fights, quieting noisy parties, and so on.

Extravagant though this statement may seem, there is contemporary evidence that turning some police work over to civilians is feasible. The phenomenal growth of the private security industry shows that the public does not insist that sworn officers handle all emergencies. Various sectors of the population are willing to pay extra, above and beyond their taxes, to obtain protection that is more responsive to their immediate needs. James Q. Wilson was farsighted when he observed in 1968 that "it is only a matter of historical accident and community convenience that [emergency services] are provided by the police: one can just as easily imagine them sold by a private, profit-making firm (Emergency Services, Inc.)" (pp. 4–5). One might also argue that the success women are having in policing shows that the heroic masculine qualities of traditional policing are unnecessary for all but a small proportion of police mobilizations.

Some departments recognize the usefulness of saving police officers for more serious work. Santa Ana, California, for example, years ago hired community service officers (CSOs) to handle calls that do not involve law enforcement (Skolnick and Bayley 1986). Dressed in uniforms similar to those of sworn officers but not carrying guns or night sticks, the CSO's do the follow-up work of mediating, referring, counseling, and advising that patrol officers are too busy to undertake. Adelaide, South Australia, and a precinct on the south side of Chicago have integrated youth workers into street patrols. Other departments have occasionally paired social and youth workers with police on patrol or made them available at police stations for ready support (Trager 1978). Most police departments have become quicker and more systematic during the last decade in referring their myriad calls for service to mental health agencies, detoxification centers, homeless shelters, homes for battered women, rape counselors, child-protection services, and so forth (Finn and Sullivan 1988).

A more dramatic proposal for simplifying police work involves giving up authoritative intervention altogether, transferring it to a civilian department run along the lines of a fire department or emergency medical service. This makes sense if the proportion of calls that involve conflict—hence the need for law enforcement—are as small as many studies have shown (Chap. 3). This proposal was explicitly rejected by the President's Commission on Law Enforcement and the Administration of Justice in 1967 (p. 98). There are several arguments against it.

First, running a 24-hour emergency service is an expensive and demanding undertaking. It would probably cost more to create a new one than to keep the existing police capacity, especially if the cost of having the police do it were reduced through the hiring of civilians. (Bittner 1970).

Second, there is the problem of predictability. How reliably could dispatchers determine whether a given call is likely to involve criminality or violence? Although some proportion of calls might clearly be safe, many would need a police officer to make an initial diagnosis.

Third, even if servicing does not always require law enforcement, successful crime prevention and effective law enforcement may require servicing. Responding to calls for service makes the police more knowledgable because such calls generate a vast amount of raw information about people, circumstances, and conditions. Although the calls are not a random selection of matters that might need police intervention, they insert the police deeply into the lives of communities (Skogan 1990). This activity may also be a necessary quid pro quo for community cooperation: It demonstrates that the police are prepared to be responsive. Paradoxically, therefore, dispatching police to calls for service may be particularly important for police forces that are committed to crime prevention.

Fourth, the practice of handling diverse calls for service prevents the police from assuming the character, in appearance as well as in their own psychology, of being a coercive, occupying force. Responding to calls for service, precisely because so many do not involve force or the application of law, provides a sympathetic human face to policing. Whether or not a police force is interested in doing more to prevent crime, it might benefit from demonstrating repeatedly that it is on the side of people in trouble.

In short, even though there may be ways of reducing the cost of emergency servicing by police, it would probably be a mistake to take this responsibility from them, *particularly* if crime prevention were to be made central to their mission.

It is important to note that if crime prevention and authoritative servicing are incompatible, it may be only in the short run. Over the long term the promise of crime prevention is that the public will need to call for police assistance less often. Crime prevention is a tool for demand management.

Substantial savings might be realized, at considerably less risk, by reducing the deployment system associated with radio dispatching— namely, random motorized patrol. Patrolling in motor vehicles is an ineffective way to prevent crime unless the concentration of vehicles is very great. Their passive presence is barely visible and does not deter crime, nor is it used for problem solving. Motorized patrolling is what police do in order to remain available for the next radio dispatch (Chap. 3).

The police might be made more efficient in crime prevention, then, if the current purposes of motorized patrol were reformulated. It would be done preventively only in concentrations that would have an effect. Directed or saturation patrols are justifiable because they are a form of "crackdown." Routine motorized patrol would be viewed exclusively as a tool for providing authoritative intervention in emergency situations that involve the possibility of physical conflict. Since these represent a small proportion of calls for service, all patrol officers would not have to be deployed for ready availability. Rather than all patrol officers being made responsible for all emergencies, police departments would deploy in rapid-response vehicles only the number of officers needed to provide emergency support to crime-prevention police and civilians who are engaged on a routine basis in working in communities. This would require the capacity to screen calls for service so that confrontational emergencies could be separated from other sorts of emergencies or from calls that can safely be postponed. Under this scheme radio cars would be deployed like ambulances, to specific holding locations close to perennial "hot spots." In effect, patrolling would become two-tiered: motorized for law-enforcement emergencies on the one hand and foot patrols, storefront offices, community police stations, and mobile problem-solving units on the other. This practice, which has been called split-force patrolling, has been tried in Wilmington, Delaware, largely as a means of saving resources (Tien, Simon, and Larson 1978). It tends to develop naturally whenever police departments commit more than token resources to community crime prevention.

Even more heretical than reducing random motorized patrols is the suggestion that criminal investigation be reorganized in the interests of crime prevention. This would be accomplished primarily through employing civilians so that police officers would be freed to concentrate on what they are uniquely trained to do—enforcing the law. There are important precedents for this. In continental Europe, criminal investigations are not carried out by people selected from the uniformed police. Instead, investigations are the responsibility of a separate service, composed of law graduates, that is responsible to ministries of justice rather than ministries of the police or the interior (Bayley 1985). Inspector Maigret, George Simenon's famous French detective, is a member of the Police Judicaire, not the Police Nationale. Maigret never walked a beat. Investigation and enforcement have been separated in Britain with respect to the control of political groups suspected of violence. The Special Branch of the London Metropolitan Police is responsible for the investigation of violent political movements, notably the ·IRA. But although its personnel are police officers, it rarely makes arrests. Instead, when arrests must be made, it calls in the uniformed branch. Thus there is a recognized division of labor between investigating and enforcing.

Increasingly in modern countries the investigation of crime, especially commercial crime, has been taken over by civilians working for insurance companies, regulatory agencies, tax offices, welfare departments, and fire departments. Private policing, which began by providing only investigative services, has in recent years developed into a large uniformed service. Police departments are themselves beginning to recruit civilians directly to their criminal investigation departments to provide expert knowledge that uniformed officers rarely have. A few departments in the United States have solicited the services of retired civilian experts. A department in Texas appealed to the American Association of Retired Persons (AARP) for a retired pilot, petroleum engineer, and insurance executive. Austin, Texas, appointed as a detective a female graduate of the University of Texas who spoke Vietnamese.

The point is that training and experience in uniformed law enforcement may not be necessary to become an effective criminal investigator. Criminal investigation can be "de-policed." Whether this achieves savings that can be devoted to crime prevention is debatable. No one is suggesting that crimes should not be investigated. Therefore, savings depend on whether employing civilians will result in lower costs. If the civilian investigators need to be experts, then they may be as expensive as uniformed officers. Although bringing civilians into crime investigations may save uniformed officers for crime prevention, it may not save money. The division of labor changes, but not the overall cost.

The aspect of policing that the police themselves are most willing to consider eliminating in the interests of efficiency is traffic regulation. Accounting generally for about 9% of police personnel, traffic regulation is the third largest specialization, after patrol and criminal investigation (Chap. 2). Traffic officers are costly because, in addition to being trained as uniformed police, they often undergo special instruction in motor-vehicle laws, high-speed chases, motor-vehicle maintenance and safety, and the operation of radar guns, video cameras, and breathalyzers. The British estimate that a traffic officer costs more than any other personnel. Furthermore, neither the police nor the public consider traffic violations serious crimes, although opinion about drunken driving may be changing in this regard. Investigations of traffic accidents is a service benefiting drivers and insurance companies that could easily be performed by civilians.

In defense of their importance to crime prevention, traffic police often point out that in enforcing traffic regulations they discover wanted persons, stolen cars, contraband drugs, and evidence pertaining to other crimes. Unfortunately, there is no evidence to support this common claim. No department that I studied (28) could cite a study of the proportion of traffic "stops" resulting in crime "hits."

For most police, traffic regulation is "chicken shit work"—trivial and resented by the public. Accounting for a large proportion of police-citizen contacts, traffic regulation rarely makes friends for the police. Police also consider traffic "stops" to be unpredictable and possibly dangerous, along with domestic disputes (Bayley 1986). For all these reasons, traffic regulation is an unpopular specialization.

Altogether, traffic regulation would seem a prime candidate for cost savings for the sake of efficient law enforcement. This could be done by creating a civilian corps to enforce laws against dangerous driving and unsafe motor vehicles, along the lines of the parking- and parking-meter police. Interestingly, in 1962 the British Royal Commission on the Police rejected this suggestion, although it approved traffic wardens for stationary offenses. Traffic regulation has been split off from policing in at least two large forces. New Zealand had a separate Traffic Safety Service run by the Ministry of Transport from 1936 to 1992.[2] The state of Western Australia assigned traffic regulation to the Road Transport Authority from 1975 to 1982. There was no saving in money, however, because the staff was made up of transferred police officers. In both New Zealand and Western Australia traffic regulation eventually reverted to police auspices.

Although traffic regulation may be ancillary to serious law enforcement, a powerful argument can be made that it should be retained as a police function if police are to undertake serious crime prevention. Reducing or eliminating police responsibility for traffic might be exactly the wrong thing to do if crime prevention is the objective. A nation's roads are a crucial part of public space; they are probably the public space shared by the largest proportion of the population. Roadways, for example, take up at least a fourth of the territory of U.S. cities. In most developed countries, where car ownership is common, people spend substantial periods of time on the roads daily. According to an article in the *New York Times* (28 February 1988), in southern California, which is only somewhat extreme, there were 8.7 million licensed drivers in 1988, making 40.2 million trips covering 221.3 million miles *each day*. The average driver commuted 10.7 miles each way. In the mid-1980s drunken driving in the United States cost almost as much as all forms of personal and household crime ($12 billion versus $13 billion; Wadman and Olson 1990). Moreover, police in all countries report that as traffic congestion has risen, so has the number of assaults and even murders arising out of minor accidents or incivilities on the highway.

If a key ingredient of crime prevention is demonstrating that a moral order exists that people should pay attention to, then it might be short-sighted to exclude the behavior of people on streets and roads. If disorder is criminogenic, as studies have shown (Skogan 1990, Wilson and Kelling 1982), then public thoroughfares cannot be allowed to become mobile "no go" areas. Traffic regulation sends messages about order, lawfulness, and civility, sensitizing people to the presence of rules that serve the community. Tailgating, speeding, making unannounced lane changes, and failing to yield may have the same effect on criminal risk taking, the fear of crime, and the public's sense of well-being as graffiti, broken windows, raucous music, and rude teenagers.

Efficient crime prevention bought at the expense of traffic regulation, then, may be counterproductive. Instead, perhaps crime prevention would benefit if the practices of CAMPS were applied determinedly to this activity that consumes so much of our daily lives. Viewed in this way, traffic regulation is not a diversion from crime prevention but simply another venue for community policing. Anthony Bouza (1990, p. 117), former chief of police in Minneapolis, sees this clearly: "There is no better way to convey the image of an aggressive law-and-order posture than through the highly visible operations of a tough traffic-enforcement program." So far, this is a minority view among police.

Traffic regulation can be viewed, then, either as irrelevant to crime prevention or central to it. One direction leads to divestment, the other to reemphasis. Is traffic regulation a candidate for efficient law enforcement or determined crime prevention? No other element of conventional policing is so ambiguously related to the crime-prevention agenda.

One other responsibility of contemporary policing that might be considered for cost cutting in the interests of efficient law enforcement is crowd control—the maintenance of order among groups of people in public places. I mention this to cover all possibilities, not because it is seriously being considered by the police. It is doubtful that any government would allow the police to relinquish this responsibility. Crowd disorder threatens governments; crimes by individuals do not. There is considerable historical evidence that the police are much more readily given the resources they need to deal with collective threats to public order than they are to fight the kinds of crimes that victimize individuals (Bayley 1985). Crime prevention by the police that does not encompass the security of government is unlikely to be supported. This does not imply that policing is a conspiracy by governments against the people (Center for Research on Criminal Justice 1975, Harring 1983). Disruption of government can be acutely unsettling to the public as well as to politicians. Without the police there may be crime; without government there is anarchy.

Furthermore, crowd control is really crime prevention. Crowds can be dangerous, so it makes as much sense to concentrate police officers on them as it does to saturate "hot spots" with directed patrols. The costs of crowd control might be reduced by substituting civilians for police at fairs, festivals, and parades as long as there is little likelihood of violence. When the police were given responsibility for crowd control in the nineteenth century, they were viewed as a humane alternative to control by the army (Silver 1967, Bayley 1975, Critchley 1967, Reith 1956). In the United States today, local police are generally considered less dangerous, and less provocative, than the National Guard.

Having examined the main possibilities for streamlining conventional policing, should efficient law enforcement be considered an important option? The answer is probably not. With the exception of mobile patrolling, all of the functions discussed here have to be done by someone, even if not by the police. So the net savings to communities, as opposed to the police, are small. Patrolling alone is a function that might be scaled back substantially. Furthermore, there do not seem to be clear advantages in having most of these functions performed by government agencies distinct from the police. Even traffic regulation seems difficult to split off, for practical as well as theoretical reasons.

Thus, reorganization of police services is not likely to be a magic formula for finding additional resources for crime prevention. The only real opportunity for cost recovery is through employing civilians to take over some police functions, rather than eliminating the functions. Altogether, crime prevention is more likely to prosper not because the police do different work but because they do the same work differently.

Option Five: Stratified Crime Prevention

Preventing crime may be consciously rejected as an important mission for the police: That is honest law enforcement. Preventing crime may simply be neglected, largely through preoccupation with other tasks: That is dishonest law enforcement. Alternatively, the police may whole-heartedly emphasize crime prevention: That is determined crime pre-vention. The police may also accommodate crime prevention through reorganizing existing work: That is efficient law enforcement.

There is one other way in which serious crime prevention might develop under police auspices. I call it stratified crime prevention. It involves concentrating responsibility for crime prevention—CAMPS—on a particular stratum of police officers, namely, uniformed frontline personnel. These might be patrol officers generally or specially created community police officers. They would be given the responsibility for determining the form of policing best suited to the crime-prevention needs of specified areas to which they are assigned. Under this option, preventing crime is limited to the activities that can be undertaken by police officers who are in closest touch with communities. It becomes a style of policing practiced by patrol officers.

The stratified-crime-prevention option is implicit in some of the community policing developments of the past few years. For example, London's sector policing, New York City's zone policing, and Japan's *koban* system depend on the creation of flexible operational groups that can consult, adapt, mobilize, and solve problems. Similarly, community policing creates a new kind of frontline officer—the community police officer—who negotiates and designs policing for particular areas. Examples include the community police officers in New York City, Edmonton, and Ontario and the neighborhood police officers in Houston.

Stratified crime prevention is quite common, occurring naturally whenever policing is effectively delegated to small commands respon-sible for local communities. It is the way policing operates in small towns, rural communities, and suburbs. Stratified crime prevention exists, for example, in most Royal Canadian Mounted Police detach-ments, in small-town subdivisions and suburbs in Britain, in Japanese residential police posts (*chuziasho*), and in outback police stations in Australia. Stratified crime prevention describes policing in most of the United States, where police departments are small—with an average of 35 sworn officers—and independent (*Sourcebook* 1991, Table 1.22). The stratification of crime prevention in the United States has not come about through devolution of command; it is the result of America's remarkably decentralized system. Stratified crime prevention is systemic in the United States. But the principle is the same: Stratified Crime Prevention occurs when policing is carried out by small, relatively autonomous commands based in distinct communities.

This proposition can be demonstrated by examining the character of policing in small towns. Without consciously doing so, small-town police incorporate naturally the elements of crime prevention into their daily operations.

Anticipation predominates over reaction in small towns. Patrol focuses on a few well-known trouble spots and stresses the development of in-depth knowledge of people and situations. Because serious crime is rare, officers spend most of their time attending to minor nuisances and disturbances, what is referred to as order-maintenance—noisy motorbikes late at night, barking dogs, after-hours drinking, teenage partying, and truancy (Murphy 1986). Patrolling is not done in order to make police available. With calls for service few and distances between points short, the police are always at hand even when sitting in the police station. Collaboration in crime prevention is easy because the police know personally the handful of service providers and authority figures in the community—clergy, doctors, visiting nurses, elected officials, welfare counselors, and so forth.

In small towns the police have the time and the knowledge to persuade, teach, warn, advise, mediate, and support. In cities, on the other hand, the police face a stark choice between ignoring offenses and enforcing the law. They are either invisible or repressive. Furthermore, in small towns police interaction with people extends from awareness of a problem to its solution; in cities, interaction goes only from complaint to arrest. Small-town police deal with familiar people; city police deal with offenders. As a Royal Canadian Mounted Police corporal said: "If I stop someone in Vancouver for a traffic violation, who cares? If I stop someone here, everyone knows and I have to live with the guy."

Apart from a few "emergency" calls, police work in small towns is determined by the voiced needs of the community. Consultation is ongoing and informal; it need not be manufactured through special meetings. Because the interdependence of the police and the community is acknowledged, the police are able to police by consent, as the British say. In the face of a crime or disruption, police do not tell the community to trust the system—they are the system. They are immediately responsible, and they are made to know it.

When dealing with strangers, police obtain compliance through the threat of force; their power must be overt and persuasive. When dealing with "neighbors," as in small towns, compliance arises out of respect. Moral status is more important than naked force. In addition, the police are made accountable by the need to preserve constructive social relationships. The consequence of hasty action in small towns is social isolation; in cities it is organizational punishment or collective disorder, both as impersonal as the weather. Accountability in a small town is achieved through membership.

The organizational culture of policing is also different in small towns. There the entire command shares responsibility for whatever needs doing—patrolling, investigating, regulating traffic, making arrests, counseling, and responding to calls for service. Each officer is necessarily a generalist, and specialization is unimportant. When backup or expertise is required, it is provided by higher levels of police organization—area and headquarters units in Australia and Britain, state and federal police in Canada and the United States (Mastrofski 1985, Henderson 1985).

Rank relations too are less formal in small towns because officers know one another as individuals. Discipline depends less on formal authority and more on interpersonal chemistry, just as it does between the police and the citizens in the community. Since the failure of one is the failure of all, problems are shared, and planning is necessarily collegial.

Underlying the differences in the character of policing between small towns and cities lies a single, critical factor—anonymity. In small towns policing is not done by strangers. Relationships are enduring and complex. Public and private lives interpenetrate. Police are never off duty, never not responsible. Even their families, especially their wives, share the burden of their position. For the police in small towns anonymity is both an opportunity and a burden (Braithwaite; Banton 1964; Jacobs 1962; Berreman 1978, Wirth 1938, Shevky and Bell 1955).

Contrary to impression, then, serious attention to crime prevention is neither new nor rare in policing. Community policing, which is what modern crime prevention is being called, developed during the 1980s in response to the inadequacies of policing in one particular social setting—cities. Community policing has been alive and well wherever operational stratification has taken place.

Ironically, however, this may not continue to be true. While city police are searching for ways to do what small-town police have been doing all along, small-town police are striving to become "professional," which means that they are trying to emulate the organizational practices of cities. Progressiveness in policing is associated with big-city practices (Murphy 1984). Sadly, therefore, what passes as professionalism pushes small towns to dismantle the practices that city forces need. To stop this deadening homogenization, a new kind of professionalism is required, one that is willing to learn from small towns. In order for crime prevention to become central to policing, then, the practices of Rutland, Vermont, must be brought to New York City; those of Cape Breton to Toronto; those of Syston to London; and those of Menindee to Sydney.

Can this be done? Community policing assumes that the small-town style of policing can work in cities. This means that this particular strategy can produce similar benefits regardless of social setting—in short, that the police tail can wag the community dog. However, if the critical determinant of the character of policing is anonymity, there may be real limits to the transferability of crime-prevention practices and of community policing from small to large communities. Social relationships are different in small towns and cities.

Is it is romantic to think that city police can emulate the practices of small towns? I think not. The mechanism for doing so is stratification of command, where crime prevention becomes the primary responsibility of frontline operational personnel. Stratification is a way of addressing the twin problems of organizational capacity and political values. Organizationally, it blends crime prevention with traditional functions by concentrating crime prevention at the bottom and placing the other functions in service to it. Politically, crime prevention is made accountable because it is focused and devised locally. Consultation is more likely to lead to accountability and less to directiveness when policing is organized on a small scale. The maximalist dangers of community policing are greater when police are restrained only by formal mechanisms of law and representative government, as is the case in impersonal cities. As Jane Jacobs (1962, p. 117) has nicely said, "Neighborhoods in cities need not supply for their people an artificial town or village life, and to aim at this is both silly and destructive. But neighborhoods in cities do need to supply some means for civilized self-government. This is the problem."

Conclusion

Dishonest law enforcement, determined crime prevention, honest law enforcement, efficient law enforcement, and *stratified crime prevention* represent the choices of people in democratic countries as they consider the shape of policing in the future. They are models that police themselves are actively considering and exploring. These models are pure types; in the real world, the practices tend to blend to various extents.

Dishonest law enforcement is still the standard. In most countries police argue vigorously that their primary functions are authoritative intervention and symbolic justice, rarely admitting that these have little effect on crime. By and large, their crime-prevention benefits must be taken on faith. Honest law enforcement, however, is an option discussed only inside policing, a response to the need to show that money is being spent efficiently.

Determined crime prevention has occurred in only a few places where police have decided to reorder the priorities of conventional policing. Probably the best examples are Newport News, Virginia; Denton, Texas; Madison, Wisconsin; and Santa Ana, California, in the

United States and Singapore and Japan abroad. Efficient law enforcement is a halfway house to determined crime prevention. It is an adaptive position taken when police try to accommodate a larger crime-prevention mission within the routines of a traditional organization. Elements of it, particularly employing civilians for core tasks, are being tried in many places. For policing generally, this option is being forced on it as privatization continues to grow.

Stratified crime prevention emerges when large police forces try to incorporate the principles of community policing (Chap. 5). It also occurs by default in very decentralized police systems or organizations. Genuine crime prevention is more likely to take place today as stratified crime prevention than in any other way.

Although the public may feel helpless about rising crime, mayhem, and disorder, the options for policing have actually been multiplying in recent years. Democratic countries are on the cusp of decision with respect to the role of the police. The issue is not whether choices will be made but whether they will be made thoughtfully and in public view.

8

A Blueprint for the Future

In modern democratic societies the police bear the primary responsibility for ensuring public safety because law enforcement is viewed as the primary solution to crime. For several reasons this total reliance on law enforcement is unwise and should not be allowed to continue.

The standing of the police is being undermined because the public is beginning to realize that the police cannot deliver what they promise. The rise of the private security industry and efforts by communities to protect themselves attest to this. Dependence on law enforcement for crime control exposes the police, as well as the entire criminal justice system, to scapegoating. Inflated expectations lead to loss of trust and eventually to the loss of resources.

Because the police are taking money ostensibly for one purpose but are actually accomplishing others, they cannot be made accountable. They are engaging in a game of obfuscation that undercuts effective oversight and control.

Experts on crime, including the police, understand very well that crime cannot be prevented exclusively through law enforcement. Police are, indeed, only a band-aid on cancer. However, as long as they monopolize crime prevention, the search for other ways of reducing crime will be half-hearted. By pretending to be the solution to crime, police become part of the problem.

Finally, giving responsibility for crime control to the police is dangerous to our liberties. When Western democratic countries are gripped by crime "crises," their habitual response is to strengthen legal controls. They enact stricter laws, reducing procedural protections for individuals accused of crimes, and make punishments harsher. In searching for remedies for crime, intensified law enforcement is the default position of liberal democratic countries. It is the only solution they know (Bayley 1985).

For these reasons, then, dishonest law enforcement, as I call the current situation, should be stopped.

What, then, should we do with the police? One possibility is to allow them to concentrate on what they do best—namely, authoritative intervention and symbolic justice, thereby explicitly making the prevention of crime someone else's responsibility. This is what I call honest law enforcement. The police would no longer monopolize crime prevention. Other institutions would have to be created to develop and implement policies for controlling crime.

This solution is impractical, in my view, for a number of reasons. First, withdrawing the police from explicit crime prevention and allowing "natural" social processes, such as markets, to create new institutions for this purpose will lead to inequities in protection. If public auspices do not provide effective crime prevention for the poor, then who will? Affluent people can always purchase protection for themselves. This leads to a dualistic system of policing, with private police preventing crime for the rich and public police enforcing laws for the poor. Furthermore, the affluent sectors of society would undoubtedly begin to object to paying twice for policing. The police, perhaps like the public schools in some cities, would be faced with dealing with society's most serious crime problems but with fewer and fewer resources. The police would become proletarianized—a poor police policing the poor.

Second, law enforcement is not irrelevant to crime prevention. It is not a cure-all, but it is a powerful tool. Order is a casualty of social disorganization, but a minimum of order is necessary for the practical implementation of crime-prevention policies. The police must often be in the vanguard of efforts at amelioration. Purely as a tactical matter, then, it is better to work with them and through them than to try to work around them.

Third, while it might be possible to reduce the police role in policing, it is not possible to remove the state from policing. Honest law enforcement does not solve the problem of combining coercion with amelioration; it merely shifts it to other institutions. Governments will inevitably remain central to crime prevention in modern societies—not because other institutions are not important but because the state cannot renounce the responsibility. The maintenance of domestic order is as crucial to the legitimacy of government as defense against external enemies. If the current situation is unsatisfactory, governments will either reform the police or will create other institutions to direct and control crime prevention. Either way, the state is going to remain important to resolving our current predicament.

Fourth, it would be harder to create new, nonpolice auspices for crime prevention than to change the police so that they become effective at it. Even though "policing" in the sense of social control and discipline depends even now on a host of nonpolice mechanisms, the public does not understand this. It would be unrealistic to ask an anxious and fearful public to entrust their security to untried institutions of crime prevention. People would have to be weaned gradually from dependence on law enforcement, which means that the police will play an important role for the foreseeable future.

Fifth, in addition to the ability to establish order in the short run, the police have resources that crime prevention needs. They have public standing, in the sense that people will listen to them. They have personnel available throughout communities day and night. They are developing expertise in the techniques and requirements of crime prevention. Most important of all, they are beginning to face up to the inadequacies of their current performance in preventing crime. The police know more about the shortcomings of law enforcement than the public does. It is likely, therefore, to be easier to reform the police than to reeducate the public about the shortcomings of law enforcement.

Sixth, it might be easier to make the police accountable for the prying intrusions of crime prevention than it would be to create a whole new set of institutions. The Anglo-Saxon tradition in policing insists on oversight. The police, correspondingly, are accustomed to being regulated by law and public opinion. They may not always like it, but they accept it as a given. Authoritarian possibilities inherent in crime prevention may be more difficult to anticipate and guard against with "committees of public safety" than with the traditional police.

All in all, I believe it would be easier, safer, and more effective to broaden the functions of the police to include the activities of crime prevention than to create new institutions to mobilize and direct society's resources against the menace of crime. This does not mean that efforts should not also be made to develop and invigorate other institutions for the same purpose. But it does mean that the police should be told that crime- prevention is their primary responsibility. Unless this is done, I fear it will not happen in ways that we will find acceptable.

There is a dilemma here. The police cannot be relied upon to prevent crime, but they cannot be excused from the responsibility either. The solution is to recognize that there are two questions here, not one. What should societies do to prevent crime? What should the police do? We cannot rely upon the police, even when they are dedicated to preventing crime, to save society from crime. No single institution can do that. At the same time, we must charge them with taking the lead in exploring what must be done. In institutional terms, they are best for the purpose.

If this reasoning is sound, then the challenge is to find ways of using the police for crime prevention without (1) losing other important functions that they perform, (2) discouraging the strengthening of other social processes that are critical to the enterprise, and (3) creating an omnicompetent police that combines coercion with consultation, amelioration, and coordination.

Can this be done? I think so. It will require policing to be demilitarized. Policing must no longer be viewed as a war, dominated by the use of force devised by senior ranks and carried out by "troops" whose primary duty is obedience. Policing will need to be stood on its head. In conventional policing, the assessment of needs and the development of strategies are done at the top, by senior staff. Lower echelons carry out the plans that headquarters formulate. In order for crime to be prevented effectively, responsibility for diagnosing needs and formulating action plans must be given to frontline personnel. Higher echelons should act in a supporting role, either by delivering the necessary resources or managing the organization in a facilitating way. In other words, the roles of staff and line personnel must be reversed. This can be accomplished through a three-tiered system.

1. Neighborhood police officers (NPOs), whose exclusive responsibility is to deliver crime prevention.
2. Basic police units (BPUs), which would be full-service command units responsible for delivering police services as needed.
3. Police forces, which would provide resources, manage the organization, and evaluate effectiveness.

Let us explore what this system would look like in detail, so that we can judge whether it might achieve more effective crime prevention while preserving existing services and avoiding excessive power.

Level 1: The Neighborhood Police Officer

The only way crime prevention can be made a core function of policing is by assigning a large number of frontline officers to it. In order for crime prevention to become important in policing, it must be staffed. A new line of work must be created, with personnel assigned to it who are deployed as extensively in communities as are conventional patrol officers. Crime prevention will not take place if it is tacked onto the existing duties of patrol officers and detectives. As long as patrol is driven by the need to be available and criminal investigation by the imperative to clear cases, crime prevention will be an afterthought. The slogan "community policing is a philosophy and not a program" is the epitaph of crime prevention, making crime prevention a matter of inward belief, not of outward activity. Similarly, if crime prevention is assigned to specialized units, then it will remain a fitful add-on to the delivery of authoritative intervention and symbolic justice.

If there is one thing social science has demonstrated, it is that roles determine behavior. People do what situations require. In policing, as well as in other modern institutions, behavior is dependent on organizational context. Unless the police make crime prevention a job that policing's front line is specifically assigned to carry out, it will not be undertaken effectively.

Therefore, the front line of policing should consist of mature, experienced, and carefully selected NPOs with the responsibility of designing policing in relatively small areas. The NPOs would assess all of the security needs of their areas and determine corrective courses of action. Such measures might involve law enforcement but would also include referral to other agencies and mobilization of the self-help capacity of each community. Each area should be small enough so that one officer, or perhaps two, would be able to consult continually with individuals and institutions about crime and disorder problems. The NPO in a community must become known to all the residents as "our police officer." NPOs would be encouraged to create local crime-prevention councils, along the lines of London's sector working groups or Edmonton's community advisory panels. Since the entire jurisdiction of any police force would be checkerboarded in this way, similar to the current beat system, the corps of NPOs would become the largest uniformed specialization within policing.

The primary function of NPOs would be the diagnosis of security needs and the formulation of plans to meet recurring needs before they become law-enforcement emergencies. It would be unrealistic for NPOs to try to prevent all crime. Rather, they would focus on incidents caused by visible circumstances within local communities. NPOs cannot be expected to reform society, but they can be expected to address local circumstances that lead to crime and disorder. They would address what Egon Bittner has called "constellations of intermediate factors that mitigate crime" (Goldstein, private communication, March 23, 1991). They would do crime prevention that is community based in a double sense. They would be based in communities, rather than entering them episodically in response to calls for service. And the problems they handle would be those based on community conditions.

NPOs would not be responsible for handling emergency calls for service. They would not be cover people, who are required to be available 24 hours a day. They would be responsible for reducing the need for residents to make emergency calls for service. For nonemergency matters, or matters that cannot be handled adequately over the telephone, residents would be encouraged to call the NPO directly and to make an appointment at a mutually convenient time. This would reduce the demand for radio car assistance and also provide pretexts for NPOs to contact citizens and inquire about recurring problems.

Neighborhood Police Officers would be the general practitioners of policing. Just as in medicine GPs are not called out to treat emergency trauma, so NPOs would concentrate on consultations with people who have incipient problems and the after-care of crime victims. In this way, they would become informed about the security problems of their areas but would be freed from the need to be available for the next emergency call. They would set their own hours. Again like doctors, it would be helpful if NPOs had a local office where they could meet "patients" and a private number where messages could be left and appointments scheduled.

Because NPOs would be doing a very different job from that of conventional patrol officers, they would need to be evaluated in a different way. Performance would not be measured in terms of the number of enforcement actions or the number of calls handled. NPOs would be evaluated in terms of their knowledge of local needs and their ability to formulate plans that lead to a reduction of those needs. It would also be unfair to evaluate NPOs in terms of crime rates. Too many factors that generate crime lie outside their ability to control. But there are two hard direct measures that could be fairly applied (Chap. 6). These are the number of problems solved to the satisfaction of the community and the reduction in the number of calls for service.

In order to appreciate the job of an NPO, one needs to see such an officer in action. NPOs are common in small towns but rare in big cities. The following describes the typical day of one such officer who was assigned to an ethnically mixed working-class neighborhood of a major U.S. city.

The Neighborhood Police Officer, who was white and 25 years old, reported for duty at 10 A.M. to a crowded, old, red-brick police station. After changing into uniform, he drank coffee and discussed ongoing problems with the supervising sergeant and his colleagues from adjacent beats. The officer was then taken by van to his neighborhood and dropped off at a small Hispanic grocery store that had been burglarized the previous night. He did not have a local office that could be used as a base.

The NPO gave the owner the complaint number of his case so that the owner could call for information when he submitted his insurance claim. He also gave the owner his personal card, carrying his police phone number, and scheduled a visit by the police security-survey team.

Consulting a list of appointments, the NPO walked several blocks to a child-care facility serving working-class African-American families. Over a cup of coffee with the female staff, he finalized plans for a visit the following week by police horses, motorcycles, and a SWAT team. Although primarily for the children, the visit would be a neighborhood event, with refreshments and a display of crime-prevention information.

On the way to his next appointment, the NPO casually inspected the street in front of a house where an Indian immigrant had repaired cars, leaving oil smears and junk all around. After repeated complaints from neighbors, the NPO had advised the man to move his repair work to his garage. When he did not, the NPO cited him for code violations carrying fines of $500. The officer noted that he might have angered one man but gained a neighborhood.

As the NPO walked slowly to his next appointment, greeting

passersby and observing conditions, he was followed along a chain-link fence by a gaggle of African-American youngsters playing in a school yard. They pestered him to recite the full Miranda warnings they had seen on television ("You have the right to remain silent. . . .") He stopped and did so, to the round-eyed delight of the kids, who mouthed the words as he spoke. The NPO pointed out the spray-painted mural on a school wall advocating "Revolucion!" The school had agreed to paint it over in the next couple of weeks. He also described the one-day painting of a nearby Catholic church that had been organized by him and the fire department. The small church, run by an elderly Polish priest, had a devoted congregation of immigrants but was very poor.

The next call was at a sheet-metal works whose foreman the NPO did not know. As the officer entered the noisy, machine-filled shed, the foreman came striding up, held out his hand, and said, "So you're our neighborhood cop!" They exchanged cards and phone numbers and discussed the theft of materials from the machine-shop yard.

After lunch in the back room of a Portuguese bar-restaurant where the NPO was well known to the owner, the officer made a social call at the local office of the city's sanitation department. The NPO had worked with the staff on several projects and wanted to bring them up to date on results. Their major project had been the cleaning of a vacant lot on a street of detached two-story houses that had been heaped six-feet deep with trash and rubbish dumped by cars, vans, and small trucks from all over the city. After three months of aggravating paper-work, the NPO had succeeded in getting the lot condemned as a health hazard. A sanitation crew had worked two days with a bulldozer and a long-bed trash truck to clean the lot. Now monitoring the lot closely, the neighborhood was prepared to report the license numbers of vehicles that dumped there. Although four months had elapsed since the clean-up, the lot was still clear.

Later in the day the NPO visited the home of an African-American woman who had organized the ongoing surveillance of the vacant lot. He warned her against encouraging residents to confront people who might try to dump in the lot: They should take down the license numbers and then call him. He also inquired whether a prostitute who had briefly solicited on the block had returned since he had warned her off two weeks before. And he promised to discuss with a local gravel company whether their trucks could use an adjacent street instead of this quiet residential one.

At 3 P.M. the NPO met four plainclothes narcotics officers at an abandoned house on a residential block. After searching the house for signs of illicit drug use, they agreed to ask the public works department to board the house up. The NPO undertook to search city records for the name of the owner and begin proceedings to get the house either fixed up or demolished.

Walking around a corner nearby, the NPO saw an African-American youth jump on his motorcycle and drive off. He was a well-known drug dealer who used the public telephone on the corner to arrange drug deliveries. At another location the NPO had persuaded the telephone company to have a public phone removed because so many dealers hung around it, frightening and inconveniencing local residents.

Late in the afternoon the NPO dropped into a Portuguese social club located in the basement of a large, decrepit brick building. Drinking free iced tea, the NPO gossiped with the manager and several elderly men who were playing cards and watching a baseball game on television. The neighborhood Portuguese newspaper had recently published a story about the NPO and his efforts to control graffiti. The NPO had worked with the local district attorney to get an ordinance passed prohibiting the display of aerosol paint cans on store shelves or their sale to people under 18 years of age. The ordinance allowed the police to warn merchants, then to issue them a summons, and, after repeated offenses, to confiscate goods.

Toward the end of the day the officer visited the two-story home of a late-middle-aged woman, whom he viewed as one of his greatest successes. Over several months the year before the woman had called the police fifty or sixty times complaining about loud music and parties in adjacent houses or in the parking lot across the street. The radio-car officers thought her a crank because they never found any parties or heard any loud music. After getting an earful from the frustrated patrol-car officers, the NPO had knocked on every door along the street trying to discover what was going on. The neighbors, too, were angry and frustrated about the repeated false calls. The officer finally had enough information to put two and two together. It turned out that the woman, widowed and poor, supported herself by caring for seven or eight elderly men and women who could no longer live alone. Being white in a neighborhood that was gradually going black, she was frightened and lonely. The false calls to the police were her way of showing she had police protection and also of finding some companionship in her narrow home-bound life. The NPO now stopped by the house at least once a week, usually at the same time, to have a short chat and a warm or cold drink depending on the weather. Since he started his regular visits, she has made no complaints about loud parties on the block. His simple solution, taking no more than a half an hour a week, has saved hundreds of hours of police time, allowing the radio cars to concentrate on more urgent matters. In addition, he provides needed reassurance to a kind soul and makes life on the block much more neighborly.

NPOs such as this one need to be more than specialists in law enforcement. Their unique role is to engage in the CAMPS that crime prevention requires. Accordingly, NPOs must be intelligent and experienced enough to be able to identify community needs; they must be skilled at talking to people and gaining their confidence; they must possess the poise to negotiate with government agencies and private service providers; and they must be responsible and self-directing. Plainly, NPOs must be the best and the brightest the police have to offer. The position should be the pinnacle of a career, one all ambitious officers aspire to.

The centrality of crime prevention to policing should be taught to all recruits. They should learn what NPOs do and serve as apprentice-helpers to NPOs for several weeks. Recruits should never be appointed NPOS, however—the position is not one for beginners. Instead, recruits should work initially in the conventional specializations of rapid response patrol, criminal investigation, traffic regulation, and crowd control. Outstanding performance in the "treatment" functions of policing should be a prerequisite for promotion to diagnosis and prescription.

NPOs should have special status in policing. They are not just police officers who do crime prevention. They are individuals of unusual skill who can be entrusted with doing crime prevention. In effect, they should have the stature of sergeants, even though the management of subordinates is not part of their job. Because the rank system is so ingrained in policing, the quickest way to accord this status would be to give NPOs sergeant rank. This rank would demonstrate that NPOs are more than spear carriers in the law-enforcement drama. Service as an NPO should also be a precondition for appointment to any higher managerial position. After qualifying for appointment as an NPO, officers would need specialized in-service training. They should probably serve an apprenticeship with an experienced NPO. Finally, because effective crime prevention requires experience and ingenuity, police organizations should facilitate the on-going sharing of tradecraft among NPOs through regular conferences where problems and solutions are compared.

The creation of a frontline corps of NPOs would institutionalize preventive diagnosis, problem solving, and demand reduction. It would also transform police-citizen contact, making it routine and low key rather than exceptional and emotionally charged. As Egon Bittner (1987) wrote: "Where once we looked for heedless heroes, [now] we would expect craftsmanship."

Level 2: The Basic Police Unit

In order for resources to be used rationally, police strategies need to be adjusted in response to information about whether desired objectives are being achieved. The problem with traditional policing has been a lockstep reliance on a few generic strategies that are used everywhere, regardless of differences in patterns of crime, disorder, and underlying social circumstances. The quantity of police resources has varied from place to place, but not the format of their use. The solution to this problem is to devise a command structure that can adapt operational strategies to local conditions. This entails the ability to assess the effectiveness of chosen strategies and programs. Police resourcing must be driven by specific, demonstrable operational needs rather than by the bureaucratic traditions of the past.

The way to achieve this sort of adaptability in the use of resources is to require operational strategies to be developed from the bottom up. Responsibility for devising appropriate strategies to accomplish police objectives should be given to the commanders of basic police units (BPUs). A BPU would be the smallest full-service territorial command unit of a police force. Similar to precincts in large U.S. cities, subdivisions in Britain, and police stations in Japan, BPUs would be responsible for delivering all but the most specialized police services. Their essential function would be to determine local needs and to devise strategies to meet those needs.

The BPUs would determine the proportion of foot beats to random motorized patrols; whether NPOs and other uniformed officers can handle most criminal investigations; the strength and staffing patterns of detectives; whether local crime problems require undercover investigation in addition to the overt probings of NPOs; whether public requests for service should be handled by appointments with NPOs, "quality-of-life" patrol cars, or fast-response radio cars; whether traffic specialists are needed or general patrol officers can occasionally be designated for traffic regulation; and what sort of supporting skills and resources NPOs most often need to resolve the problems on their beats.

In short, BPUs would determine what resources localities require, stock them for use, and oversee their coordinated deployment. They would be the primary center for operational planning.

Police budgets, then, would represent an aggregation of local needs, based on evaluations of local effectiveness. This would lead to new mixtures of resources. As we saw in Chapter 3, local commanders generally use only one resource—personnel. Moreover, this resource comes prepackaged in a limited number of assignments—patrol, detectives, traffic. Flexibility is further restricted by the ranks assigned. The police are not well equipped to prevent crime because they have never seriously inventoried all of the resources that might be needed. The primary function of a BPU would be to match police resources to needs, marshaling them in advance according to a strategic plan and then organizing them in appropriate and flexible ways to meet shifting problems. As things are now, police say they are fighting a war against crime, but it's a war they often fight with rifles when they need artillery or with airplanes when they need ground troops.

When strategies are developed from the ground up rather than from the top down, it will become apparent that skills and competence are more important than uniforms and ranks. Confronting needs firsthand, BPUs would request personnel who collectively possess whatever skills the crime problems of their localities require. These might be the ability to build a community organization, engender trust in ethnic communities, counsel troubled families, mediate neighborhood disputes, clandestinely watch potential criminal activity, respond rapidly to crime emergencies, manage case files on computers, determine crime "hot spots," investigate allegations of child abuse, advise businesses about security equipment, and so on. By stocking skills rather than specialist assignments such as patrol, investigation, and traffic, commanders would gain flexibility in the use of their basic resource.

With BPUs command would be located at a level where the effectiveness of crime prevention could reasonably be assessed. BPUs should be large enough, on the one hand, so that resources allocated to them are sufficient for most of their needs without being underused for substantial periods of time. They should be small enough, on the other hand, so that the problems they face will be reasonably homogeneous. This means that BPUs should be smaller than most city-wide or state/province-wide forces, but larger than individual beats. BPUs could properly be held accountable for crime and disorder because they would have the opportunity, now generally lacking in policing, to fit strategies to particular criminal circumstances. Police forces are generally unable to do this now because the authority to command and the knowledge of circumstances are separated. NPOs can fit strategies to circumstances, but they cannot collect and use all the resources available in policing. The BPU is the right level at which to make this discriminating fit.

The boundaries of BPUs should be made coincidental with those of local government or, where local government is weak, of communities that have a sense of identity and common purpose. Local people are in the best position to balance the usefulness of what the police propose against the costs of a too intrusive police presence. The BPU would concentrate at a single organizational level police responsibility for developing strategies, evaluating their effectiveness, and consulting with communities. This tripartite interaction would avoid the current problem, especially acute in large forces, of accountability divorced from effective operational command and the potential problem of coupling crime prevention with coercion. In short, locating operational responsibility for devising appropriate policing at the lowest level of effective self-government is the best protection against the danger of an omnicompetent police growing out of the crime-prevention mandate.

Creation of BPUs in touch with local government provides an arena for "authoritative negotiations" about the coordination of all community resources for purposes of crime prevention (Robert Dingwall, private communication, January 13, 1993). Just as police strategies for the prevention of crime and disorder are likely to be devised more successfully at community levels, so too is the coordination of police strategies with other resources. Community strategies need to involve private institutions as well as nonpolice government agencies. Individual officers, such as NPOs, find this difficult to do because their ambit of operation is small. The top command of police forces, especially when forces are large, cannot do this because they are not in close enough touch with operational needs. The BPU can provide just the right combination of government and community liaison with the practical assessment of needs.

The crime-prevention mandate of the police, therefore, becomes limited by the territory of its application. It focuses on crime and disorder that has local origins. This system would give the police a reasonable chance to succeed but would limit their authority to local conditions. It follows that the performance of BPUs should be evaluated in terms of direct indicators, both hard and soft (Chap. 6).

Although BPUs must be adaptable operational commands, their autonomy cannot be unlimited, even when checked by vigorous public opinion. Policing cannot become wholly a matter of local convenience or even local effectiveness. Some aspects of policing are neither negotiable nor discountable. Three such areas are: justice, equity, and discipline. Police actions must always conform to the law, regardless of the shortcuts communities might like to take. Equal degrees of protection must also be available to all sections of the populace. There cannot be different standards for the poor and the rich, for blacks and whites. Strategies should vary from place to place, but commitment to demonstrably effective action cannot vary. Similarly, standards governing the conduct of individual officers must transcend local necessities. Brutality, for example, cannot be tolerated where crime is severe but punished where it is not. Justice, equity, and discipline, therefore, must be off limits to the command initiative of BPUs as well as to local public opinion.

Where then does the responsibility for making operational decisions begin and a community's desires leave off? It can be argued that the assessment of local needs and the devising of appropriate crime-prevention responses are matters for trained professionals, not laymen. Should the police have to defer to political opinion? When and when not? The British have defended the operational autonomy of the police by arguing that because the constable is appointed by the sovereign and is responsible for maintaining "the Queen's peace," police are accountable only to the law. Celebrated court decisions have supported this view, and the matter is still highly controversial (Lustgarten 1986). In the United States, the major accomplishment of the so-called reform era in the early twentieth century was to insulate the police from partisan politics. This was accomplished largely through the creation of civil service boards that appoint, regulate, and dismiss police officers. Politicians in the United States are very wary about being caught "meddling" in operational matters. This reluctance, coupled with vagueness in specifying the mission of the police, has made the institution of the police virtually unaccountable with respect to performance, apart from the area of misconduct by individual police officers.

This conundrum between necessary autonomy and necessary accountability is unlikely to be resolved through abstract discussion. But one practice can harmonize both: publication of the results of evaluations of police effectiveness. The public does not have the expertise to tell the police how to meet the challenges of crime and disorder. The innumerable surveys that ask people what they think the police should do are worthless.The public always wants more of the same because that is all the public knows. However, people should be given enough information so that they know whether the police are performing well. Then they can ask the police to explain why they are not doing better. Accountability is best obtained through open processes of evaluation, not through directed policies. Embarrassment for being ineffective is a much better incentive for improving performance than inexpert opinions from the public and its political representatives. If operationally autonomous BPUs are subject to regular evaluations of effectiveness, they will become accountable almost without further effort.

The essential function of a BPU is to devise a coordinated approach to the crime problems of particular areas, consulting with both NPOs and communities through representative bodies. A BPU should *not* be viewed as a command responsible for carrying out the orders of others. The chief function of a BPU is to develop operational plans, to carry them out, and to adjust them in response to evaluations of their effectiveness. A BPU is not like an army platoon. It is more like a university, a hospital, or a law firm, in which professionals with many skills work together under collegial leadership for a common purpose. It follows that the commander of a BPU must be more than a supervisor. The commander must be a leader in the intellectual sense, treating crime and disorder as problems that must be solved. The BPU would be the place in police organizations where true professionalism can at last develop because in it policing would be created out of practical needs, programmatic feedback, and the concerns of the public.

Level 3: The Police Force

BPUs look very much like miniature police forces, but with one vital difference. They cannot provide several crucial ingredients that are required for effective operation. These are support, organization, and evaluation. These needs must be met by a higher level of organization—namely, the police force.

First, police forces must supply the physical, technical, financial, and human resources that frontline operations require, and they need to do so in a timely way. They need to recruit, train, equip, build, maintain, and generally administer the housekeeping functions of policing.

Second, police forces should be responsible for creating an organization that operates in the decentralized, prevention-focused fashion recommended here. Organizations are not perpetual-motion machines that function reliably once they have been started. Police forces must develop the bureaucratic systems that produce the kinds of activities required of BPUs and NPOs. They create the roles that determine the behavior of frontline personnel. They do so by organizing the working world of operational personnel, which involves setting levels of pay and benefits, evaluating personnel, transferring and promoting individuals, drawing up job descriptions and performance standards, inculcating values, supervising performance, and providing in-service counseling and education.

Third, police forces must evaluate the performance of constituent units and personnel. They carry out the studies that demonstrate whether the strategies developed by BPUs are paying off. Evaluation cannot be delegated to BPUs because it requires specialized skills that would be costly to duplicate across operational commands. Moreover, evaluation needs to be objective and needs to be separated from operational decision making. Police forces must provide the feedback that allows BPUs to determine whether what they are doing should be changed. They must also monitor the nonnegotiable aspects of policing—justice, equity, and discipline.

The distinct function of police forces is organizational management. They do not command operations, and they do not diagnose or develop strategies. They provide the infrastructure that effective crime prevention requires.

It follows, therefore, that the performance of police forces needs to be judged in different terms than that of BPUs and NPOs. NPOs should be judged by the vitality of their community-based assessments and problem solving and BPUs by their success in reducing crime. The performance of police forces should be judged in terms of management skills. Has the force created a system that can reasonably be expected to lead to vigorous decentralized problem solving while at the same time serving justice, equity, and discipline?

Currently, senior managers of police forces are evaluated as if they were operational officers, in terms of crime rates or complaints about police brutality. Strange as it may seem, a police chief in a large force is not directly responsible for lowering crime rates; she or he is responsible for creating *an organization* that lowers crime rates. The commanders of BPUs are the ones who should be evaluated in terms of crime rates as well as other hard direct performance measures. Daryl Gates, former chief of police in Los Angeles, was not responsible for the beating of Rodney King. The officers and sergeant on the scene were. Gates was responsible for managing an organization that made the Rodney King episode likely (Bayley 1992). When commanders of large police organizations are held accountable for particular outcomes, they quickly and plausibly shift the blame to circumstances beyond their control, such as changes in demography or unemployment in the case of crime or "a few bad apples" in the case of individual misconduct. Instead, they should be evaluated in terms appropriate to their responsibilities. Do they know what is going on in their organizations? Have they anticipated likely shortcomings? Can they propose and carry out reforms that solve organizational problems? Do they insist on evaluation? Do they adjust organizational practices as new needs develop? Is the organizational culture supportive of crime prevention? And so forth.

In the case of police forces that accept crime prevention as their core mission, the performance of senior managers should be judged by whether they have elevated the operational status of crime prevention; subordinated service delivery to problem solving; developed middle-level managers who are both comfortable with and competent in deciding how police functions should be mixed in particular communities; developed a system for the flexible and prompt allocation of resources according to local needs; and balanced the exercise of local discretion against the maintenance of nonnegotiable standards.

Running a police force requires the ability to solve a different order of problem than confronts BPUs and NPOs. One of the great shortcomings of modern policing is that force managers are not required to be reflective in terms appropriate to their positions. They are almost never asked to present a coherent philosophy of policing, justified in terms of the conditions they face. Nor are they examined about the organizational requirements of their vision and their skill in implementation.

A New System

In order to prevent crime, modern policing must be reorganized so that thinking takes precedence over reaction. The conventional police organization is preoccupied with the delivery of a small set of prepackaged services—patrol, rapid-response, and criminal investigation. Police forces are dominated by line functions. Senior officers command, middle ranks supervise, lower ranks execute. As a result, once delivery decisions are made by force commanders, the intricately rank-stratified organization has nothing to do except share the work of implementation.

Police have not recognized that effective crime prevention requires qualitatively different activity at different levels of organization. Crime problems are best analyzed by frontline personnel; delivery problems by small full-service commands; and management problems by force headquarters. In conventional policing, analysis and decision making are regarded as higher-order functions. The brains of policing are concentrated, implicitly, at the top, and this situation is reinforced by the rank system. In order for crime and disorder to be anticipated and reduced, however, analysis and decision making must be spread throughout the levels of police organization, with each level accepting responsibility for different sorts of decisions.

In short, the levels of police organization should be distinguished by their responsibilities and functions, not simply by the authority they have to make decisions. As it is now, the functions of crime prevention are being forced to conform to an organization created for another purpose—namely, the implemention of operational decisions, the following of orders. When organizational form is allowed to follow the function of crime prevention, then an entirely new kind of police institution will be created. At each level there will be police officers who can think, decide, and act. They will differ only in what they think about, decide to do, and carry out. It follows that the police do not need ranks; they need levels of organization distinguished by function. In truly professional organizations, the crucial hands-on work is performed by high-status practitioners, such as professors, doctors, and attorneys. The organizations of which they are a part—universities, hospitals, and law firms—are "commanded" by people who are distinctive in function. They are managers. Their authority attaches to function; formal rank is not necessary. In policing, however, authority flows from rank, and ranks are not connected to organizational needs.

Stratifying police organizations by functions has important implications for performance evaluation and the exercise of accountability. Police, as I have argued, should be held responsible for reducing crime and maintaining public safety. But every level of police organization cannot be held responsible for these functions. The performance of each level must be evaluated in terms appropriate to it. NPOs should be judged by indirect performance indicators, that is, by what they do, and by the two hard direct indicators of problems solved and demand reduced. BPUs, however, can appropriately be judged in terms of objective public safety. Police are not succeeding unless communities become safer. Police forces, meaning headquarters and support units, should be evaluated in terms of what they do to facilitate the functions delegated to BPUs and NPOs. Have they created an organization that performs as effective crime prevention requires? Their responsibility is to manage the vision.

The new police organization will recognize multiple functions, multiple responsibilities—and the need for multiple auditors. The performance of NPOs should be evaluated by BPUs. BPUs are in the right position to determine whether NPOs are performing well because they use the diagnoses prepared by NPOs in formulating their delivery plans. They also rely on the NPOs to implement specific problem-solving strategies. NPOs are also accountable in a disaggregate way to their communities, since effective crime prevention requires ongoing consultation with citizens.

BPUs should be evaluated by force headquarters in terms of the success they are having with the strategies they have chosen and the dispositions they have made. This means reductions in crime and disorder. BPUs should be accountable, as well, to local communities, either through local governments or advisory panels.

Finally, the managerial performance of senior officers, working out of force headquarters, can be judged only by government officials at their level or by specially designated boards of commissioners or supervisors. Their public accountability comes through the usual mechanisms of democratic oversight, supplemented by public tribunals dealing with complaints of misconduct.

In summary, effective crime prevention requires police systems that are stratified according to function, performance indicators, auditors, and accountability (see Table 8.1).

In order for policing to become effective in preventing crime, it must develop linked systems, not autonomous forces, that provide these stratified capabilities. Not all forces, as currently constituted, can do all of this. Large forces, like those of Australian states or Canadian provinces, can encompass all three levels within their existing organization, as can forces in large U.S. cities. The multitude of small U.S. departments cannot include several levels, nor can some of the smaller Canadian and British forces. On the other hand, these smaller forces have already developed vital crime-prevention activity at levels 1 and 2 of Table 8.1. Most U.S. forces are really BPUs, with their patrol officers often operating like NPOs.

The implication of this line of reasoning is that there is no optimal size for a police force. Each size has distinct advantages and disadvantages. Large forces have trouble delegating strategic decision making, but they are very good at providing managerial support. Small forces

TABLE 8.1
Elements of a New Police System

Level	Function	Performance Indicators	Auditor	Public Accountability
1 NPO	Diagnosis	Indirect	BPU	Local citizens
2 BPU	Delivery	Direct	Force	Local government
3 PF	Management/ support	Indirect	Government	General public

tend to be more effective in preventing crime at the grassroots, but they tend to have trouble developing managerial expertise. The capabilities required for successful and responsible crime prevention by the police need to be distributed at different levels of organization and territory, regardless of the current size of existing forces. Except in its large cities and in some states, the United States needs to develop level 3 (Table 8.1), providing skilled management, support, and evaluation to its myriad small forces. "Support your local police" is a popular slogan in the United States, but local forces cannot be expected to provide all the services that crime prevention requires. The United States could learn from Britain and Australia about the coordination of level 3 services. The United States also lacks the specialized auditors of police force performance that Britian has in its police authorities and Canada in its provincial police commissions. It relies on oversight exercised by local politicians rather than appointed boards of experts. Britain's forces are generally large enough to provide management, support, and evaluation, but they are struggling at the present time with delegating command to BPUs and are very unsure about the role they want beat police officers to play. They could learn from outback stations in Australia and small towns in the United States. The Japanese system accommodates levels 1 and 2, but its *koban* patrol officers have not yet learned to diagnose and solve problems. They could learn from small U.S. forces and community-policing experiments in large U.S. cities.

The structure of a nation's police system is deeply rooted in tradition (Bayley 1985), with its character changing very little over time. The result is that countries are pretty well stuck with the size forces they have. The United States is unlikely to abolish its patchwork of small forces; Australia is unlikely to create autonomous local police forces; and Japan is unlikely not to remain relatively centralized. Therefore, countries must develop organizational expedients that provide the crime-prevention capabilities their systems lack—frontline diagnosis and problem solving, adaptive service delivery, and managerial support—whatever the size of their existing forces. The key is learning to see policing stratified in terms of space and learning to fit organizations to the distinct needs of each level.

Toward a Rational Police System

Police systems in democratic countries cannot prevent crime effectively as they are currently organized for four major reasons. First, police actions are not closely related to publicized objectives. Police promise one thing but do something else (Chap. 2). Second, strategies are too generic and are not adaptable to different circumstances. Police forces turn all their resources into a few traditional activities regardless of the problems they face (Chap. 3). Third, police forces are preoccupied with one kind of activity: the delivery of a small set of services. Their organizational capabilities have been reduced to the requirements of command, very much like the military. As a result, the police have not developed the capability to do what crime prevention requires (Chap. 4). Fourth, the evaluation of police performance is narrow and superficial, which in turn undermines meaningful public accountability (Chap. 5).

The blueprint set forth here addresses these shortcomings. It commits police to the prevention of crime, but not all by themselves. The unique mission of the police is to reduce crime and disorder within particular localities by drawing up plans for the utilization of all community resources. Their preventive role must be focused and concrete. Macrosocial solutions should be left to governments as a whole.

The blueprint institutionalizes the diagnosis of crime and the formulation of solutions at community levels. It expands the capabilities of the police from the delivery of authoritative intervention and symbolic justice to the management of crime. It subordinates authoritative intervention and symbolic justice to crime prevention.

The blueprint creates an organization with layered capacities, each one tied to the needs of crime prevention. Personnel at each level must display intelligence, responsibility, and adaptability, but they do so in order to accomplish different sets of tasks related to effective crime prevention.

Finally, the blueprint increases public accountability, even while it increases the scope of the police mission. The intrusive activities of crime prevention are monitored through multilayered consultation within communities. In addition, the top levels of a police system are made explicitly responsible for collecting and publicizing information about the effectiveness of strategic programs, as well as the legality, fairness, and rectitude of actions.

This blueprint is more than a theoretical plan. Each element already exists somewhere in the world of democratic policing. If the blueprint makes sense, it is due to the hard-won experience of many farsighted and public-spirited police officers. Its lessons are widely recognized, even if their implementation is far from assured. The blueprint shows how contemporary self-criticism and experimentation can be drawn together to create systems of policing that can control crime—as the police currently promise and as the public desperately wants.

Notes

Chapter 1: The Myth of the Police

1. Based on the Uniform Crime Reports' so-called index crimes: murder and non-negligent manslaughter, forcible rape, robbery, aggravated assault, burglary, larceny-theft, and motor vehicle theft. Arson was not included. *Sourcebook of Criminal Justice Statistics*, 1988, Table 3.119.

2. San Antonio tied with San Diego for the lowest number of police per capita, and it had a significantly higher crime rate (12,929) than either Chicago or San Diego.

3. Data furnished by each police department. Violent crime, a subcategory of index crime, includes murder and non-negligent manslaughter, forcible rape, robbery, and aggravated assault.

4. Data furnished locally from official sources in each country.

5. The incidence of crime can be measured in two ways: the number of crimes that are reported to the police and the number of crimes people report that have occurred to them even if they did not report the crimes to the police. The first are referred to as reported rates and the second as victimization rates. Official statistics provided by police agencies and governments are almost always reported rates. Data on victimization began to be collected nationally in the United States beginning in 1973. Victimization rates are always higher than reported rates, the magnitude of difference between them varying with the seriousness of the crime. The proportion of serious crimes reported to the police is higher than the proportion of minor crimes. Although victimization surveys provide a fuller picture than reported rates, they do not perfectly reflect the incidence of crime. Their accuracy is limited by the faulty memories of people and the inability of people to know exactly what sorts of offenses, if any, they were the victims of.

6. DNA identification procedures may change the situation. This technology considerably enhances the ability of the police to identify criminals from physical clues left at the scene of a crime. Fingerprint identification serves the same function but is easier to foil.

7. Japan is the other major developed democracy that retains the death penalty. In recent years it has executed fewer than 5 persons a year.

8. They also included the ratio of cars per capita and consumer expenditure per capita on consumer goods other than automobiles.

Chapter 2: What Do the Police Do?

1. The figures represent averages for the years 1987–1990 for the sample of police forces studied in Australia, Britain, Canada, Japan, and the United States. In Japan national data are collected by the National Police Agency.

2. A comparable figure cannot be calculated for Japan because crime reports do not distinguish serious larcenies—that is, thefts with a monetary value over a certain threshold—from all others, as U.S. figures do.

3. The calculation is based on 12,384,300 arrests, excluding arrests for traffic offenses and drunk driving. The total number of full-time police officers was 649,037. See note 1 chapter 3.

4. A more definitive test is difficult for two reasons. First, many police forces have very poor records of the number of officers in different assignments. Second, the boundaries of police-station jurisdictions, which would be most informative for cross-sectional analysis, often do not coincide with the boundaries for gathering other sorts of information, especially census data.

Chapter 3: How Much Is Enough?

1. I estimated the number of full-time sworn police personnel in the United States at all levels (federal, state, municipal, local) to have been 649,037 in 1990. Government agencies do not publish a figure for total police officers. There is one for all personnel, lumping together sworn officers and civilians; another for sworn personnel at state and local levels but none for the federal level; and another for full-time equivalent police officers—that is, including part-timers, at all levels of government. As a result, one is forced to estimate the total number of sworn officers from several sources. The published data allow this to be done in two ways.

(a) The LEMAS (Law Enforcement Management and Administrative Statistics) survey estimates the number of full-time police officers in state, sheriff's, local, and special police agencies at 595,869 (*Sourcebook* 1991, Table 1.22). The Bureau of the Census, by the way, puts the number of full-time state and local police at 520,000 (1990). The U.S. Bureau of Justice Statistics estimates that 8.2% of all persons (civilians and sworn officers) employed by police agencies at all levels of government are federal. Assuming that civilians make up a similar proportion of total personnel at the federal level as they do at all others, it is possible to calculate the number of federal officers and, hence, the total number of U.S. police officers: $8.2/91.9 = x/595,869$, where x represents the total number of U.S. police. The figure is 649,037.

(b) The Bureau of Justice Statistics estimates that the total number of full-time employees in U.S. law enforcement in 1990 was 746,736 (*Sourcebook* 1991, Table 1.16). The LEMAS studies for all law-enforcement agencies except federal give figures on civilians and sworn personnel. Of all employees 75.1% are sworn. If the percentage is the same at the federal level, then the total number of full-time police in the United States in 1990 was 75.1% of 746,736, or 560,799.

So we have two figures—649,037 and 560,799—that differ by 90,000 officers. By the way, the *Uniform Crime Reports* estimates the number of full-time officers in 1991 at 348,070, not including those in federal law enforcement. And the Bureau of the Census puts the number of full-time equivalent officers at all levels of government at 625,000 (1990, Table 1). What does it say when a super-power does not know the number of its police officers within a margin of error of almost 100,000 (14%)?

I have chosen to use the larger of the two Justice Department figures because the smaller one is less than the estimate produced by LEMAS through its survey of only state, sheriff's, local, and special police departments. More-over, this figure is also larger than either the FBI's or the Bureau of the Census's figure. The LEMAS survey covered all police agencies, except federal, with more than 100 officers, plus a representative sample of those with less than 100. In all, LEMAS estimates its information covers over 17,000 law-enforcement agencies. This seems to me to be the most direct measure available of the num-bers of police personnel. Therefore, I consider this number to be a floor for esti-mating the police population of the United States. In other words, the total number of police in the United States at all levels has to be larger than the num-ber estimated by the most rigorous survey of only state and local law-enforce-ment agencies.

I am indebted to Kathleen Maguire, editor of the *Sourcebook of Criminal Justice Statistics*, for helping me make this determination.

The U.S. population in 1990 was 249,924,000 (*Statistical Abstract of the United States 1992*, Table 2).

2. Australia: 41,921 police, 16,676,800 population; Britain, 124,979 police, 50,718,600 population; Canada, 56,034 police, 26,584,000 population; Japan, 221,800 police, 121,371,798 population.

3. For an explanation of the Japanese "secret," see Bayley 1991a, Chap. 9, "Lessons in Order."

4. I calculate the number of people per police officer in 1970 to be 588 in Australia, 538 in Britain, 561 in Canada, 570 in Japan (1972), and 519 in the United States. The U.S. figure was calculated by others from a variety of sources (*Sourcebook* 1973, Table 1.26).

5. The rate of expansion attributed to Parkinson varies considerably, from 4.0 to 6.65%. His own writing is inconclusive. The exact rate appears to have been less important for him than the fact that increases are automatic.

6. The United States, unlike many other countries, does not publish a total crime figure. The *Uniform Crime Reports* give figures for Part I offenses (serious crimes) but not Part II, despite the fact that the reports publish the number of persons arrested for both Part I and Part II crimes.

7. The comparison is misleading with respect to Canada. Assault figures in Canada lump together aggravated, or serious, assault and simple assault, while rape includes indecent assault. Therefore, the Canadian violent crime rate is substantially exaggerated compared with similar data in the other countries. I am indebted to Professor Robert Silverberg, University of Alberta, for explain-ing this to me.

8. I have omitted Canada because of legal differences in what are counted as rapes and assaults. See note 7. At face value, the violent crime rates would be higher than in the United States, at 990 per 100,000 persons.

9. The data reflect calls for service made to the police, not the number of times officers were actually dispatched to the call. Many of these calls were

undoubtedly handled over the telephone, without a police vehicle being dispatched.

10. There is a discrepancy between the average number of calls for service per officer calculated using data collected for forces as a whole and calculated using data for the sample of constituent police stations. The station averages are less than the force averages.

11. A great deal more study needs to be done of variations in workloads in different social settings. On the basis of research in Nova Scotia, Canada, Christopher Murphy (1986) has argued, as I have, that large towns tend to have more crime per officer than small towns. Dick Hobbs and Joanna Shapland (1989), on the other hand, studied 15 police forces in Britain in 1984 and found that workloads were greater in rural areas, where officers also had greater distances to cover on each call.

12. Terminological differences in the way police refer to themselves, their work, and their environment may contain important clues about police mindsets and attitudes, which in turn could affect the character of operations. This is a topic that deserves further study. One wonders, for example, whether the phrase "at the coal face" indicates that Australian officers view their work as manual labor rather than as a fight or war as U.S. officers seem to. Could this difference in terminology be related to the greater importance of weapons in U.S. than in Australian policing? Australian police have only recently begun routinely to carry visible weapons on duty; weapons among U.S. police are a prized badge of membership in the police fraternity.

13. This generalization is true for Australia, Britain, Canada, and the United States but not for Japan. Most Japanese patrol personnel are deployed in *koban*, operate on foot, and receive a large proportion of their requests on the spot in person. For these reasons, I have excluded Japan from the analysis.

14. The New York data were especially detailed. The patrol incidents handled were 70% radio dispatched, 17% on-view, and 12.5% traffic. These were distributed over an average of 216 patrol cars per shift.

15. In one of the few older studies on this point, Boydstun (1975) found that Kansas City, Missouri, had 5.3 calls per patrol unit in the mid-1970s.

16. Christopher Murphy (1986) has argued that when small-town police departments shift to a more professional style, emulating big-city forces, crime rates rise, largely because such forces concentrate on offenses against public order.

17. Total state and local expenditures on law enforcement were $27.8 billion. The October payroll was $1.9 billion, making an estimated yearly total of $22.4 billion. State and local outlays accounted for 87% of total national expenditures on law enforcement. (*Sourcebook* 1991).

18. The high proportion of expenditures devoted to personnel has been consistent in the United States throughout the twentieth century. It was 90% in both 1902 and 1960 (Bordua and Haurek 1971).

19. Some of the data and arguments in this and the following sections appeared in a paper written for the Centre of Criminology at the University of Toronto, which was presented at a conference on police resourcing in October 1992.

20. Los Angeles requires such approval for all expenditures over $25,000.

21. Some forces have adopted the "Ottawa system," which involves ten-

hour shifts. Studies have shown that this practice does not result in more officers being available for street duty or for any other kind of work.

22. Allison (1969) presents three models for understanding bureaucratic behavior. He calls these the rational process model, which is ends oriented; the organizational model, which emphasizes smooth internal functioning; and the bureaucratic politics model, which involves competition among agencies.

Chapter 4: The View from Inside

1. Australian data are based on the seven state police forces; the British data was provided by the Audit Commission; and Japanese data are from the National Police Agency. Canadian data come from my sample, the respective ratios being 1/4.9 for the RCMP, 1/3.5 for the OPP, 1/2.6 for Montreal, and 1/3.9 for Toronto.

2. The Australian figure is based on the seven state police forces; Britain, on Leicestershire, Northumbria, and the London Metropolitan police forces (90.2%, 91%, and 91.9%, respectively), and Japan on national figures (Bayley 1991a).

3. I first heard this story from Patrick V. Murphy, former New York City police commissioner, but have heard similar versions in other places.

4. Australian data from the states of New South Wales, South Australia, Northern Territory, Victoria, Tasmania, and Western Australia (1988); Canadian data from Philip Stenning (Bayley 1991b); U.S. data from *Sourcebook* 1992. Information on felonious fatalities is not available for Britain.

5. I am grateful to Professor Philip Stenning, Centre of Criminology, University of Toronto, for providing this information, which is part of a larger study to be published shortly.

6. The relative death rates per 100,000 employees in 1990 were 48 in agriculture, 34 in construction, 27.7 in law enforcement, 25 in mining/quarrying, and 24 in transportation/utilities (*Sourcebook* 1990, *Statistical Abstract of the United States* 1990). I am grateful to Ed Maguire for putting this information together.

7. Apologies to P. D. James, whose book *An Unsuitable Job for a Woman* (London: Faber and Faber, 1972) was about a female private detective.

8. About 1% of Canadian police were female in 1970 (Canadian Centre for Justice Statistics 1991a).

Chapter 5: Agendas for Change

1. Britain has 43 regional forces, plus the London Metropolitan Police and the City of London Police.

2. Her Majesty's Inspectorate of Constabulary is not responsible for overseeing the performance of the London Metropolitan Police. However, the Met agreed in 1992 to merge its performance database with HMIC's. They will soon be published together, giving Britain the only fully national police reporting system I know of that is available to the general public.

3. An earlier version of this discussion appeared in my essay "Back from Wonderland, or the Rational Use of Police Resources" that was prepared for a

conference on police resources at the Centre of Criminology, University of Toronto, October 1992.

Chapter 6: Taking Crime Prevention Seriously

1. It is also referred to as community-oriented policing and neighborhood-oriented policing. Although the phrase "community-oriented policing" makes a nice acronym—COP—it is redundant. I prefer the shorter "community policing" (Skolnick and Bayley 1988).

2. The situation is complicated further because spokesmen for community policing have emphasized different sorts of changes. Different people employ different languages of discourse. The languages are not really alternatives, but they often seem so. Lee Brown, for example, former New York City police commissioner, continually stresses that community policing is a philosophy, not a specific program (Brown 1989). Mark Moore of Harvard University says that community policing is a new management process. Community policing represents a change in the basic process by which police services are delivered (Executive Session on Police 1991). I have generally taken a third line, arguing that community policing must be defined in terms of activity at the point at which police services are delivered (Bayley 1988). If philosophy and management do not produce new practices at the coal face, then community policing is empty.

3. Discussions of the new developments in crime prevention by the police are made more difficult by the fact that problem-oriented policing, developed by Herman Goldstein, is often presented as if it were an alternative to community policing or community-oriented policing. I view problem-oriented policing as a part of community policing, for two reasons.

First, each approach leads to the other in practice (Goldstein 1990, pp. 24–27). A police department that seriously tries to establish close community contact will immediately discover that communities have particular agendas of problems they want the police to solve. Alternatively, if a department sets about solving particular problems, it will soon discover that it must involve communities. In other words, consultation and mobilization lead to adaptation and problem solving; and adaptation and problem solving lead to consultation and mobilization.

Second, the same people developed both approaches. They were associated with, or closely connected to, the Executive Session on Policing at Harvard University in 1985–1991 and with the Police Foundation and the Police Executive Forum in Washington, DC.

The phrase "community policing" has more popular appeal than "problem-oriented policing." It sounds less technical and more friendly. On the other hand, "problem-oriented policing" draws attention to the programmatic implications for police of improving crime prevention; it concentrates attention on concrete activities that police need to undertake. Since community policing and problem-oriented policing cannot be untangled in practice, I prefer to use the more resonant phrase "community policing" but to insist that "community policing" be understood to include problem solving.

4. In their survey of community policing in the U.S. cities of Seattle, Los Angeles, Portland, Minneapolis, St. Louis, and Savannah, Feden and Klinger

(1991, p. 30) report that most such squads do not handle emergency calls for service.

5. It is instructive that the Japanese developed their modern *koban* system—the archetype of community policing—shortly after World War II, but did not describe it as community policing until the late 1980s (Bayley 1991). At that time they translated several works on community policing produced in the United States and imported the phrase "community policing" into Japanese. Visitors to Japan are sometimes startled to hear the English phrase "community policing" crop up when Japanese police discuss their system of policing. The Japanese police are like the man who took a college literature class and was surprised to discover that he had been speaking prose all his life.

Chapter 7: Options for Policing

1. I wonder as well whether this volte-face by intellectuals in the last generation, especially academic scholars, might be explained by cooptation. In the 1960s intellectuals knew next to nothing about the police; scholarship in the area was rare. Now scholars are deeply involved with police forces (Chap. 5). This may have affected their perspective, making them less suspicious, more sympathetic, and more protective. In other words, having viewed the world through the eyes of the police, they are beginning to see the creative potential in coercive force.

2. The story is a bit more complicated. In 1929, when the Ministry of Transport was created, regulation of traffic was spread among several departments and over 300 local authorities. Gradually all of these surrendered traffic regulation to the Ministry of Transport. This process was completed in 1989.

References

Ahern, James F. 1972. *Police in Trouble*. New York: Hawthorne Books.

Alderson, John. 1979. *Policing Freedom*. Plymouth, UK: Macdonald and Evans.

Allison, Graham T. 1969. "Conceptual Models and the Cuban Missile Crisis." *American Political Science Review*. September, pp. 689–717.

Arkell, P. J., and Knight, R. W. 1975. "The Analysis of a Territorial Division." *Police Research Bulletin*. London: Home Office, Summer, pp. 14–26.

Ashbury, Kathryn E. 1990. "Private Security, Public Police, and Mass Residential Space: A Case Study." *Canadian Police College Journal*. 145(1):1–27.

Audit Commission of Local Authorities and the National Health Service. 1990a. "Calling All Forces: Improving Communications Rooms." *Police Papers*, June, No. 5.

———. 1990b. "Footing the Bill: Financing Provincial Police Forces." *Police Papers*, June, No. 6.

———. 1990c. "Effective Policing—Performance Review in Police Forces." *Police Papers*, December, No. 8.

———. 1991. "Reviewing the Organisation of Provincial Police Forces." February, No. 9.

Avison, W. R., and Loring, P. L. 1986. "Population Diversity and Cross-National Homicide." *Criminology* 24:733–749.

Banas, Dennis W., and Trojanowicz, Robert C. n.d. *Uniform Crime Reporting and Community Policing: An Historical Perspective*. East Lansing, MI: National Neighborhood Foot Patrol Center, Community Policing Series No. 5.

Banton, Michael. 1964. *The Policeman in the Community*. New York: Basic Books.

Bayley, David H. 1975. "The Police and Political Development in Europe." In Tilly, Charles (ed.), *The Formation of National States in Western Europe*. Princeton, NJ: Princeton University Press.

———. 1978. "Crime Prevention in the Context of Criminal Policy." *Police Studies*. June, pp. 3–9.

———. 1985. *Patterns of Policing*. New Brunswick, NJ: Rutgers University Press.

———. 1986. "The Tactical Choice of Police Patrol Officers." *Journal of Criminal Justice* 14:329–348.

———. 1988. "Community Policing: A Report from the Devil's Advocate." In Greene, Jack, and Mastrofski, Stephen (eds.), *Community Policing: Real or Rhetoric?* New York: Praeger Publishers.

———. 1989. *A Model of Community Policing: The Singapore Story*. Washington, DC: National Institute of Justice.

———. 1991a. *Forces of Order: Policing Modern Japan,* rev. ed. Berkeley: University of California Press.

———. 1991b. *Managing the Future: Prospective Issues in Canadian Policing.* Ottawa, Canada: Ministry of the Solicitor General.

———. 1992a. *Back from Wonderland, or Toward the Rational Use of Police Resources.* Toronto: Centre of Criminology.

———. 1992b. "Comparative Organization of the Police in English-Speaking Countries." In Tonry, M., and Morris, N. (eds.), *Modern Policing.* Chicago, IL: University of Chicago Press.

———. Forthcoming-a. "Getting Serious about Police Brutality." In Stenning, Philip (ed.), *Police Accountability.* Toronto: University of Toronto Press.

———. Forthcoming-b. "Police Brutality Abroad." In Toch, Hans, and Geller, William A. (eds.) *Police Use of Excessive Force and Its Control: Key Issues Facing the Nation.* Washington, DC: National Institute of Justice.

Bayley, David H., and Garofalo, James, 1989. "The Management of Violence by Police Patrol Officers." *Criminology* 27(1): 1–25.

Bennett, Richard R. 1983. "The Effect of Police Personnel Levels and the Incidence of Crime: A Cross-National Investigation." *Criminal Justice Review* 8(2):32–39.

Bennett, Trevor. *The Effectiveness of Community Crime Prevention in Britain.* London: The Home Office, forthcoming.

Bennett, Trevor, and Lupton, Ruth. 1992. "A Survey of the Allocation and Use of Community Constables in England and Wales." *British Journal of Criminology* 32(2):167–182.

Berreman, Gerald D. 1978. "Scale and Social Relations: Thoughts and Three Examples." In Barth, Frederik, (ed.), *Scale and Social Organization.* Oslo: Universitetsforlaget.

Bieck, William, and Kessler, David A. 1977. *Response Time Analysis.* Kansas City, MO: Board of Police Commissioners.

Bittner, Egon. 1970. *The Functions of the Police in Modern Society: A Review of Background Factors, Current Practices, and Possible Role Models.* Chevy Chase, MD: National Institute of Mental Health.

———. 1987."Establishing Criteria of Excellence in Policing." Appendix to Police Foundation, *Policing Atlanta in the Year 2000.* Washington, DC: Police Foundation.

———. 1990. *Aspects of Police Work.* Boston, MA: Northeastern University Press.

Bordua, David J., and Haurek, Edward W. 1971. "The Police Budget's Lot: Components of the Increases in Local Poice Expenditures, 1902–1960." In Hahn, Harlan (ed.), *Police in Urban Society.* Beverly Hills, CA: Sage Publications, pp. 57–70.

Bouza, Anthony V. 1990. *The Police Mystique.* New York: Plenum Press.

Boydstun, John E. 1975. *San Diego Field Interrogation Final Report.* Washington, DC: Police Foundation.

Bradley, David, Walker, Neil, and Wilkie, Roy. 1986. *Managing the Police: Law, Organisation and Democracy.* Brighton, UK: Wheatsheaf Books Ltd.

Braithwaite, John. 1989. *Crime, Shame, and Integration.* Cambridge, UK: Cambridge University Press.

Bright, Jon. 1991. "Crime in America: Towards a Preventive Stragegy." New York: Commonwealth Fund, unpublished paper.

Brown, Lee P. 1989. "Community Policing: A Practical Guide for Police Officials." *The Police Chief* August: 72–82.

———. 1991. *Public Employment 1991*. Washington, DC: Department of Commerce.

Bureau of the Census. 1990. *Public Employment 1990*. Washington, DC: Department of Commerce, Series GE No. 1.

Bureau of Justice Statistics. 1987. "Police Departments in Large Cities." Washington, DC: Government Printing Office.

Burrows, J. 1986. "Investigating Burglary: The Measurement of Police Performance." London: Home Office Research Study.

Butler, Tony. 1992. "Police and the Citizens' Charter." *Policing* 8:40–50.

Bynum, Timothy S., Worden, Robert E., and Frank, James. Forthcoming. *Police Control of Drug Markets*. Washington, DC: National Institute of Justice.

Cahn, Michael, and Tien, James. 1979. *An Evaluation Report on an Alternative Approach to Police Response*. Washington, DC: National Institute of Justice.

Canada, Correctional Services. 1991. *Basic Facts About Corrections in Canada*. Ottawa: Ministry of the Solicitor General.

Canadian Centre for Justice Statistics. 1991a. *Juristat*, October, p. 7.

———. 1991b. *Juristat*, November, p. 27.

Center for Research on Criminal Justice. 1975. *The Iron Fist and the Velvet Glove*. Berkeley, CA: Center for Research on Criminal Justice.

Chaiken, Jan M., and Chaiken, Marcia R. 1983. "Crime Rates and the Active Criminal." In Wilson, James Q. (ed.), *Crime and Public Policy*. San Francisco, CA: Institute for Contemporary Studies.

Chevigny, Paul. 1969. *Police Power: Police Abuses in New York City*. New York: Random House.

CIPFA (Chartered Institute for Public Finance and Accountancy). Yearly. *Police Statistics*. London.

Clairmont, Donald. 1988. "Community Based Policing and Organizational Change." Halifax, Nova Scotia: Atlantic Institute of Criminology.

Clarke, Ronald V., and Hough, Mike. 1984. *Crime and Cost Effectiveness*. London: Home Office, Research Study 79.

Clinard, Marshall B. 1978. *Cities with Little Crime*. Cambridge, UK: Cambridge University Press.

Cohen, Stanley. 1985. *Visions of Social Control*. Cambridge, UK: Cambridge University Press.

Cohen, L. E., Felson, M., and Land, K. C. 1983. "Property Crime in the United States: A Macrodynamic Analysis." *American Journal of Sociology* 86:90–118.

Cordner, Gary W. 1985. *The Baltimore County Citizen-Oriented Police Enforcement (COPE) Project: Final Evaluation*. Report to the Florence V. Burden Foundation. Baltimore, MD: Criminal Justice Department, University of Baltimore.

———. 1988. "A Problem-Oriented Approach to Community-Oriented Policing." In Greene, Jack, and Mastrofski, Stephen, (eds.), *Community Policing: Real or Rhetoric?* New York: Praeger Publishers, pp. 135–153.

Couper, David C. 1983. *How to Rate Your Local Police*. Washington, DC: Police Executive Research Forum.

Cramer, James. 1964. *The World's Police*. London: Cassell and Co.

Critchley, T. A. 1967. *A History of the Police in England and Wales, 1000–1966*. London: Constable.

Cunningham, William C., and Taylor, Todd H. 1985. *The Hallcrest Report: Private Security and Police in America.* Portland, OR: Chancellor.

Cunningham, William C., et al. 1991. "Private Security: Patterns and Trends." *Research in Brief.* Washington, DC: National Institute of Justice.

Currie, Elliot. 1985. *Confronting Crime.* New York: Pantheon Books.

Eck, John E. 1982. *Solving Crimes: The Investigation of Burglary and Robbery.* Washington, DC: Police Executive Research Forum.

Eck, John E., et al. 1987. *Problem Solving: Problem-Oriented Policing in Newport News.* Washington, DC: Police Executive Research Forum.

Edmonton, Canada, Police Department. 1989a. *Interim Reports.* February–April.

———. 1989b. Beat Officers' Reports.

Elliot, J. F. 1973. *The "New Police."* Springfield, IL: Charles C Thomas.

Emsley, Clive. 1983. *Policing and Its Context, 1750–1870.* London: Macmillan.

Engstad, Peter. 1988. Speech to the Police Resources and Effectiveness Seminar, Australian Institute of Criminology, Canberra, June.

Ericson, Richard V., and Shearing, Clifford D. 1986. "The Scientification of Police Work." In Bohme, G. and Stehr, N. (eds.), *The Knowledge Society.* Dordrecht: D. Reidel Publishing Company, pp. 129–159.

Ericson, Richard V. 1982. *Reproducing Order.* Toronto, Canada: University of Toronto Press.

Executive Session on Police, John F. Kennedy School of Government, Harvard University, 1985–1991.

Farmer, Michael T., and Furstenberg, Mark H. 1979. "Alternative Strategies for Responding to Police Calls for Service: State of the Art, Literature Review, and Preliminary Survey Results." Unpublished manuscript.

Feden, Nicholas, and Klinger, David. 1992. *The South Seattle Crime Reduction Project.* Washington, DC: National Institute of Justice.

Felson, Marcus. 1987. "Routine Activities and Crime Prevention in the Developing Metropolis." *Criminology.* 25:911–932.

Fielding, P. 1991. *The Police and Social Conflict: Rhetoric and Reality.* London and Atlantic Highlands, NJ: Athlone Press.

Finn, Peter E., and Sullivan, Monique. 1988. "Police Respond to Special Populations: Handling the Mentally Ill, Public Inebriate, and the Homeless." Washington, DC: National Institute of Justice Reports, May/June, No. 209, pp. 2–8.

Fogelson, Robert M. 1977. *Big-City Police.* Cambridge, MA: Harvard University Press.

Forst, Brian, et al. 1982. "Arrest Convictability as a Measure of Police Performance." Washington, DC: National Institute of Justice.

Fosdick, Raymond. [1915] 1969. *European Police Systems.* Reprint, Montclair, NJ: Patterson Smith.

Frisbie, Douglas W., et al. 1978. *Crime in Minneapolis: Proposals for Prevention.* Minneapolis: Minnesota Crime Prevention Center.

Furstenberg, Frank F., Jr., and Wellford, Charles F. 1973. "Calling the Police: The Evaluation of Police Service." *Law and Society Review* (Spring): 393–406.

Fyfe, James. 1988. "Police Use of Deadly Force: Research and Reform." *Justice Quarterly* 5:165–205.

Garner, Joel, and Clemmer, Elizabeth. 1986. "Danger to Police in Domestic Disturbances." *Research in Brief.* Washington, DC: National Institute of Justice.

Gilsinian, James F. 1989. "They Is Clowning Tough: 911 and the Social Construction of Reality." *Criminology* 27:329–344.

Giner, James D. 1987. *Policing Atlanta in the Year 2000.* Washington, DC: Police Foundation, Appendix.

Glazer, Nathan. 1987. *The Limits of Social Policy.* Cambridge, MA: Harvard University Press.

Goldsmith, Andrew (ed.). 1991. *Complaints Against the Police.* Melbourne, Australia: Oxford University Press.

Goldstein, Herman. 1979. "Improving Policing: A Problem-Oriented Approach." *Crime and Delinquency* 25:236–258.

———. 1987. "Toward Community-Oriented Policing: Potential, Basic Requirements, and Threshold Questions." *Crime and Delinquency* 33:6–30.

———. 1990. *Problem-Oriented Policing.* Philadelphia, PA: Temple University Press.

Goldstein, Herman, and Susmilch, Charles E. 1982. "Experimenting with the Problem-Oriented Approach to Improving Police Service: A Report and Some Reflections on Two Case Studies." Madison: University of Wisconsin Law School.

Grabosky, Peter. 1990. "Crime Control and the Citizen: Non-Governmental Participants in the Criminal Justice System." Paper presented at the International Crime Conference, Bali, Indonesia, December 10–13.

———. 1992. "Crime Control and the Citizen: Non-Governmental Participants in the Criminal Justice System." *Policing and Society* 2:249–272.

Greenberg, Reuben. 1989. *Let's Take Back Our Streets!* Chicago, IL: Contemporary Books.

Greenwood, Peter F. 1982. *Selective Incapacitation.* Santa Monica, CA: Rand Corporation.

Greenwood, Peter W., Petersilia, Joan, and Chaiken, Jan. 1977. *The Criminal Investigation Process.* Lexington, MA: D. C. Heath.

Gurr, Ted R. 1979. "On the History of Violent Crime in Europe and America." In Graham, H. D., and Gurr, Ted R. (eds.), *Violence in America: Historical and Comparative Perspectives.* Beverly Hills, CA: Sage Publications.

Hagan, John. 1988. *Structural Criminology.* Cambridge, UK: Polity Press.

Harries, Keith. 1976. "Cities and Crime: A Geographic Model." *Criminology.* November, pp. 369–386.

Harring, Sidney L. 1983. *Policing a Class Society: The Experience of American Cities, 1865–1915.* New Brunswick, NJ: Rutgers University Press.

Henderson, Lori M. 1985. "Intergovernmental Service Arrangements and the Transfer of Functions." In Ridley, C. E., and Nolting, O. F. (eds.), *The Municipal Yearbook.* Washington, DC: International City Management Association.

Henry, Vincent E. 1990. "Police Reform: The Overseas View." Brisbane, Australia: Griffiths University, unpublished paper.

Hobbs, Dick, and Shapland, Joanna. 1989. "Police Chiefs Don't Talk About Indians." *Policing* 5:107–120.

Home Office. 1975. *Study of Urban Workloads.* London: Police Research Services Units.

———. 1991. *Safer Communities.* London: HMSO.

Home Office–Treasury Department. 1989. *Police Manpower: Report of a Joint Home Office/Treasury Working Group.* HMSO, June.

Hoogenboom, B. 1991. "Grey Policing: A Theoretical Framework." *Policing and Society* 2:17–30.

Hornick, Joseph P., et al. 1989. *An Evaluation of the Neighbourhood Foot Patrol Program of the Edmonton Police Service.* Ottawa, Canada: Ministry of the Solicitor General.

Hudzik, J. 1989. "Financing Australian Police Forces: Issues Relating to Organisation and Workloads." In Chappell, Duncan, and Wilson, Paul (eds.), *Australian Policing: Contemporary Issues.* Sydney: Butterworths, Chap. 12.

Jacobs, Jane. 1962. *The Life and Death of Great American Cities.* New York: Vintage Books.

Kelling, George L. 1985. "Order Maintenance, the Quality of Urban Life, and Police: A Line of Argument." In Geller, William A. (ed.), *Police Leadership in America.* Chicago, IL: American Bar Foundation; New York: Praeger Publishers.

———. 1987. "Acquiring a Taste for Order: The Community and the Police." *Crime and Delinquency* 33:90–102.

———. 1988. "Police and Communities: The Quiet Revolution." In National Institute of Justice, *Perspectives on Policing.* Washington, DC: National Institute of Justice and Harvard University.

———, and Moore, Mark H. 1988. *The Evolving Strategy of Policing.* Washington, DC: National Institute of Justice.

———, et al. 1974. *The Kansas City Preventive Patrol Experiment: A Summary Report.* Washington, DC: Police Foundation.

Kennedy. Leslie W. 1991. "The Evaluation of Community-Based Policing in Canada." Unpublished manuscript.

Kent Constabulary, 1992. "Monthly Operational Management Information Package," March.

Kinsey, Richard, and Lea, John. 1986. *Losing the Battle Against Crime.* New York: Basil Blackwell.

Klein, Stuart M., and Ritti, R. Richard. 1982. *Understanding Organizational Behavior,* 2nd ed. Belmont, CA: Kent.

Koenig, Daniel J. 1991. *Do Police Cause Crime? Police Activity, Police Strength and Crime Rates.* Ottawa, Canada: Canadian Police College.

Koller, Katherine. 1990. *Working the Beat: The Edmonton Neighbourhood Foot Patrol.* Edmonton, Canada: Edmonton Police Service.

Krahn, Harvey, and Kennedy, Leslie. 1985. "Producing Personal Safety: The Effects of Crime Rates, Police Force Size, and Fear of Crime." *Criminology* 23:697–710.

Lane, Roger. 1980. "Urban Police and Crime in Nineteenth-Century America." In Morris, N., and Tonry, M. (eds.), *Crime and Justice.* Chicago, IL: University of Chicago Press.

Langworthy, Robert H. 1986. *The Structure of Police Organizations.* New York: Praeger Publishers.

Larson, Richard C. 1988. "Rapid Response and Community Policing: Are They Really in Conflict?" Paper presented the Seventh Meeting of the Executive Session, Community Policing, Harvard University, Kennedy School of Government, Cambridge, MA, June.

Laurie, Peter. 1970. *Scotland Yard.* New York: Holt, Rinehart and Winston.

Lee, W. L. Melville. [1901] 1971. *A History of Police in England.* Reprint, Montclair, NJ: Patterson Smith.

Lincoln, Nebraska, Police Department. 1991. Statement of the Mission of the Department.

Loftin, Colin, and McDowall, David. 1982. "The Police, Crime, and Economic Theory: An Assessment." *American Sociological Review* 47:393–401.

Loree, Donald J. (ed.). 1989. *Future Issues in Policing: Symposium Proceedings.* Ottawa, Canada: Canadian Police College.

Loveday, Barry. 1990. "The Road to Regionalisation." *Policing* 6:639–660.

Lunney, Robert. 1989. "Police Management: The Past Twenty Years and the Next Twenty." In Loree, Donald J. (ed.), *Research Leaders in Policing: Symposium Proceedings.* Ottawa: Canadian Police College.

Lustgarten, L. 1986. *The Governance of the Police.* London: Sweet and Maxwell.

Maas, Peter. 1973. *Serpico.* New York: Viking Press.

Maguire, M., and Corbett, C. 1989. "Patterns and Profiles of Complaints Against the Police." In Morgan, Rod, and Smith, David J. (eds.), *Coming to Terms with Policing.* London: Routledge.

Mangan, Terence C., and Shanahan, Michael G. 1990. "Public Law Enforcement/Private Security—a New Partnership." *Law Enforcement Bulletin* (January): 18–22.

Manning, Peter K. 1977. *Police Work.* Cambridge, MA: M.I.T. Press.

Margarita, Mona. 1980. "Killing the Police: Myths and Motives." *The Annals of the American Academy of Political and Social Science* (November): 63–71.

Martin, Susan E., and Sherman, Lawrence W. 1986. *Catching Career Criminals: The Washington, DC, Repeat of Offender Project.* Washington, DC: Police Foundation.

Marx, Gary T. 1988. *Undercover Police Work: The Paradoxes and Problems of a Necessary Evil.* Berkeley: University of California Press.

———, and Reichman, Nancy. 1984. "Recent Research on 'The New Police Undercover Work': Review and Critique." Paper presented at the annual meeting of the Law and Society Association, June 1984.

Mastrofski, Stephen D. 1985. "Police Agency Consolidation: Some Lessons from a Case Study." In Fyfe, James J. (ed.), *Police Practices in the 90s: Key Management Issues.* Washington, DC: International City Management Association.

McCabe, Sarah, and Sutcliffe, Frank. 1978. *Defining Crime: A Study of Police Decisions.* Oxford, UK: Centre for Criminological Research.

McClure, James. 1980. *Spike Island: Portrait of a British Police Division.* New York: Pantheon Books.

McElroy, Jerome E., Cosgrove, Colleen A., and Sadd, Susan. 1992. *Community Policing: CPOP in New York.* Newbury Park, CA: Sage Publications Inc.

McGahey, Richard M. 1986. "Economic Conditions, Neighborhood Organization, and Urban Crime." In Reiss, Albert Jr., and Tonry, Michael (eds.), *Communities and Crime.* Chicago, IL: University of Chicago Press.

McIver, John P., and Parks, Roger B. 1981. "Evaluating Police Performance." In Bennett, Richard (ed.), *Police at Work: Policy Issues and Analysis.* Beverly Hills, CA: Sage Publications.

Meyer, John W., and Brown, Brian. 1977. "Institutionalized Organizations: Formal Structure as Myth and Ceremony." *American Journal of Sociology* 83:340–363.

Miyazawa, S. 1991. "The Privatization of Law Enforcement in Japan: A Critical Appraisal." In Gormley, William (ed.), *Privatization and its Alternatives*. Madison: University of Wisconsin Press.

Morgan, R. 1989. "Policing by Consent: Legitimating the Doctrine." In Morgan, R., and Smith, D. J. (eds.), *Coming to Terms with Policing*. London: Routledge.

Morris, Pauline, and Heal, Kevin. 1981. *Crime Control and the Police: A Review of Research*. London: Home Office, Research Study 67.

Mukherjee, Satyanshu K., and Dagger, Dianne. 1991. *The Size of the Crime Problem in Australia*, 2nd ed. Canberra: Australian Institute of Criminology.

Murphy, Christopher. 1984. "Community Based Policing: A Review of the Critical Issues." Ottawa: Royal Canadian Mounted Police and Programs Branch of the Ministry Secretariat, working paper.

―――. 1986. *The Social and Formal Organization of Small-Town Policing: A Comparative Analysis of RCMP and Municipal Policing*. Toronto, Canada: University of Toronto, unpublished Ph.D. dissertation.

―――. 1992. "Thinking About Police Resources: A Discussion Paper." Toronto, Canada: University of Toronto, Centre for Criminology, unpublished conference paper.

Nalla, Mahesh, and Newman, Graeme. 1991. "Public versus Private Control: A Reassessment." *Journal of Criminal Justice* 19:537–549.

New York Police Department. 1991. "911 Communications Division."

New York State, Legislative Commission on State-Local Relations. 1985. *New York's Police Service: Perspective on the Issues*. Albany: Interim Report.

Oostoek, A. 1990. "Estimating 'Minimum' Police Personnel Levels Using PARR." Unpublished manuscript.

Ostrom, Eleanor, et al. 1977. *Policing Metropolitan America*. Washington, DC: Government Printing Office.

―――, et al. 1978. "The Public Service Production Process: A Framework for Analyzing Police Services." *Police Studies Journal* 7:381–389.

Parker, William H. 1954. "The Challenge of Crime in Our Great Cities." *The Annals* (January): 5–13.

Pate, Anthony, and Hamilton, Edwin E. 1991. *The Big Six: Policing America's Largest Cities*. Washington, DC: Police Foundation.

Pearson, Geoffrey. 1983. *Hooligan: A History of Respectable Fears*. London: Macmillan.

Percey, Stephen. 1980. "Response Time and Citizen Evaluation of the Police." *Journal of Police Science and Administration* 8:75–86.

Petterson, Warner E. 1991. "Police Accountability and Civilian Oversight of Policing." In Goldsmith, Andred J. (ed.), *Complaints Against the Police: The Trend to External Review*. Oxford, UK: Clarendon Press.

Pfuhl, Erdwin, Jr. 1983. "Police Strikes and Conventional Crime." *Criminology* 21:489–503.

Pierce, Glen, Spaar, S. A., and Briggs, L. R. 1984. *The Character of Police Work: Implications for the Delivery of Police Services*. Boston, MA: Northeastern University Press.

Police Foundation. 1981. *The Newark Foot Patrol Experiment*. Washington, DC: Police Foundation.

―――. 1986. *Reducing Fear of Crime in Houston and Newark: A Summary Report*. Washington, DC. Police Foundation.

Portland, Oregon, Police Department. 1991. "Summary of Findings of Five Community Police Meetings."

President's Commission on Law Enforcement and the Administration of Justice. 1967a. *The Challenge of Crime in a Free Society*. Washington, DC: Government Printing Office.

———. 1967b. *Task Force Report: The Police*. Washington, DC: Government Printing Office. U.S. Government Printing Office.

Reiner, Robert. 1985. *The Politics of the Police*. New York: St. Martin's Press.

———. 1990. "Multiple Realities, Divided Worlds: Chief Constables' Perspectives on the Police Complaints System." Unpublished manuscript.

Reiss, Albert J., Jr. 1971. *The Police and the Public*. New Haven, CT: Yale University Press.

———. 1982. "Forecasting the Role of the Police and the Role of the Police in Social Forecasting." In Donelan, Rita (ed.), *The Maintenance of Order in Society*. Ottawa: Royal Canadian Police College.

———. 1992. "Police Organization in the Twentieth Century." In Tonry, M., and Morris, N. (eds.), *Modern Policing*. Chicago, IL: University of Chicago Press.

Reith, Charles. 1948. *A Short History of the British Police*. London: Oxford University Press.

———. 1956. *A New Study of Police History*. London: Oliver Boyd.

Reuss-Ianni, Elizabeth, and Ianni, Francis. 1983. "Street Cops and Management Cops: The Two Cultures of Policing." In Punch, Maurice (ed.), *Control in the Police Organization*. Cambridge, MA: M.I.T. Press.

Richardson, James F. 1970. *The New York Police: Colonial Times to 1901*. New York: Oxford University Press.

Robinson, Jan, et al. 1988. *Measuring Police Effectiveness: A Literature Review*. Wellington, New Zealand: Wellington Univesity, Institute of Criminology.

Rosenbaum, Dennis P. 1987. "The Theory and Research Behind Neighborhood Watch: Is It a Sound Fear and Crime Reduction Strategy?" *Crime and Delinquency* 33:103–134.

———. 1988. "Community Crime Prevention: A Review and Synthesis of the Literature." *Justice Quarterly* 5:323–395.

Rosenbaum, Dennis P., and Heath, Linda. 1990. "The 'Psycho-Logic' of Fear-Reduction and Crime-Prevention Programs." In Edwards, John, et al. (eds.), *Social Influence Processes and Prevention*. New York: Plenum Press.

Royal Commission on Criminal Procedures. 1981. Research Study 17. London: HMSO.

Sampson, R. J. 1987. "Urban Black Violence: The Effect of Joblessness and Family Disruption." *American Journal of Sociology* 93:348–382.

Scott, Eric J. 1980. "Calls for Service: Citizen Demand and Initial Police Response." Bloomington, IN: Workshop in Political Theory and Policy Analysis. Mimeo.

Shapland, Joanna, and Hobbs, Dick. 1989. "Policing Priorities on the Ground." In Morgan, Rod, and Smith, David H. (eds.), *Coming to Terms with Policing*. London: Routledge.

Shearing, Clifford D. 1991. "Taking the Police Out of Policing: The Discovery of Social Policing." Unpublished manuscript.

———. 1992. "The Relation between Public and Private Policing." In Tonry, M., and Morris, N. (eds.), *Modern Policing*. Chicago, IL: University of Chicago Press, pp. 399–434.

Shearing, Clifford E., and Stenning, Phillip C. 1980. "The Quiet Revolution: Future Prospects for Research." Unpublished manuscript.

Sheehy Commission. 1993. Report. London: HMSO.

Sherman, Lawrence W. 1986a. "Policing Communities: What Works." In Reiss, Albert J., and Tonry, Michael (eds.), *Communities and Crime*. Chicago, IL: University of Chicago Press, pp. 343–386.

———. 1986b. "Uncertain Risks, Uneasy Criminals." *Wall Street Journal*, September 11.

———. 1987. "Uncertain Punishment: Crackdown and Backoff in Crime Control." Unpublished manuscript.

———. 1991. "The Results of Police Work: A Review of Problem-Oriented Policing by Herman Goldstein." *Criminal Law and Criminology* 82:401–418.

Sherman, Lawrence W., Gartin, Patrick, R., and Buerger, Michael E. "Hot Spots and Predatory Crime: Routine Activities and the Criminology of Place." *Criminology* 27:27-55.

Shevky, Eshref, and Bell, Wendell. 1955. *Social Area Analysis*. Stanford, CA: Stanford University Press.

Silberman, Charles. 1978. *Criminal Violence, Criminal Justice*. New York: Random House.

Silver, Alan. 1967. "The Demand for Order in Civil Society: A Review of Some Themes in the History of Urban Crime, Police, and Riot." In Bordua, David J. (ed.), *The Police: Six Sociological Essays*. New York: John Wiley & Sons.

Skogan, Wesley G. 1990a. *Disorder and Decline*. New York: Free Press.

———. 1990b. "Police and the Public in England and Wales: A British Crime Survey Report." London: HMSO, Home Office Research Study No. 117.

Skolnick, Jerome H., and Bayley, David H. 1986. *The New Blue Line*. New York: Free Press.

———. 1988. *Community Policing: Issues and Practices Around the World*. Washington, DC: National Institute of Justice.

Skolnick, Jerome H., and Fyfe, James. 1993. *Beyond the Law*. New York: Free Press.

Smith, David H., and Gray, Jeremy. 1983. *Police and People in London*, Vol. 4, *Police in Action*. London: Policy Studies Institute.

Sourcebook of Criminal Justice Statistics. 1988/1990/1991. Washington, DC: Bureau of Justice Statistics, Government Printing Office.

Southgate, Peter, and Eckblom, Paul. 1984. "Contacts between Police and Public: Findings from the British Crime Survey." London: Home Office Research Study No. 77.

Sparrow, Malcolm K., Moore, Mark H., and Kennedy, David M. 1990. *Beyond 911: A New Era for Policing*. New York: Basic Books.

Spelman, William, and Brown, Dale K. 1981. *"Calling the Police": Citizen Reporting of Serious Crime*. Washington, DC: Police Executive Research Forum.

Statistical Abstract of the United States. 1992. Washington, DC: Government Printing Office.

Stenning, Philip C. 1989. "Private Police and Public Police: Toward a Redefinition of the Police Role." In Loree, Donald J. (ed.), *Future Issues in Policing: Symposium Proceedings*. Ottawa: Canadian Police College.

Sykes, Gary W. 1986. "Street Justice: A Moral Defense of Order Maintenance Policing." *Justice Quarterly* 3:497–512.

Tarling, Roger. 1988. "Police Work and Manpower Allocation." London: Home Office Research and Planning Unit, Paper No. 47.

Thames Valley Police. 1991. *Annual Report of the Chief Constable.*

Tien, James M., Simon, James W., and Larson, Richard C. 1978. *An Alternative Approach in Police Patrol: The Wilmington Split-Force Experiment.* Washington, DC: Government Printing Office.

Toronto Police Department. 1989. "Evaluation of Phase I of the Implementation of Community Policing."

———. 1990. "1990 Environmental Assessment and Force Goals and Objectives for 1991."

Trager, Harvey. 1978. "Wheaton-Niles and Maywood, Police-Social Service Projects." In Cranfield Institute of Technology, *The Cranfield Papers.* London: The Peel Press, pp. 107–117.

Tremblay, P., and Rochon, C. 1991. "Police Organizations and Their Use of Knowledge." *Police and Society* 1:269–284.

Van Maanen, John. 1988. *Tales from the Field.* Chicago, IL: University of Chicago Press.

Vancouver, Canada, Police, Research and Planning and Audit Section. 1990. "First Quarter 1990 Deployment."

Victoria, Canada, Police. 1983. "The Broadmeadows Study: An Analysis of Police and Community Attitudes Relative to Crime Control and the Police Role in Society."

Wadman, Robert C., and Olson, Robert K. 1990. *Community Wellness.* Washington, DC: Police Executive Research Forum.

Walker, Samuel. 1977. *A Critical History of Police Reform: The Emergence of Professionalism.* Lexington, MA: Lexington Books.

———. 1989. *Sense and Nonsense About Crime,* 2nd ed. Pacific Grove, CA: Brooks/Cole Publishing Co.

———, and Bumpus, Vic W. 1991. *Civilian Review of the Police: A National Survey of the 50 Largest Cities, 1991.* Omaha: University of Nebraska Press.

Weatheritt, Mollie. 1986. *Innovations in Policing.* London: Croom Helm.

———. 1988. "Community Policing." In Greene, J. and Mastrofski, S. (eds.), *Community Policing: Real or Rhetoric.* New York: Praeger Publishers.

———. 1992. "Getting More for Less: Thinking About the Use of Police Resources." Draft paper prepared for the Workshop on Police Resources, Centre of Criminology, University of Toronto, October.

Weick, Karl. 1976. "Educational Organization as Loosely Coupled Systems." *Administration Science Quarterly* 21:1–19.

Wellford, Charles R. 1974. "Crime and the Police." *Criminology* 12:195–213.

Whitaker, Gordon, et al. 1981. "Measuring Police Agency Performance." Washington, DC: Law Enforcement Assistance Administration. Mimeo.

Wilks, Judith A. 1967. "Ecological Correlates of Crime and Delinquency." In President's Commission on Law Enforcement and the Administration of Justice, *Task Force Report: Crime and Its Impact—An Assessment.* Washington, DC: Government Printing Office, pp. 138–156.

Williams, K. R. 1984. "Economic Sources of Homicide." *American Sociological Review* 49:283–289.

Wilson, James Q., and Kelling, George L. 1982. "Broken Windows: The Police and Neighborhood Safety." *Atlantic Monthly,* March, pp. 29–38.

Wilson, James Q. 1968. *Varieties of Police Behavior.* Cambridge, MA: Harvard University Press.

Wirth, Louis. 1938. "Urbanism as a Way of Life." *American Journal of Criminology* 44:1–24.

Wolfgang, Marvin R., Figlio, R., and Sellin, Thorsten. 1972. *Delinquency in a Birth Cohort*. Chicago, IL: University of Chicago Press.

Worden, Robert E. "The 'Causes' of Police Brutality." In Toch, Hans, and Geller, William A. (eds.), *Police Use of Excessive Force and Its Control: Key Issues Facing the Nation*. Beverly Hills, CA: Sage Publications (forthcoming).

Wycoff, Mary Ann. 1982. "Evaluating the Crime-Effectiveness of the Municipal Police." In Greene, Jack R. (ed.), *Managing Police Work*. Beverly Hills, CA: Sage Publications.

Index

DISCARD